IMAGES
of America

BAYLOR COUNTY

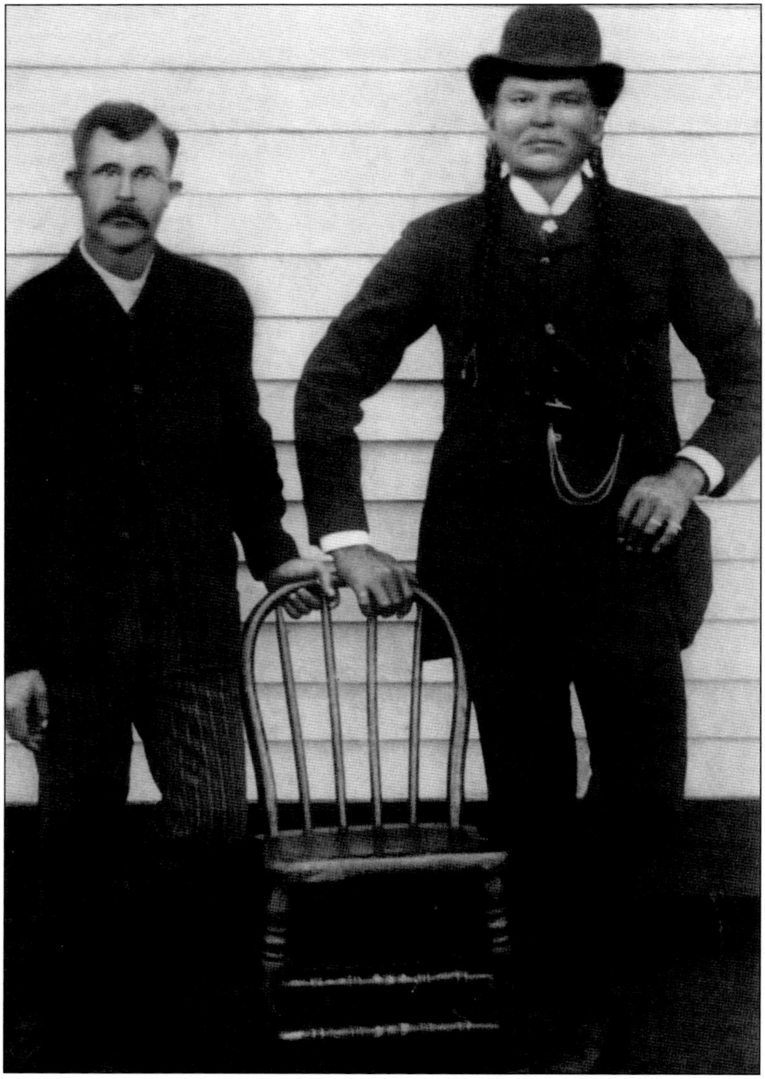

W.H. Portwood and Quanah Parker. W.H. Portwood (left) became acquainted with Quanah Parker during the years he worked for Waggoner Ranch, when his job entailed living in a dugout in Indian Territory. Quanah Parker, the last of the Comanche chiefs, was the son of Cynthia Ann Parker, a captured white woman, and Comanche chief Peta Nocona. Quanah Parker adapted to the white man's ways and became a leader and spokesman for Indian rights. (Courtesy of Sammie Portwood Morris.)

On the Cover: Randal Hamby, the foreman of the Criswell Ranch in Baylor County, is shown in this undated photograph with some of the Criswell registered Herefords in Baylor County. J.S. Criswell had ranches in Scurry, Fisher, and Baylor Counties. Herefords used to be a staple in Baylor County pastures but have given way to crossbred cattle. (Courtesy of Ann Criswell Tucker.)

IMAGES
of America

BAYLOR COUNTY

Carolyn Bomberger with the Baylor
County Historical Commission

ARCADIA
PUBLISHING

ISBN 978-0-7385-7966-5

Published by Arcadia Publishing
Charleston, South Carolina

Printed in the United States of America

Library of Congress Control Number: 2011923771

For all general information, please contact Arcadia Publishing:
Telephone 843-853-2070
Fax 843-853-0044
E-mail sales@arcadiapublishing.com
For customer service and orders:
Toll-Free 1-888-313-2665

Visit us on the Internet at www.arcadiapublishing.com

To the pioneers and early settlers of Baylor County who made courage, strength, determination, and faith a way of life

Contents

ACKNOWLEDGMENTS

The Baylor County Museum is fortunate to have many original 19th- and early-20th-century photographs. Sadly, many are in fragile condition, and it is a challenge to preserve them. The financial position of many county museums, ours included, precludes professional museum restoration of these fine old photographs. Arcadia Publishing offered us an opportunity to present these photographs to a larger audience, and we are grateful to the company for adding *Baylor County* to its Images of America series.

We are indebted to earlier publications that deal extensively with the history of Baylor County, notably the two-volume *Salt Pork to Sirloin: The History of Baylor County from 1878 to 1930*, published in the 1970s by the Baylor County Historical Society. These books represented a Herculean undertaking and are unsurpassed in their contribution to preserving the history of the county. Nor must we forget the *Early History of Baylor County* by Sara Ann Britton, published in 1955. More recently, we are indebted to a series of articles entitled "Museum News" published by the *Baylor County Banner* and written by the late Jack Jones. Finally, special thanks to Janice Vita Thornhill, who contributed the chapter on the one-room schoolhouse. We also recognize the many private individuals who stepped forward with cherished photographs and stories of their ancestors and the way life used to be. We regret that editorial limitations prevent all of the photographs from being published.

We have made every effort to ensure historical accuracy but recognize that, at times, the records themselves are inaccurate, incomplete, or in conflict. We also know that there are frustrating gaps in the pictorial history of Baylor County. Few families owned cameras in the county, and the lenses of professional photographers, with the exceptions of family portraits, were frequently focused on high-profile people and events.

The Baylor County Historical Commission has tried to provide a glimpse of life in Baylor County and a reflection of life on the southern edge of the great American prairie. For its inhabitants, it was—and is—a land of challenging weather, eternal paradoxes, and beautiful wide-open spaces.

INTRODUCTION

The history of Baylor County is a tale of the American West. It is action-packed and full of conflict, hostilities, gunfights, adventure, and the remarkable accomplishments that were to become the legacy of the West. The story took place on a hostile stage. The land in Baylor County was wild, unplowed, and fraught with danger. Establishing the most basic trappings of American civilization took determination and courage and at times seemed an impossible dream.

For the early farmers and ranchers, everyday hardship was also part of the equation. They took personal tragedies with stoicism and no complaints and were ever mindful of the greater vision that brought them to Baylor County—land. Three major groups of settlers occupied Baylor County following shortly after the ranchers arrived: refugees from the Civil War, settlers from other counties in Texas, and immigrants. They came to North Texas because of the Homestead Act of 1862. This legislation offered free land, usually 160 acres, to qualified homesteaders. Land ownership was the driving force for enduring hardship. The elements that shaped their lives were death, drought, failed crops, dangerous pests, blue northers, scouring wind, and the availability of water. Much of the county had underground water provided by the Seymour Aquifer. The rest of the county had to rely on the few natural water holes or springs or on creeks.

The early years of settlement were tenuous and often violent. Brothers Eugene, Alonzo, and Hiram Millett were among the first men to recognize the opportunities provided by the Western Trail cattle drives in 1874 in which tough, two-fisted, hard-riding cowboys were obligated to ride armed over 200 square miles of open range and live in an armed fortress to protect the cattle herds. The first two county attorneys were run off, and an irritated saloon keeper killed the first county judge, E.R. Morris, and was never to be caught for the murder. Sporadic violence persisted even into the 20th century, and in August 1916, a prisoner killed sheriff Will Ellis.

Ordinary residents also suffered. Late in the summer of 1897, Bull Turner and J. Lazarus were returning to Seymour with a livery team belonging to J.D. Peeler. Looking through field glasses a few miles outside of Seymour, they saw a group of men on horseback. A mile from town, the horsemen shifted directions, cut off Turner and Lazarus's route, and attacked the two men. Turner's body fell from the buggy as it crossed Plants Creek just west of where Highway 277 traverses the creek today. The horses struggled into town and on to the Peeler livery, but they were mortally injured and were destroyed. Turner was later found with 15 bullet holes in his body.

In 1911, drought hit the Shawver community located southeast of Seymour. Water holes and creeks dried up. Water could have been brought from Seymour, but the freight charge was so high, nobody in the community could afford it. Men from the community banded together, dug, and found water in the Brazos riverbed, but it was 10 miles away, and the teams were so weakened from lack of grazing and feed that they could not pull the loaded water wagons. Eventually, farmers and ranchers learned to compensate for this lack of water. In the southwest part of the county where much of the land is red clay, it is possible to dig a tank that drains off the land and catches rainfall. Tanks are still in use today and have the added benefit of providing water for the county's bountiful wildlife.

Sadly, the premature death of loved ones also shaped survivors' lives. James Anderson Henyan and his wife moved to Baylor County in 1884. They had 18 children; only eight survived. Most of the others are buried in the Cache Creek Cemetery. Remnants of many of these early community graveyards still exist scattered throughout the county, but only five—Round Timber, Cache Creek, Bomarton, Red Springs, and Westover—are maintained regularly.

Nevertheless, progress was rapidly made. After drought and an exceptionally severe winter in 1886–1887, the county had a string of good weather, and the land produced bumper wheat crops. The county was prospering, and by 1890, Seymour had a bridge across the Brazos River, a railroad, 24 streetlights, a jail, courthouse, and all the businesses necessary for a prosperous town. Many fine homes were built of native rock or lumber, which had to be hauled by wagon from Fort Worth or Weatherford, adding substantially to the cost of a house. Settlers continued to flow into Baylor County, and by the first quarter of the 20th century, the county had 38 small communities located within its 30-square-miles. Each had a school, church, and cemetery. These communities prospered until after World War II, when they began to contract. By the 1960s, the number of farms had decreased, but the average size of farms had increased. This trend continues in the 21st century, with many of the smaller farms also being sold for recreational hunting.

During the 1920s, Baylor County and the City of Seymour continued to improve the infrastructure; they paved roads, built a hospital, city park, and city hall. Oil discovered in 1924 helped the county through the Great Depression. In December 1953, oil was discovered in the south and southwest parts of the county as well. The Baylor County Regular oil field helped alleviate the effects of the severe drought of the 1950s. Over 57,407,611 barrels of oil have come out of the county since its discovery in 1924.

While historians and descendants of the area may see the settling of the county as full of hardship, turbulence, and notorious events, the pioneers themselves did not. The early family histories that have been preserved are positive and optimistic. An individual might occasionally acknowledge it was a hard life, but he did not dwell on the fact. Instead, settlers chose to speak fondly of the closeness of the communities, the entertainment offered by socials and dances, and the solace provided by country churches. They were especially thankful for how neighbors helped neighbors, regardless of the task, and marveled at the kindness of a table well set for friends and strangers alike; and the antics of the one-room schoolhouse are especially cherished.

These small communities and villages have slowly disappeared, and of the 38 rural schoolhouses, only one, Mary's Creek, still stands as a testament to their educational endeavors. The early settlers accomplished their goals. They civilized a wild land. Their legacy is fields that are still plowed and fertile, ranches that still run cattle, neighbors that still help neighbors, and a faith that has sustained generations of their descendants.

Once an isolated prairie town, Seymour today sits at the intersection of five major highways.

One

Baylor County Organizes

In 1874, buffalo roamed the county, the Comanches and Kiowa raided settlements regularly, and the Millett Ranch cowboys rode armed with pistols, carbines, and rifles to protect the ranch's cattle herds.

In 1879—just five years later—the buffalo were gone, the Indians had been relocated to Indian Territory in what is now the state of Oklahoma, and the county was safe for settlement. The population had grown sufficiently to merit organization. With nine families in 1875, the community of Round Timber is recognized as the oldest community in Baylor County.

The county's organization was presided over by judge W.B. Clements, of Clay County; at that time, Baylor County was attached to Clay County for judicial purposes. County officials were elected at the home of W.A. Fancher. Four men agreed to donate land for the public square: E.P. Miller, J.R. McClain, E.R. Morris, and E. Reiman.

The county may have been officially determined to be safe for settlement, but there were still frequent differences of opinions. So, in February 1882, county commissioners voted to award a contract to C.B. Greene to build a jail. Greene's bid was $6,700, and the courthouse was built in 1884 by Aubrey and Sloan.

The city of Seymour was organized in 1890. Theories relating to the origin of the town's name include one that alleges it is named after Horatius Seymour, who, according to the 1977 two-volume history of Baylor County *Salt Pork to Sirloin*, was governor of Indiana and a candidate for the United States presidency. The second and most popular theory is that the city was named after cowboy Seymour Munday, who often camped on what is now Seymour Creek.

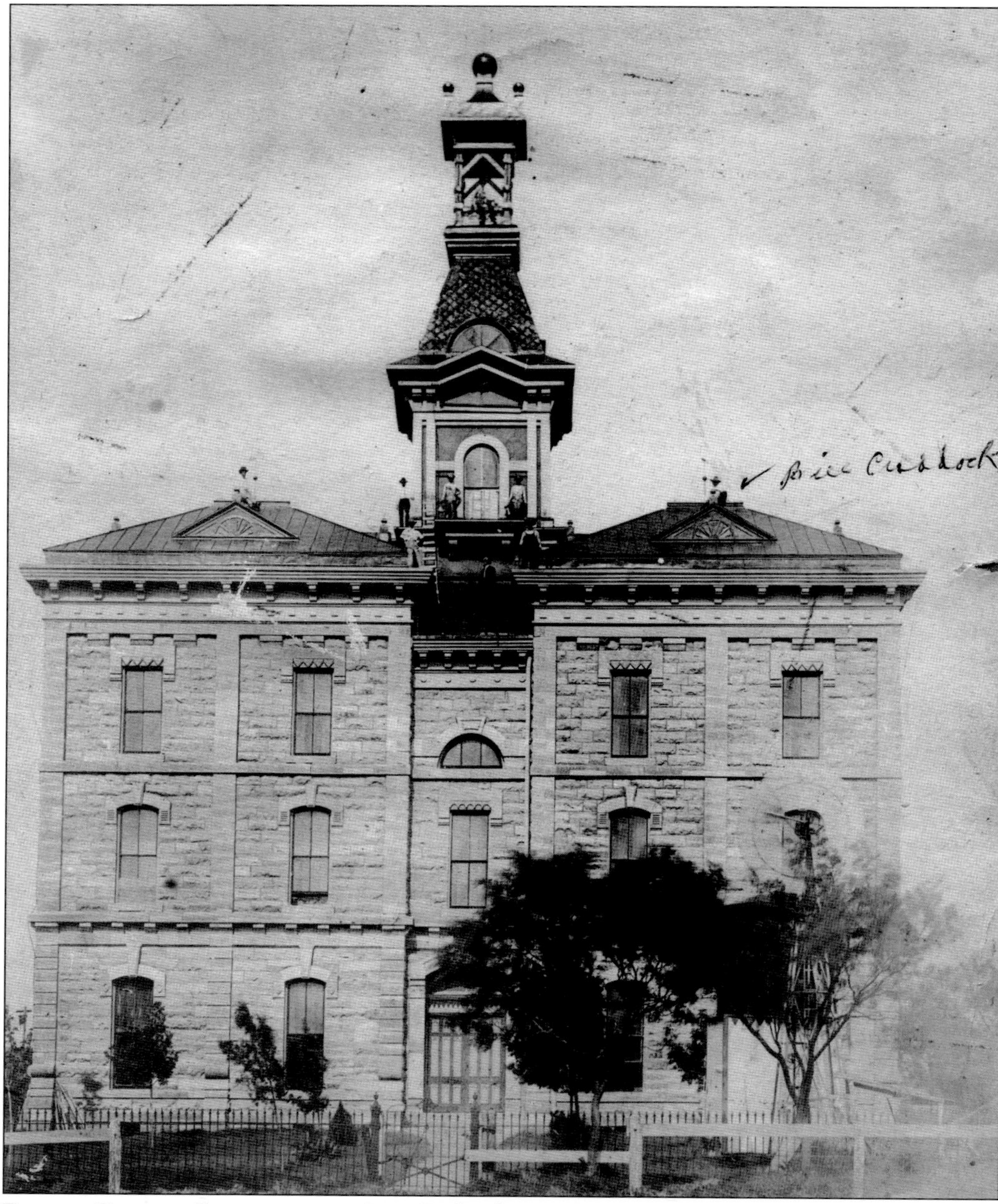

BAYLOR COUNTY COURTHOUSE, 1910. Built of native stone taken from the bed of the Brazos River, the county's first courthouse was constructed in 1884 at a cost of $40,500. The walls were three feet thick. A dome took the place of the cupola in 1912. This courthouse was torn down in 1967 and replaced with a modern structure. (Courtesy of Baylor County Museum.)

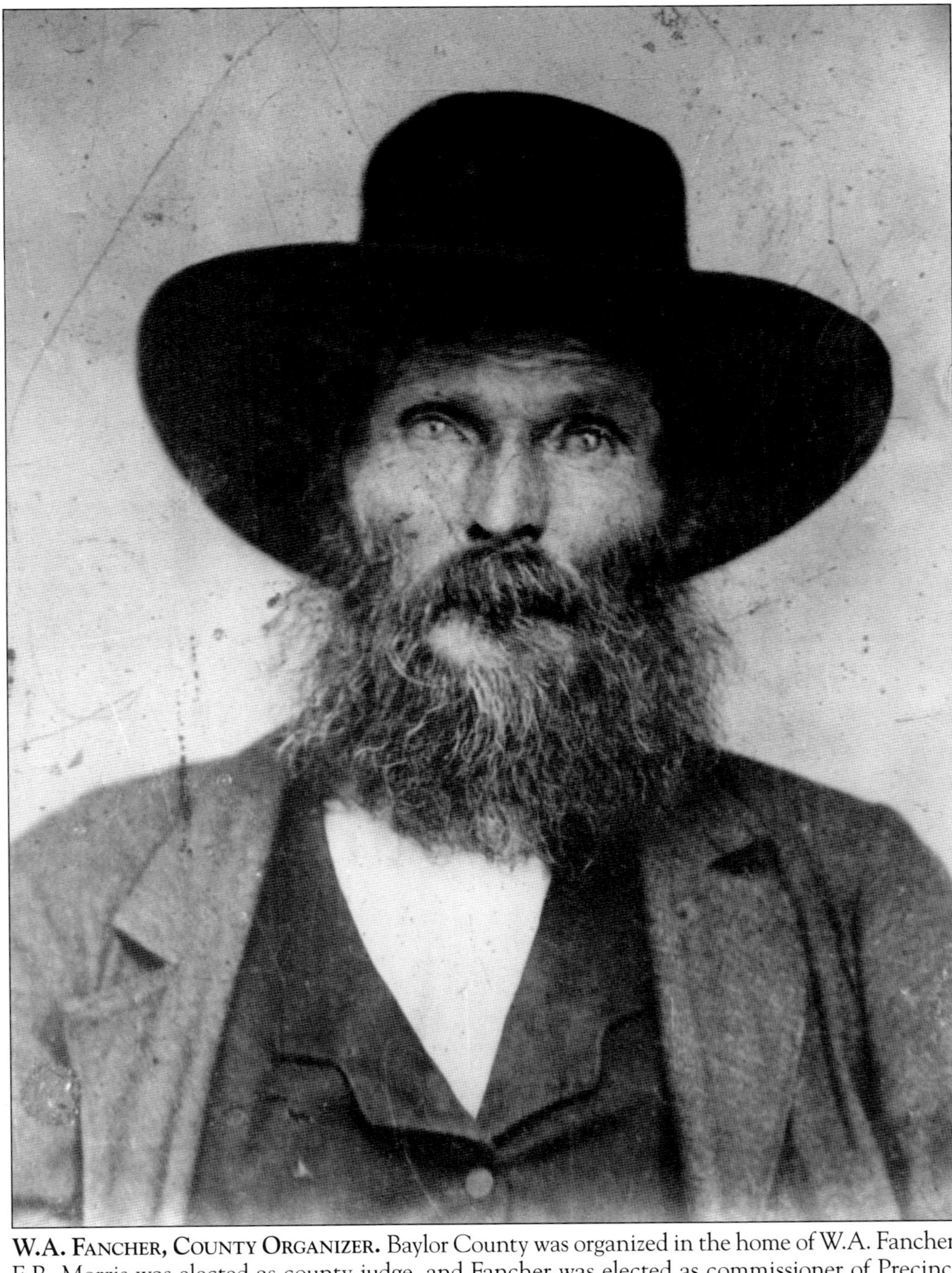

W.A. FANCHER, COUNTY ORGANIZER. Baylor County was organized in the home of W.A. Fancher. E.R. Morris was elected as county judge, and Fancher was elected as commissioner of Precinct 2. On June 27, 1879, the first term of commissioners court convened in a portion of a mercantile store operated by Ingram and Perrin. Fancher later served as county treasurer from 1896 to 1903. (Courtesy of Baylor County Museum.)

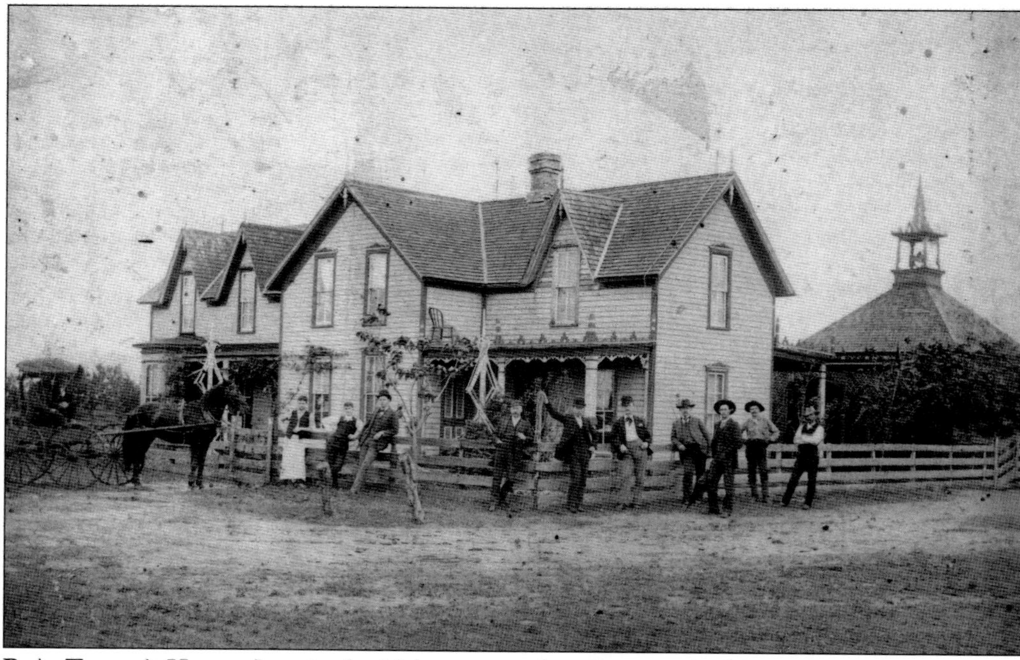

R.A. Talley's Hotel. Late in the 19th century when Seymour had fewer than 2,000 people, it boasted no less than seven hotels. They included the Bandy, the McClain, the Commercial, the Eureka, the Washington, and the Seymour. Rooms were also available in several of the town's boarding houses. Eventually, all of the hotels burned, except for the Commercial, which was razed to build a private home. (Courtesy of Baylor County Museum.)

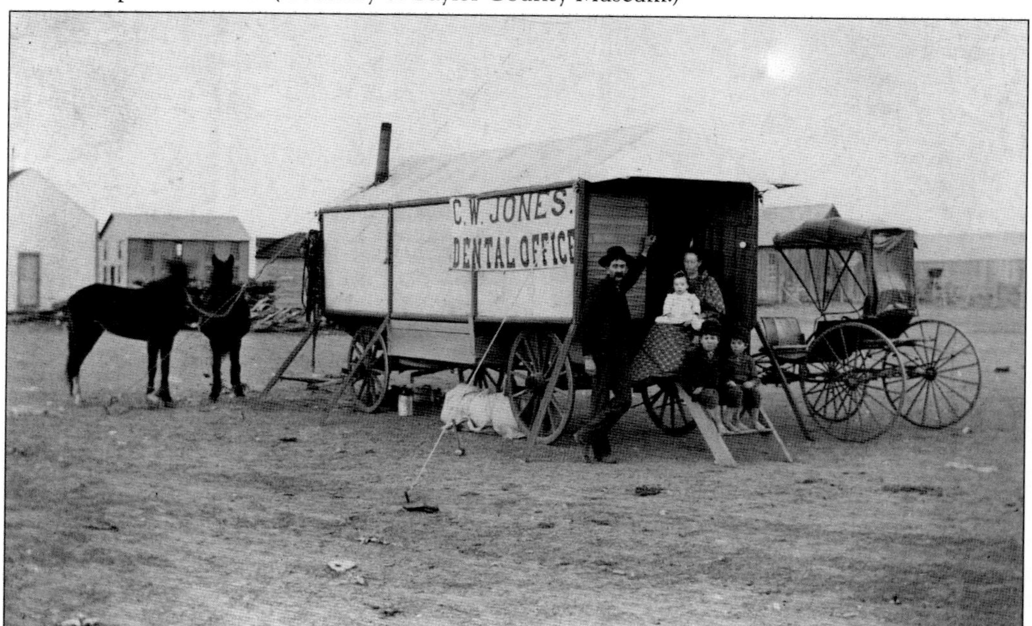

C.W. Jones's Dental Office. Baylor County had plenty of doctors and up-to-date medical advancements. Nevertheless, a tooth extraction prior to modern anesthetics was an excruciating experience. Painkillers were most often either opium or whiskey. Another physician, Dr. Johnson, purchased the first car in the county, a 1905 Maxwell. (Courtesy of Baylor County Museum.)

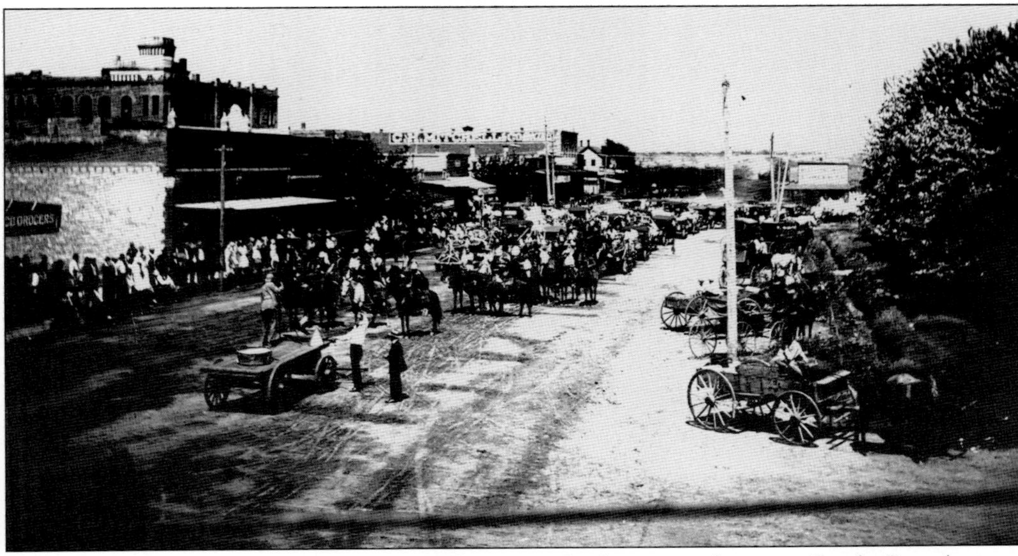

Seymour Street Scene, "Smoky Row." The original reference to the name Smoky Row (written on a mat surrounding this photograph) is unknown. However, the street it refers to is north of the courthouse and was the location of the town's numerous blacksmiths, who were among the first businessmen in town. The hot forges, flying sparks, and steam produced from dunking hot iron in water would have produced plenty of smoke. (Courtesy of Baylor County Museum.)

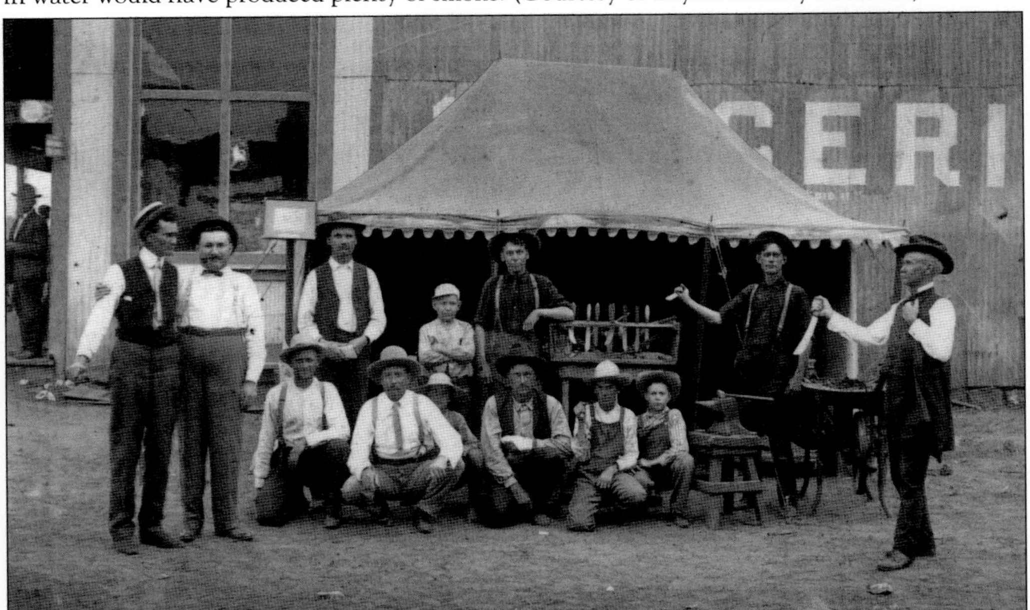

Itinerant Knife Peddler. This picture, taken about 1910, is an enigma. Presumably it is an itinerant knife-sharpening operation, and the tent and knife display would seem to support this theory. However, close inspection of the composition and content of the photograph raises many questions, including why the picture was taken. Who owns the business? The man standing on the right, posed formally in the three-piece suit with a knife in hand, the man standing informally behind the anvil, or the man in the center front row with the bandaged hand? Finally, does the disparity in ages and dress of the men suggest customers or an audience? (Courtesy of Baylor County Museum.)

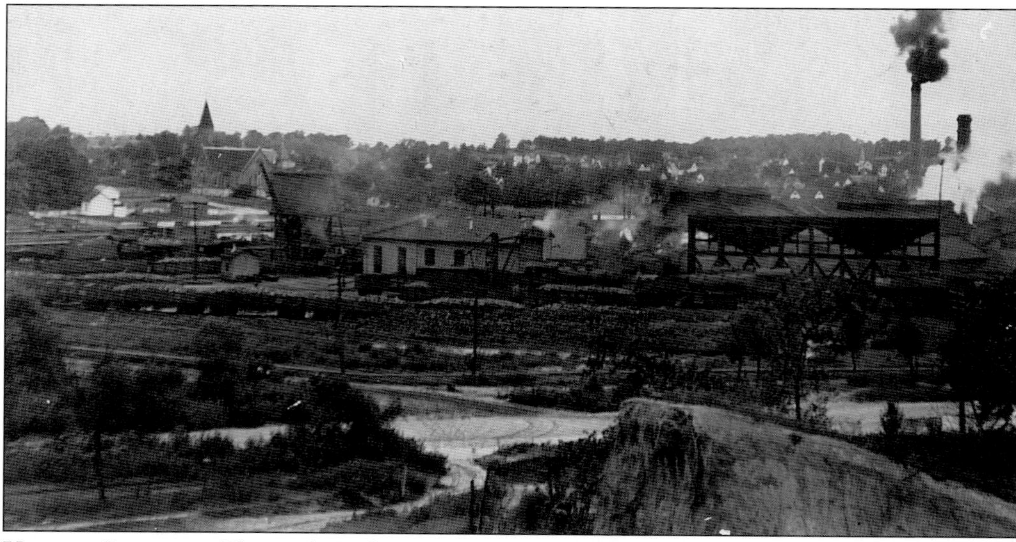

VIEW OF SEYMOUR. This early-20th-century view of Seymour shows one of the town's railroad depots and tracks. The trains are loaded with either coal or rocks from the riverbed or a local quarry. Seymour's early industries are indicated by the smokestacks. The first manufacturing in the county was a brick factory in 1893. Other early industries included a cotton gin and compress, a cotton oil mill, and a Coca-Cola bottling plant. (Courtesy of Baylor County Museum.)

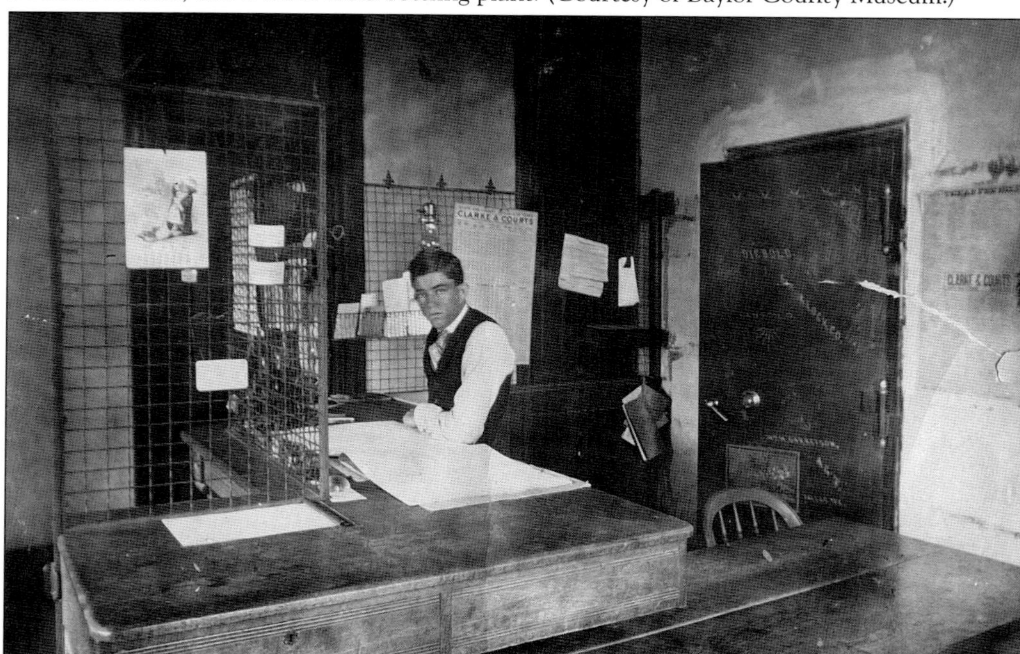

W.E. CRADDOCK IN SHERIFF'S OFFICE. The Craddock family has contributed significantly to the history of Baylor County. W.E. Craddock served as sheriff from 1885 to 1900 and again from 1906 to 1910. W.E.'s brother T.E. Craddock was instrumental in the development of the Rural Electrification Agency (REA). The Craddock Ranch is one of a handful of 19th-century ranches still operating in the county by family descendants.(Courtesy of Baylor County Museum.)

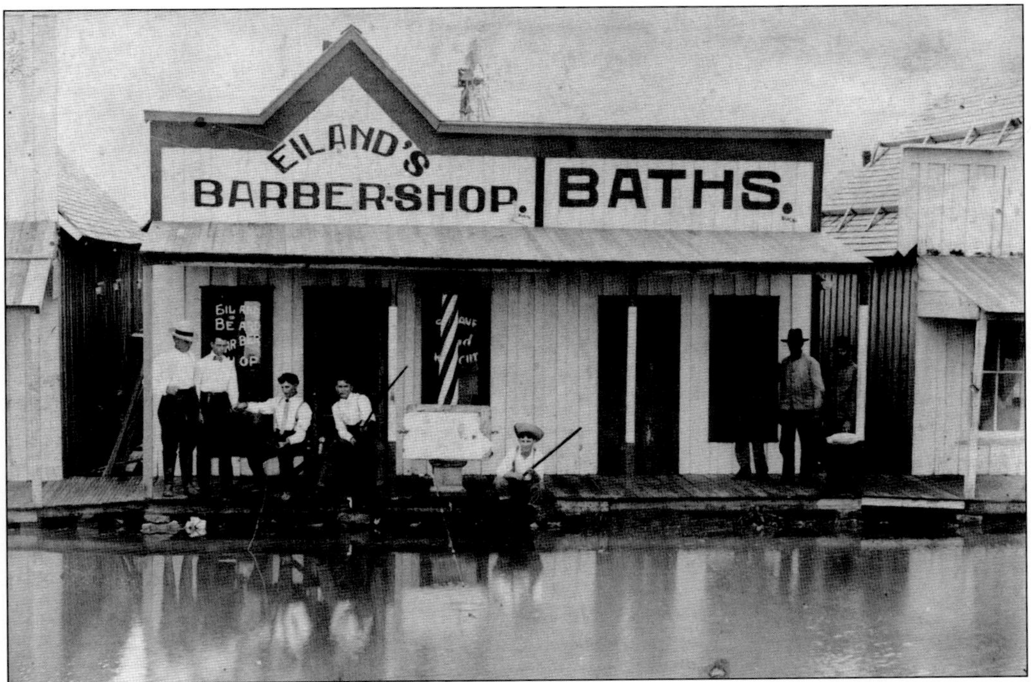

EILAND'S BARBERSHOP ON WASHINGTON STREET. Dusty cowhands and travelers often needed and welcomed the services of a barbershop and bath, and fishing has always been a popular pastime in the county. Seymour is situated near the Brazos River, but these enterprising fishermen are probably taking advantage of flooding from Seymour Creek. (Courtesy of Baylor County Museum.)

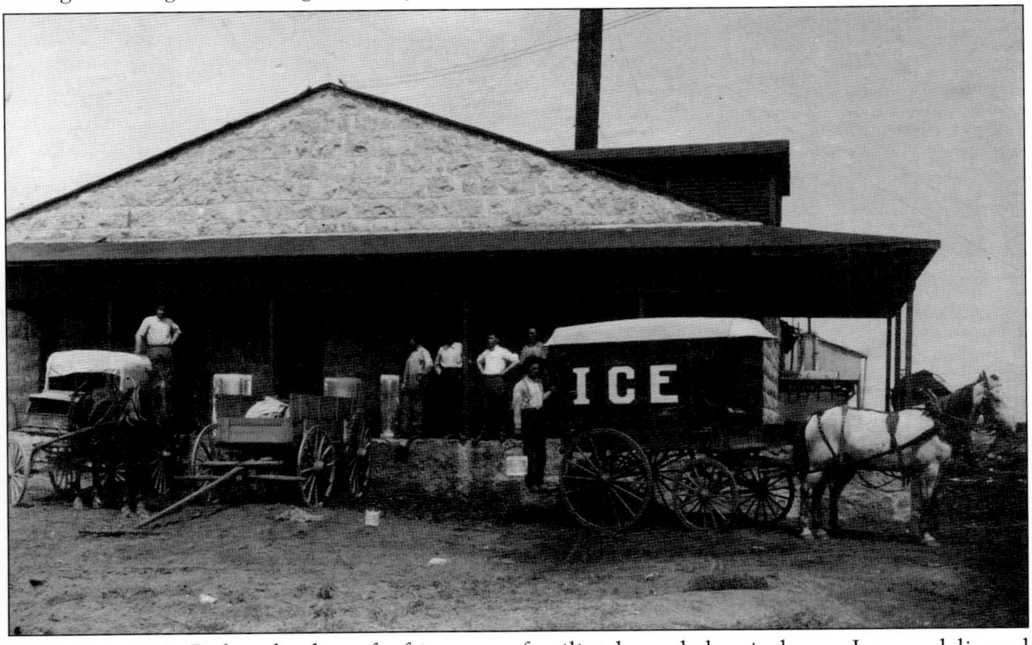

ICEHOUSE, 1910. Before the days of refrigerators, families depended on iceboxes. Ice was delivered from the icehouse to individuals for storage in an icebox. Pieces of ice were then chipped off as needed. This photograph is a good example of the sizes of ice blocks, the ice tongs used for moving them, and the type of vehicles used for deliveries. (Courtesy of Baylor County Museum.)

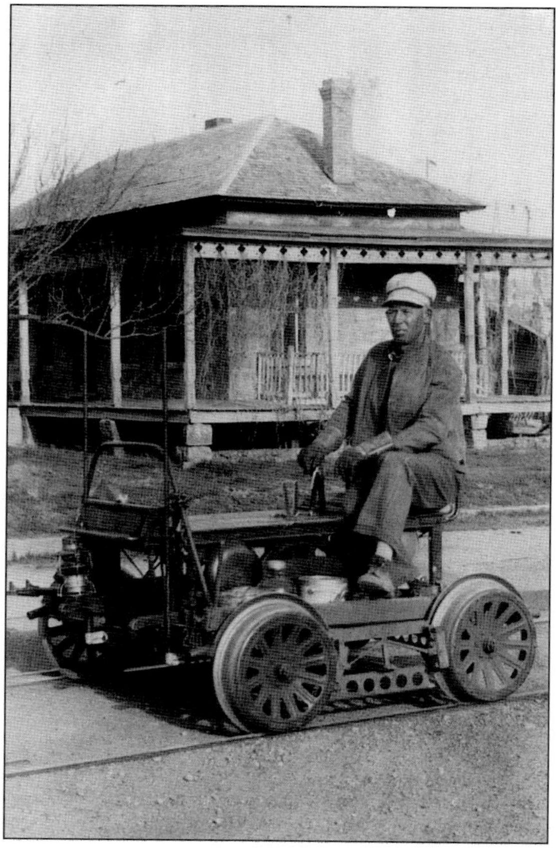

O. (Oscar) Cole, Section Foreman. Cole was the section foreman for the Wichita Valley Railway. The extension of the Wichita Valley line through Seymour to Abilene gave the county a better outlet for crops and cattle to be shipped south. The town of Bomarton was founded as a railroad stop in 1906. Cole is pictured in front of the Harvey House, one of the oldest residences in Baylor County and the first home of the Baylor County Museum. (Courtesy of Baylor County Museum.)

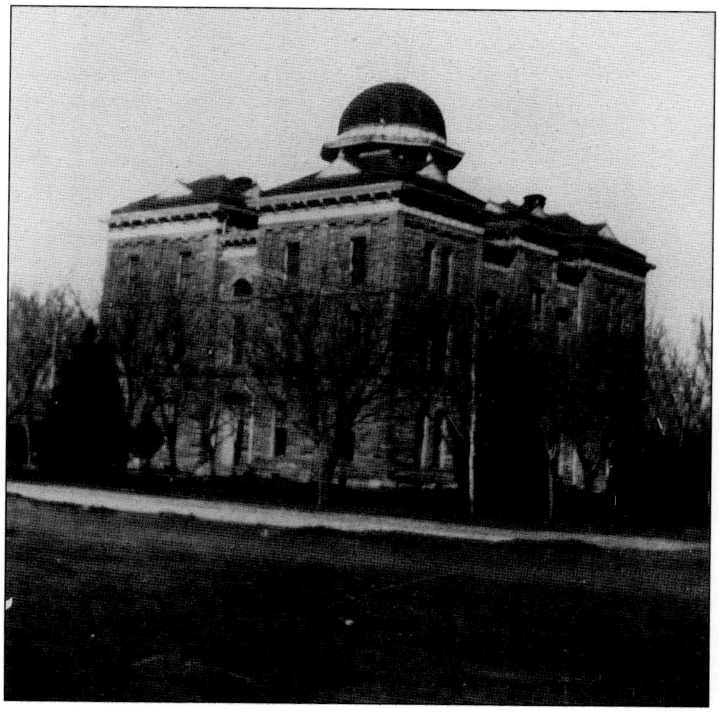

Baylor County Courthouse with Dome. In this photograph, the cupola on the courthouse has been replaced by a dome. The dome remained on the courthouse until it was torn down in 1967 and replaced with the current courthouse. It took two years to build the original structure and eight hours with a wrecking ball to tear it down. The new courthouse was funded with a $350,000 bond issue. (Courtesy of Baylor County Museum.)

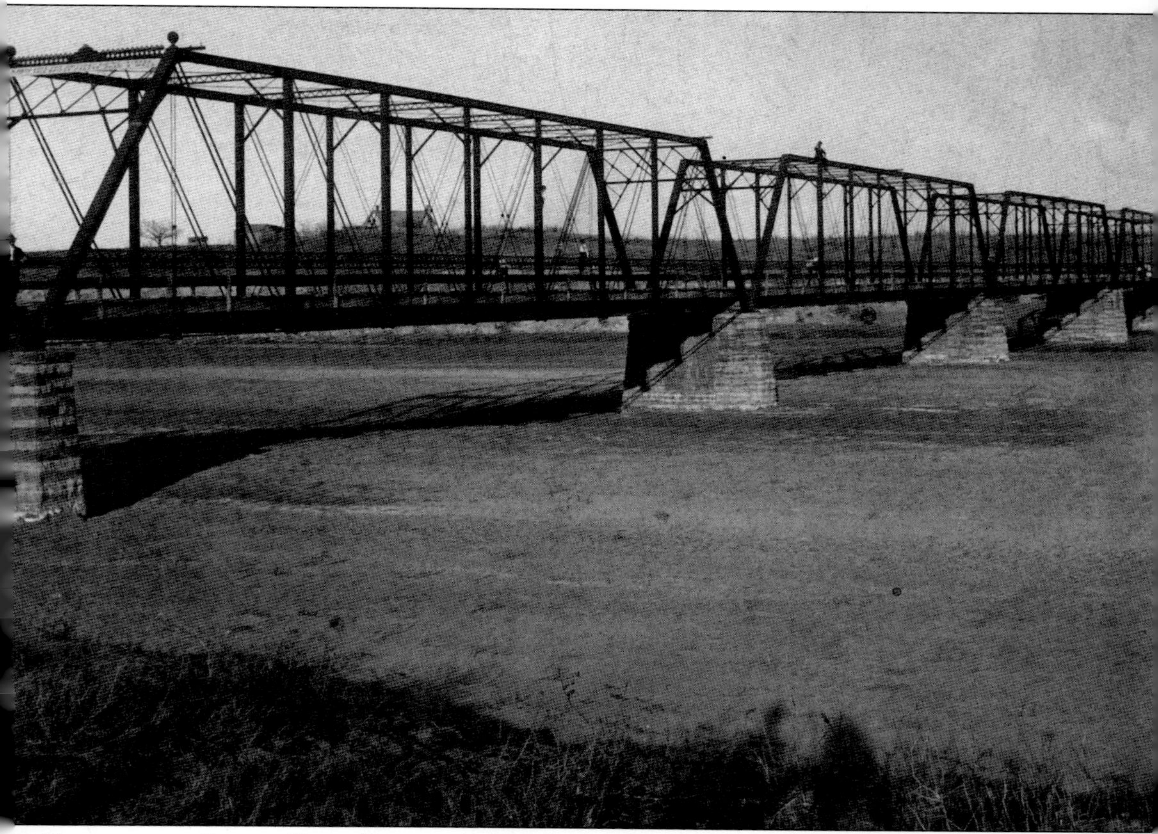

CROSSING THE BRAZOS RIVER BRIDGE. At least five bridges have been built over the Brazos River since the county's organization in 1879. The trestle bridge pictured above was built in 1889 by the military. It washed away about 1898. Photographs of the second bridge are available, but no information concerning its construction is known. The third span, still a trestle bridge, was built sometime in the mid-1930s at a cost of $168,000. The third bridge was replaced by a concrete bridge in the 1960s, and since then two, more concrete bridges have been constructed. The latest, built by the Texas Department of Transportation, was completed in 2009. (Courtesy of Baylor County Museum.)

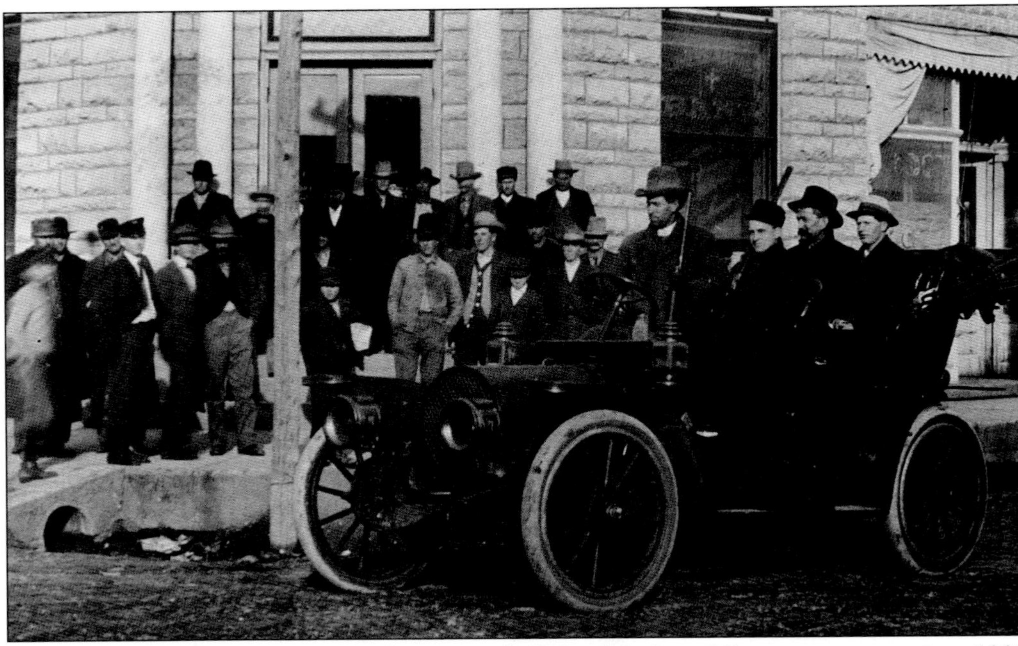

1909 FRANKLIN CAR. Messrs. Dickson, Mitchell, Lankford, and Browning appear in a 1909 Franklin car in front of the Farmer's National Bank, which was formed in 1904. From 1904 to 1907, the bank was located in the McClain Hotel. In 1907, it moved to the corner of Washington and McClain Streets, where it is still located. These gentlemen were all prominent residents of the day. The circumstances of the photograph, however, are unusual. The men are armed, and a curious crowd of onlookers suggests that it was not a routine drive down the street. (Courtesy of Baylor County Museum.)

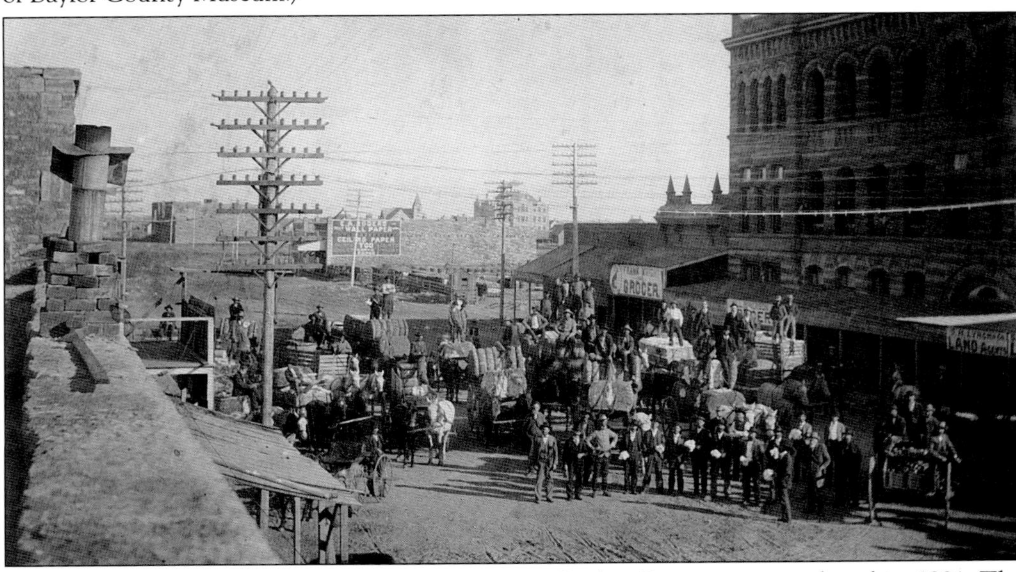

A GOOD COTTON CROP. The first cotton crop in Baylor County was produced in 1891. The cotton was ginned, baled, and weighed and then sold to buyers. Seymour was a popular place to sell cotton because of the well known integrity of Mann Tackitt, a cotton buyer for the firm of Johnson and Bussell. This photograph was taken about 1905 on Main Street in front of the McClain Hotel. (Courtesy of Baylor County Museum.)

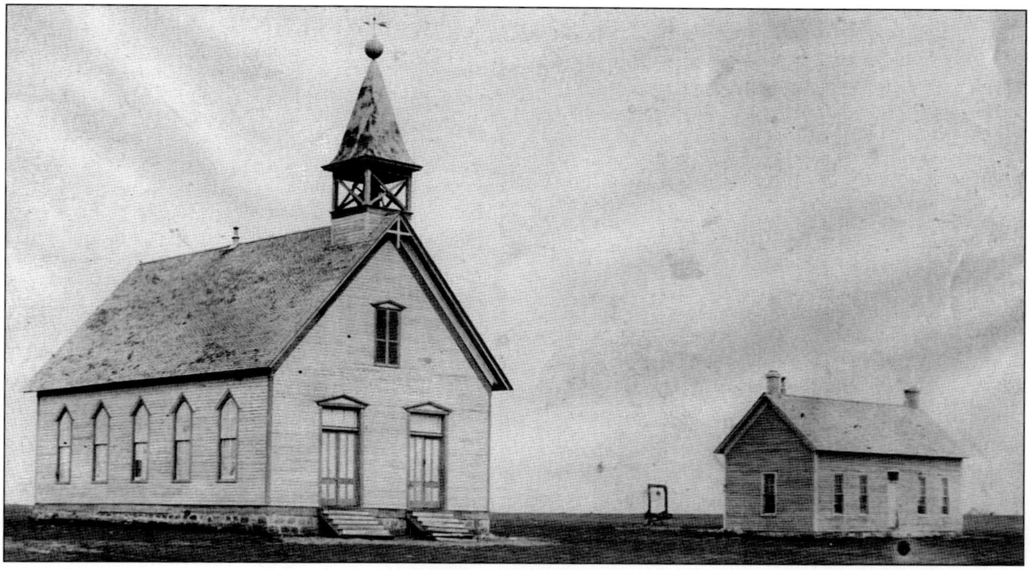

Unidentified Community Church And Parsonage. Early pioneer families possessed a strong Christian ethic, and churches were often the first public buildings constructed in the communities of Baylor County. In Seymour, the Methodist and First Christian congregations were organized in 1880 and the Presbyterians in 1883. The first evidence of a sermon is from the winter of 1879 when elder E.S. Colthorp spoke to the Baptists. St. John's Catholic Church of Bomarton was built in 1909. (Courtesy of Baylor County Museum.)

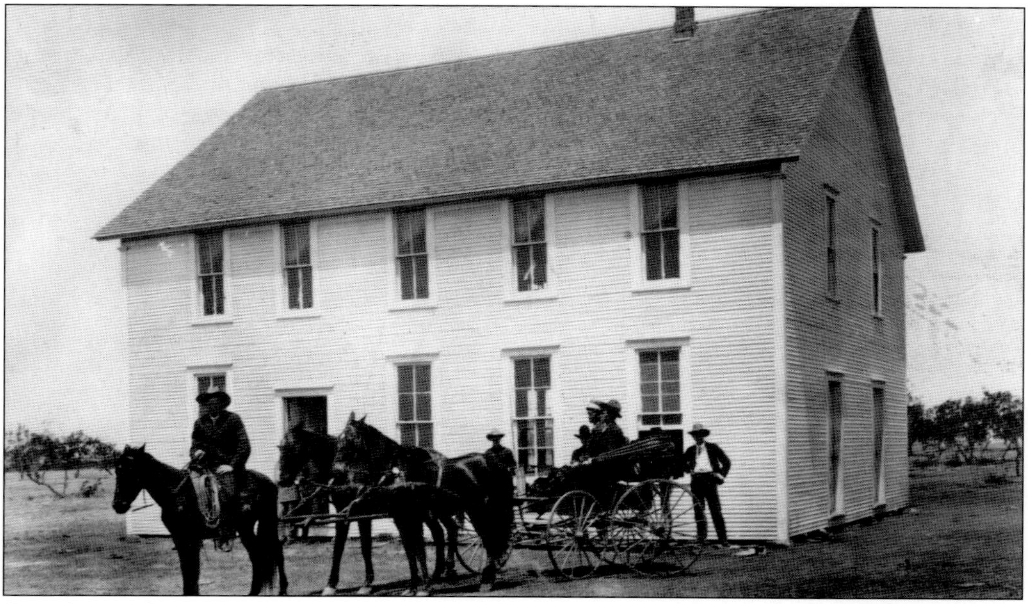

Old Ample Community Building. Annie Thurman married Frank Allen in 1906. Thurman and her family had come to Texas from Tennessee in a covered wagon and crossed the Mississippi River on a barge. They settled in the now vanished community of Old Ample. Old Ample was located on the adjoining corners of Baylor, Knox, Throckmorton, and Haskell Counties. When bridges over Miller Creek and the Brazos River made travel to Seymour and Munday easier, Old Ample declined. This structure served as church, school, and community building. (Courtesy of Sammie Portwood Morris.)

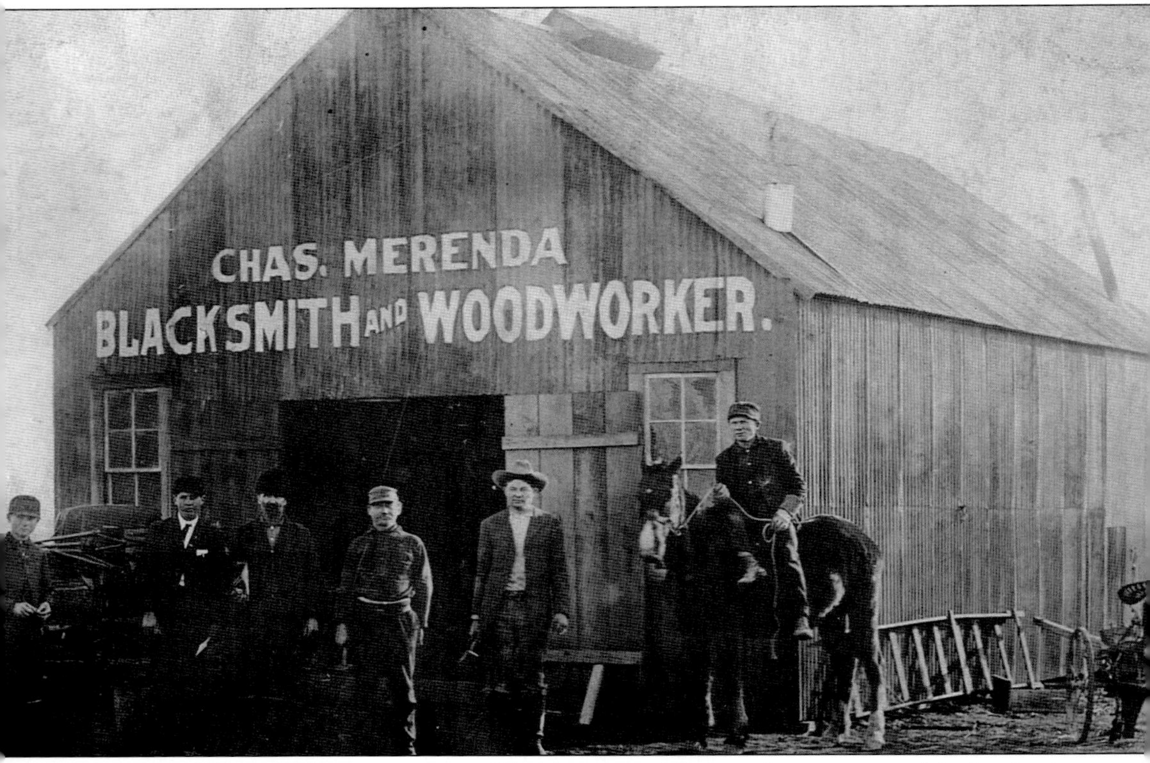

CHARLES MERENDA BLACKSMITH AND WOODWORKING. Blacksmiths were some of the first businesses to open in Seymour and surrounding communities. This photograph was taken in Bomarton in 1909. Two other blacksmiths, John Morris and Adolph Pavlicek, were operating in that community at the time. It was a natural progression for many blacksmiths to become automobile mechanics once horses and wagons began to be supplanted by cars. (Courtesy of Baylor County Museum.)

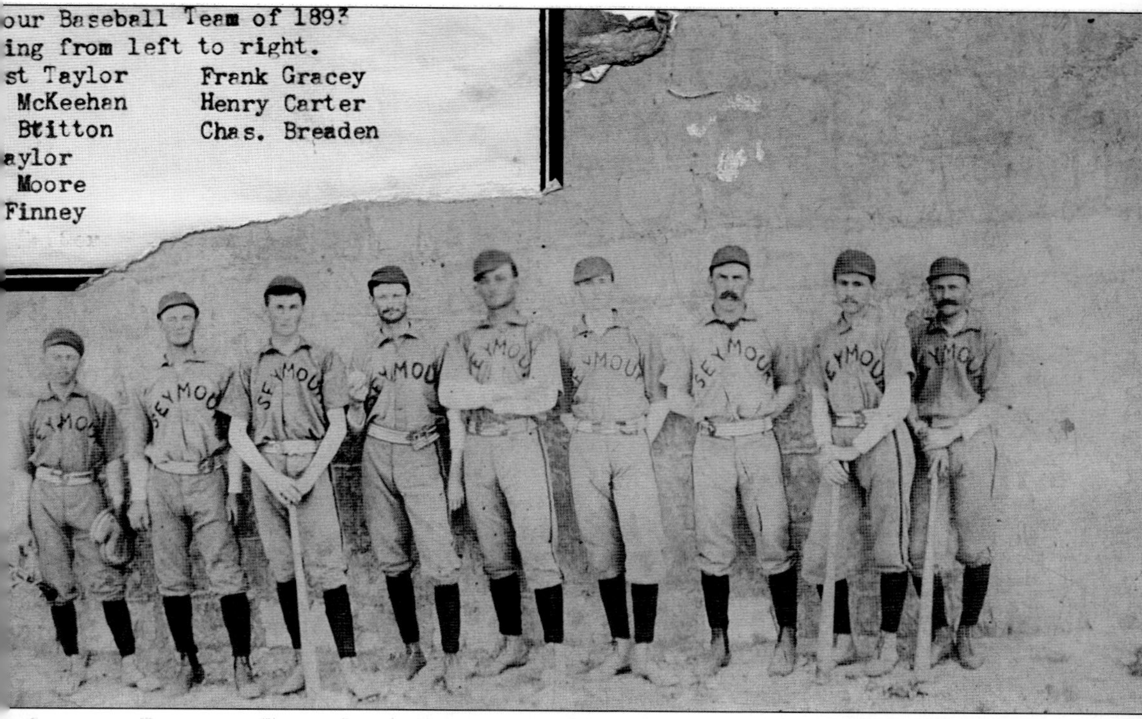

SEYMOUR BASEBALL TEAM. Baseball was a popular sport in Seymour and the surrounding communities during the 1890s. The Cache Creek community fielded strong teams, and two players from Cache Creek—Powell Burnett and Troy Stallings—went on to play professional baseball. Burnett ultimately played for the New York Giants and Stalling for the Brooklyn Dodgers. From left to right in this photograph of the Seymour team are Forrest Taylor, Claud McKeehan, Bill Britton, George Caylor, Billy Moore, John Finney, Frank Gracey, Henry Carter, and Charley Breaden. (Courtesy of Baylor County Museum.)

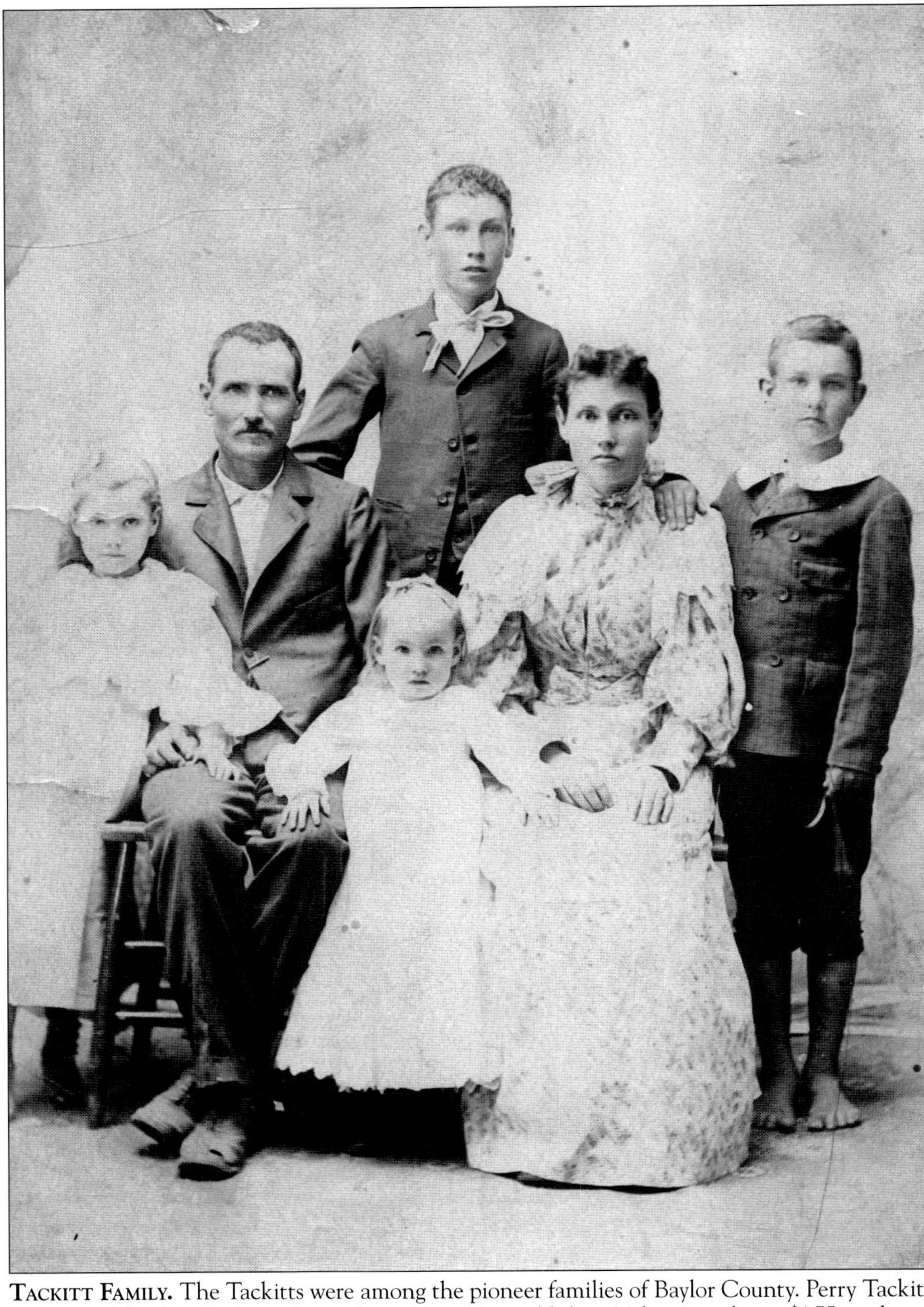

TACKITT FAMILY. The Tackitts were among the pioneer families of Baylor County. Perry Tackitt was one of the first blacksmiths in the county. He could shoe 30 horses a day at $1.75 per horse and also made branding irons, bridle bits, and spurs for the local ranchers. According to *Salt Pork and Sirloin* (vol. 1, page 256), he was also the first groom in the county when he married Matilda Hethie Miller. (Courtesy of Sharon Gaines.)

Two

WESTERN TRAIL DAYS

Baylor County owes its initial growth to the development of the Western Trail and the great cattle drives. Seymour was a stop and supply point for this trail. The dust created by over seven million longhorn cattle was on the horizon when the last of the buffalo were driven form North Central Texas. The drives on the Western Trail formed not only the basis of the county's prosperity but also the developmental seed for the nascent cattle industry and the county's ranching heritage.

The first Hereford bull to come to the county was brought to the Irby and Davis place on Deep Creek, southeast of Seymour. His name was Mote. The first black cattle introduced in the county were a long-haired breed called Galloway. European shorthorns were introduced into America with the fencing of the open range.

An enduring tradition that sprang from the Western Trail was the Seymour Rodeo and Old Settler's Reunion. First held in 1896, it was the suggestion of Seymour resident and retired Pitchfork (King County) cowboy Jeff Scott. The first reunion and rodeo lasted three days, closed with a grand ball, and drew 10,000 people. The second reunion in 1897 was even more spectacular, lasted four days, and attracted 20,000 people. One of the major draws was Chief Quanah Parker, accompanied by one of his wives and 300 to 500 of his braves. W.J. Sullivan, a Texas Ranger, was brought in from Austin to maintain order. During the 1940s, the rodeo was large enough to have two arenas working simultaneously. Bucking events were held on the east side and roping events on the west.

The Old Settlers Rodeo and Reunion still reunites people from the far corners of the globe to visit with friends and renew old acquaintances.

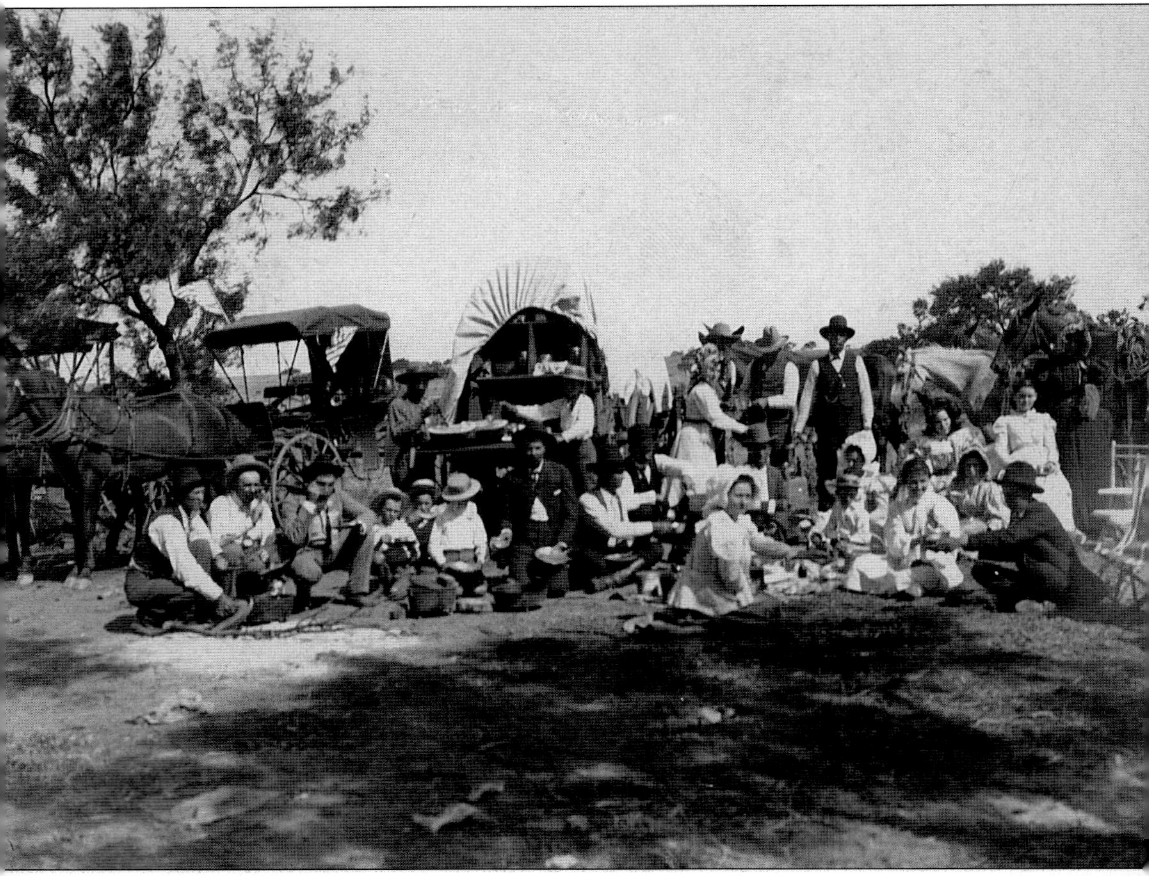

The G.S. Plants Family at Camp. The Plants family was prominent in the early development of West Texas and Seymour. G.S. Plants came to Seymour in 1890, and in 1891, he became the cashier in the newly founded First National Bank. In 1895, Plants was named to the board of directors. In 1915, he assumed the office of president and served in this position until his death in 1939. This photograph was taken in Haskell County during the Haskell Cowboy Reunion in 1898. (Courtesy of Baylor County Museum.)

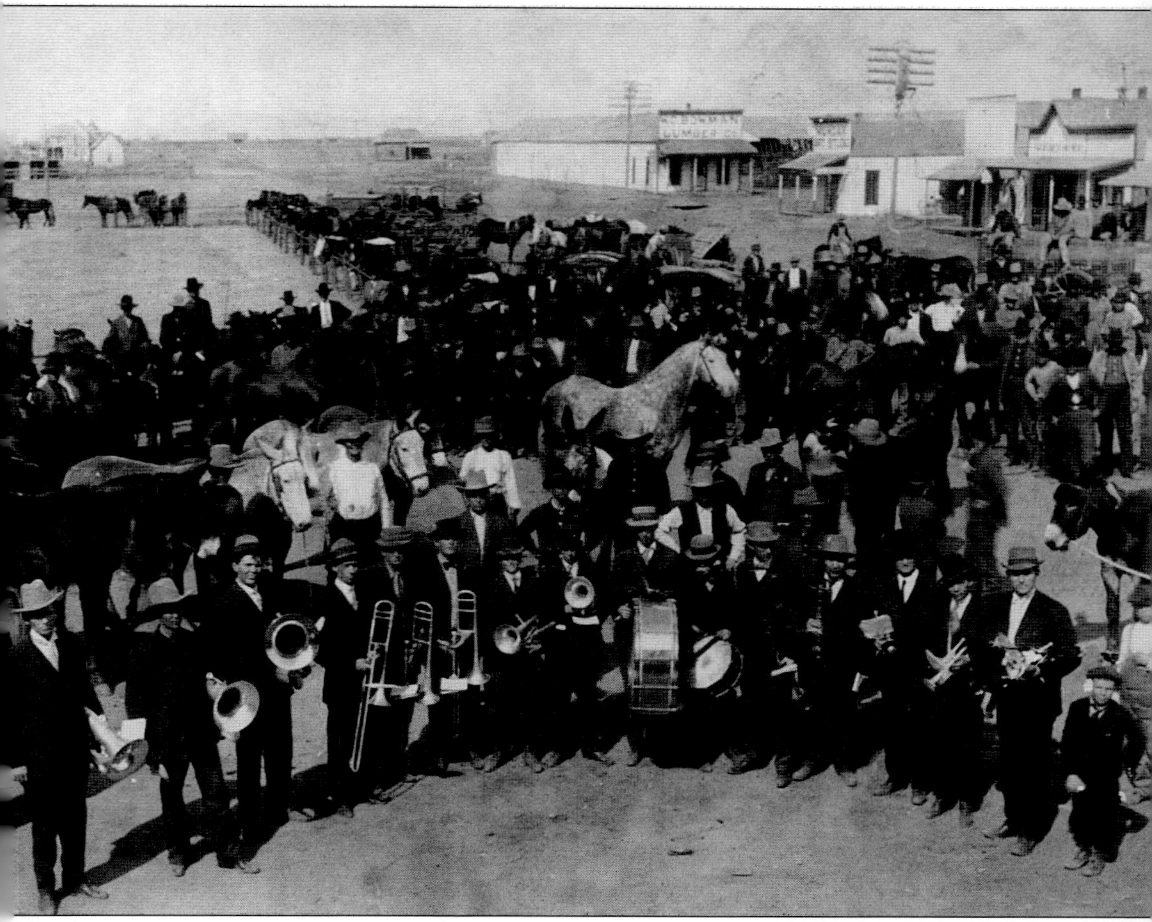

BOMARTON BREEDERS BARN. During World War I, many hundreds of horses and mules were bought out of Baylor County for duty in the armed forces. The presence of the 15-member band indicates sale of these animals was cause for celebration. In the early 20th century, Bomarton had two brass bands. One was composed of farmers and merchants who played for dances and bohemian wedding celebrations. (Courtesy of Margaret Higgins Johnson.)

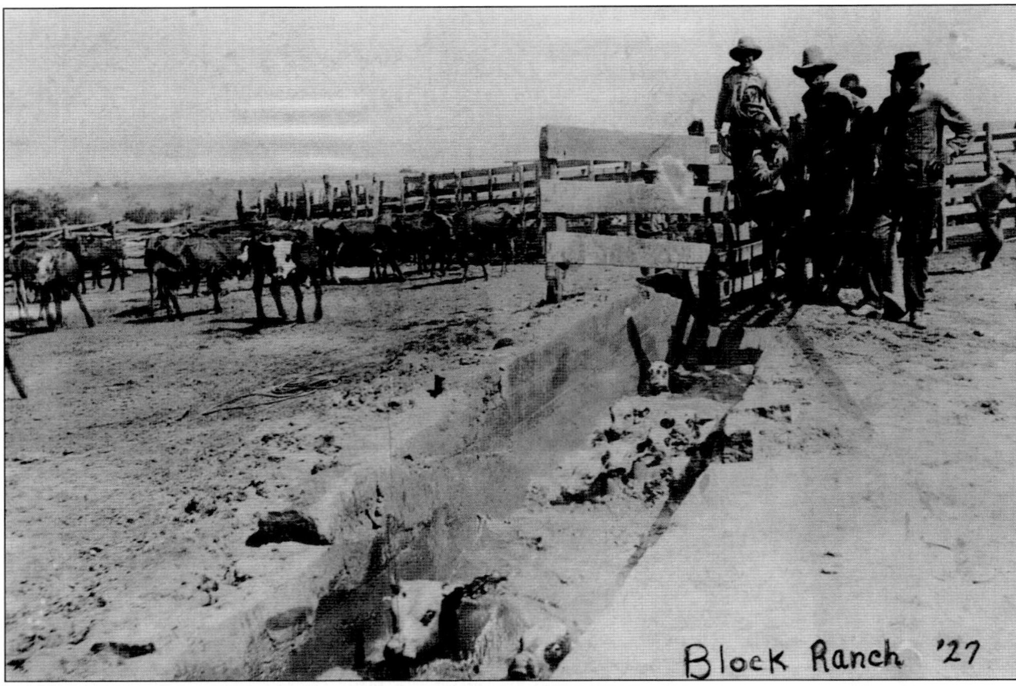

Dipping Vat on Three Block Ranch. Around 1890, tick fever was causing huge losses in Texas cattle herds. The United States Department of Agriculture (USDA) passed a tick eradication program in 1906 requiring inspection and dipping in problem areas. The disease was successfully eradicated in 1943. Dipping vats were usually about 20 feet long, two-and-one-half to three feet wide, and deep enough for the cattle to be completely submerged. They were lined with cement and filled with medicated water. This dipping vat was on W.H. Portwood's Three Block Ranch in southern Baylor County in 1927. The cowboys are unidentified. (Courtesy of Sammie Portwood Morris.)

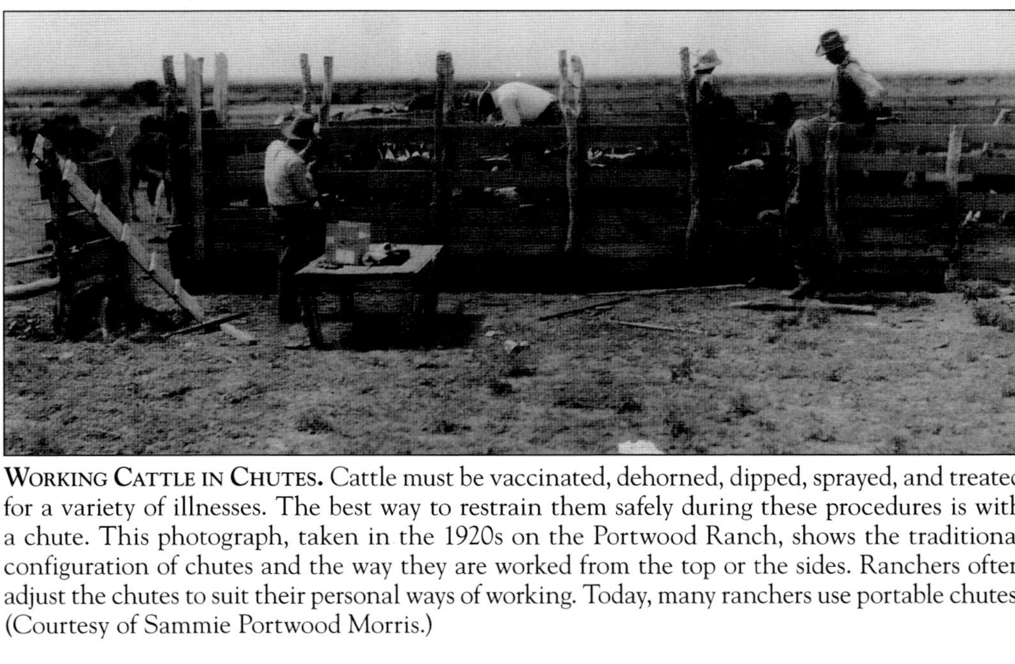

Working Cattle in Chutes. Cattle must be vaccinated, dehorned, dipped, sprayed, and treated for a variety of illnesses. The best way to restrain them safely during these procedures is with a chute. This photograph, taken in the 1920s on the Portwood Ranch, shows the traditional configuration of chutes and the way they are worked from the top or the sides. Ranchers often adjust the chutes to suit their personal ways of working. Today, many ranchers use portable chutes. (Courtesy of Sammie Portwood Morris.)

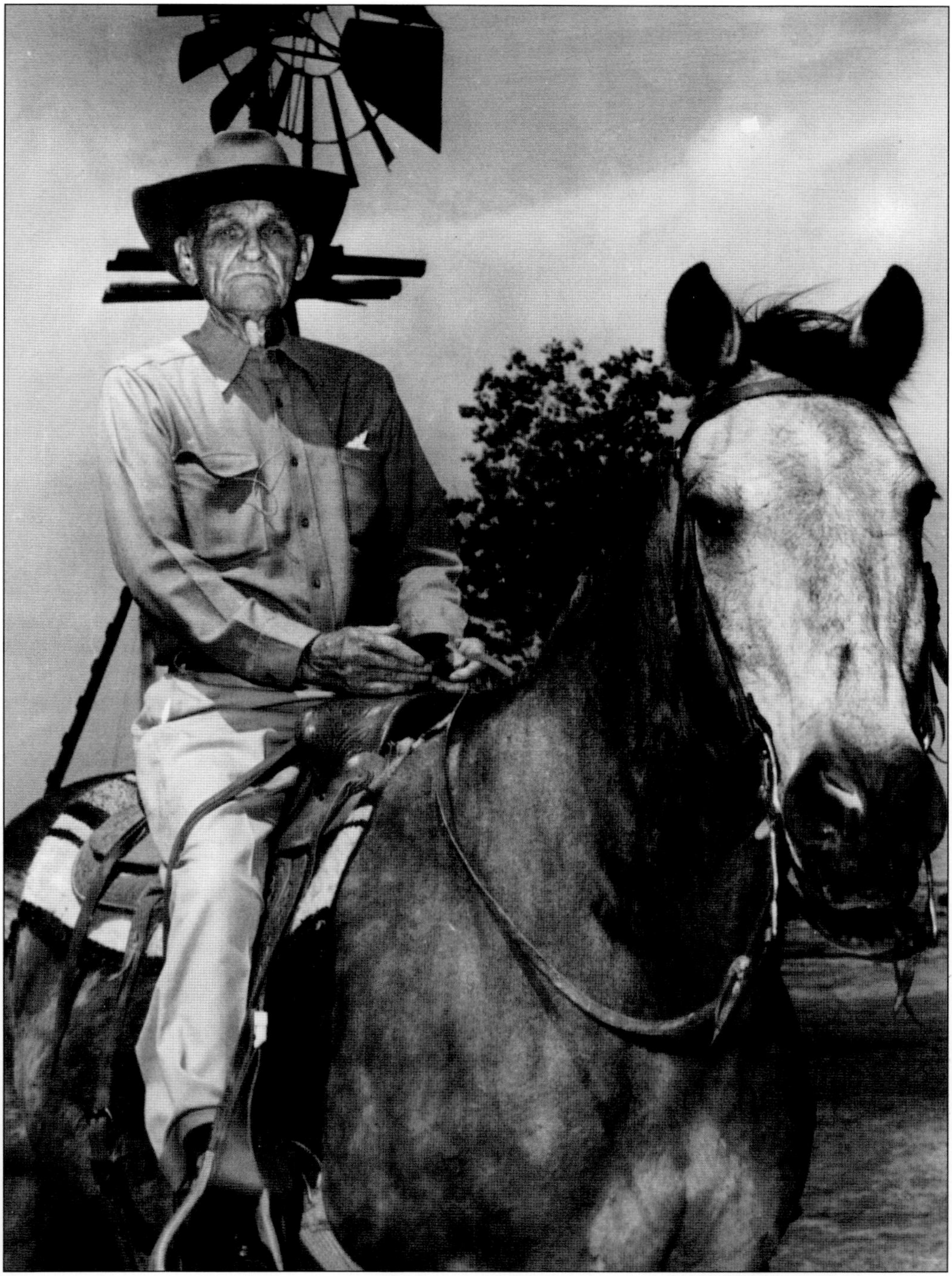

PIONEER RESIDENT FRANK ALLEN. Pictured is Frank Allen on his faithful horse Moonshine. Allen was still cowboying at age 92 until his horse fell with him shortly after this photograph was taken. Buying 14,000 acres of patent land in Baylor and Throckmorton Counties from the state of Texas at $2 an acre, his family settled here in 1878. The original Hereford herd was purchased from Frank Houston, brother of Sam Houston, and driven from Brenham, Texas. (Courtesy of Sammie Portwood Morris.)

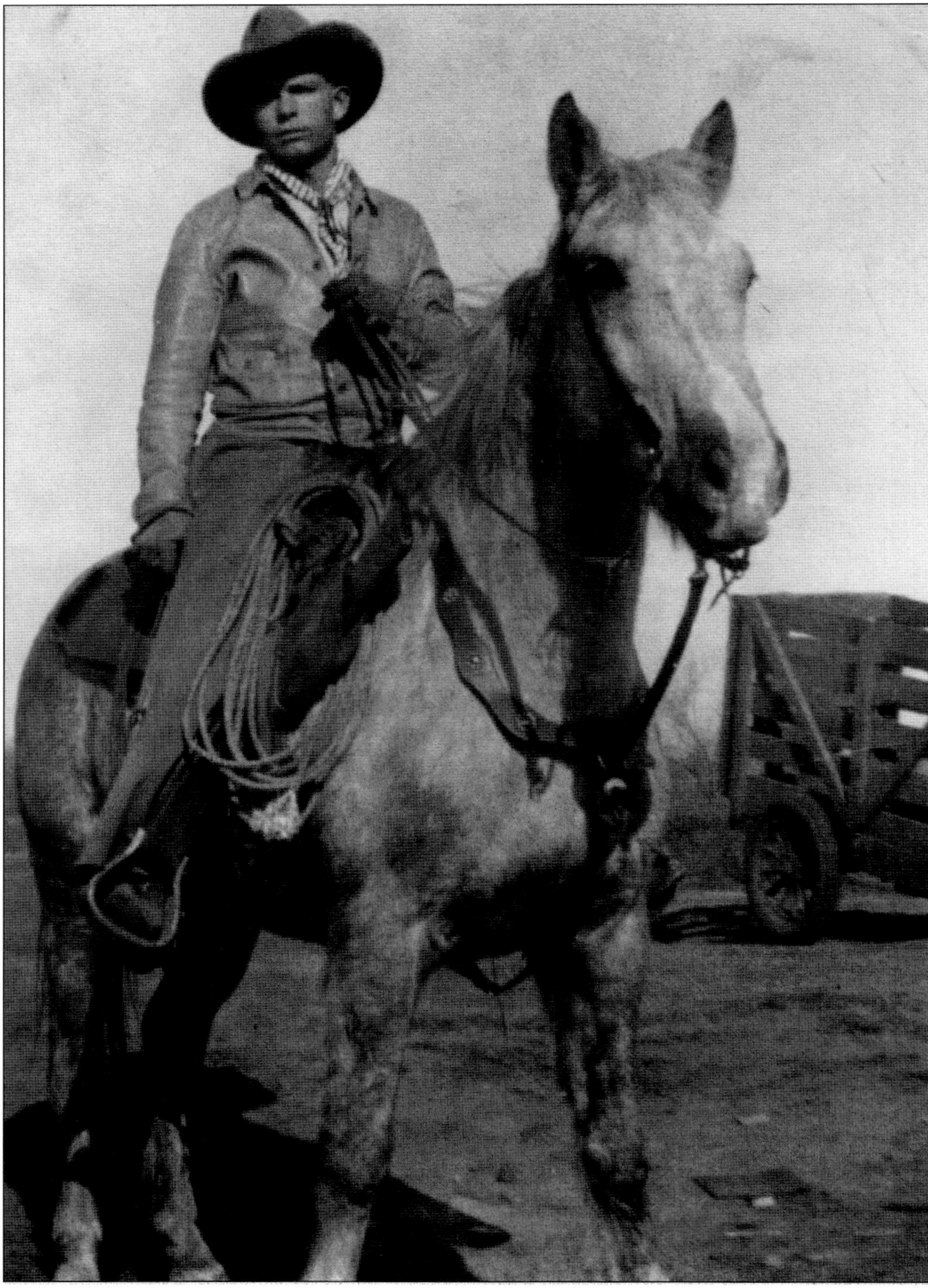

Rancher Sam Portwood. Sam Portwood is equipped for a day on the range. This photograph was taken at the Stevens Ranch in Baylor County, now part of the Portwood holdings. J.W. Stevens purchased a large tract of land in the Round Timbers community in Baylor County. By 1884, he had 3,600 head of cattle and owned 7,000 acres of land with an additional lease of 6,000 acres. (Courtesy of Sammie Portwood Morris.)

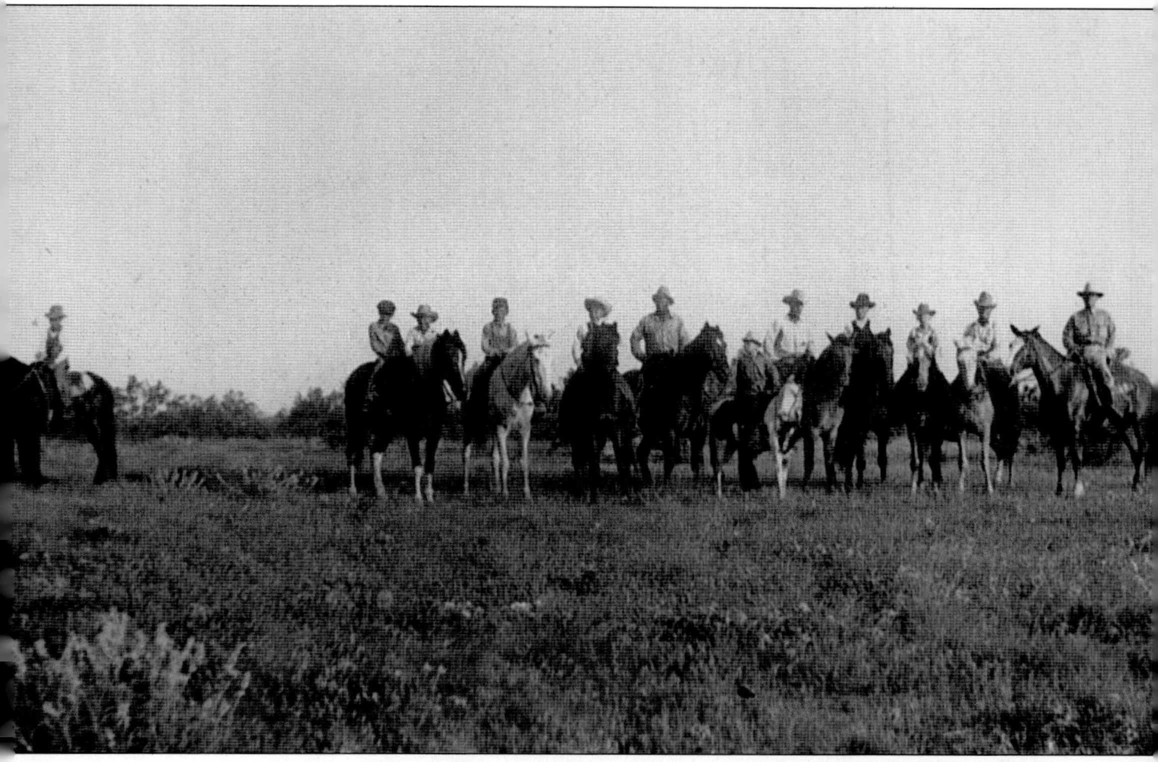

Riders on the Stout Ranch. This timeless photograph of riders was taken on the Stout Ranch in the southwest part of the county in the 1930s. Near the end of the 19th century, over 1,700 cattle brands were registered with the county clerk in Baylor County. Many operating ranches in Baylor County today had their origins in the late 19th or early 20th centuries. (Courtesy of Mac Stout.)

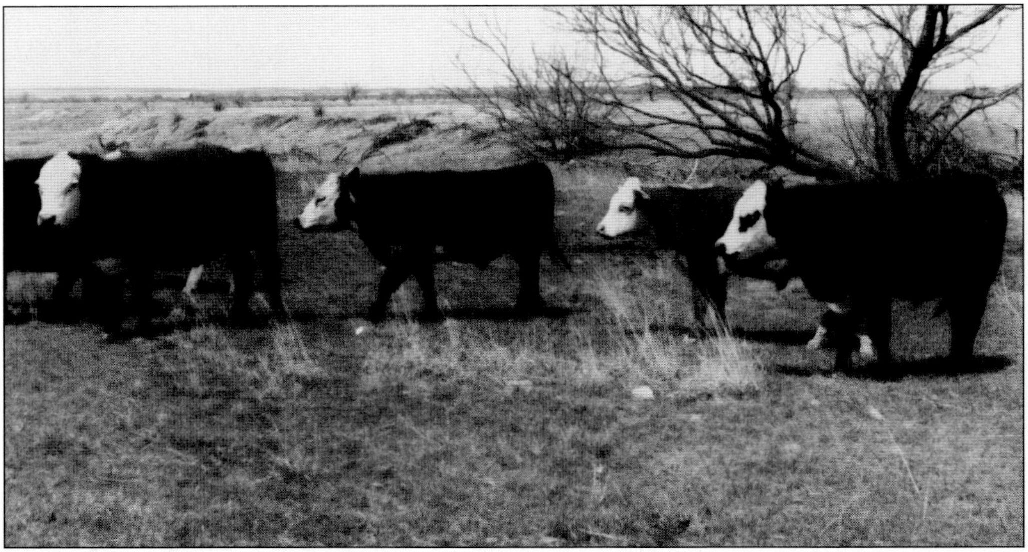

Black Baldy Cattle. These stocker calves in a pasture are known as Black Baldies because of their white face. Black Baldies are the result of Hereford cattle crossed with Angus cattle. They are very hardy cattle and popular with today's cowmen. The term *stocker* refers to calves that are purchased as weanlings, overwintered for weight gain, and then resold. (Courtesy of Baylor County Office of the USDA.)

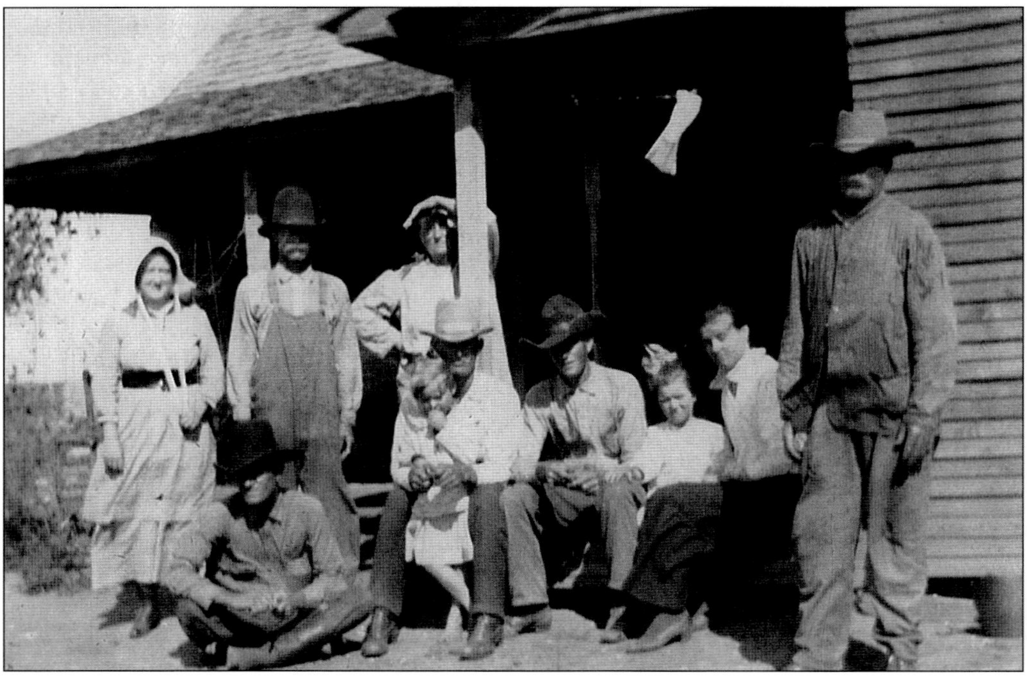

Echols Family Homestead. John W. and Mary Woods Echols and their children moved from Hale to Baylor County in about 1920. Many families from this era were large, and the Echols raised seven sons and two daughters. A bachelor brother Henry also lived with them. John ran a café for several years, and it was known for its exceptional chili, which was cooked by Willie Mae, an Echols daughter. John eventually returned to farming in the Round Timber community. (Courtesy of Mac Stout.)

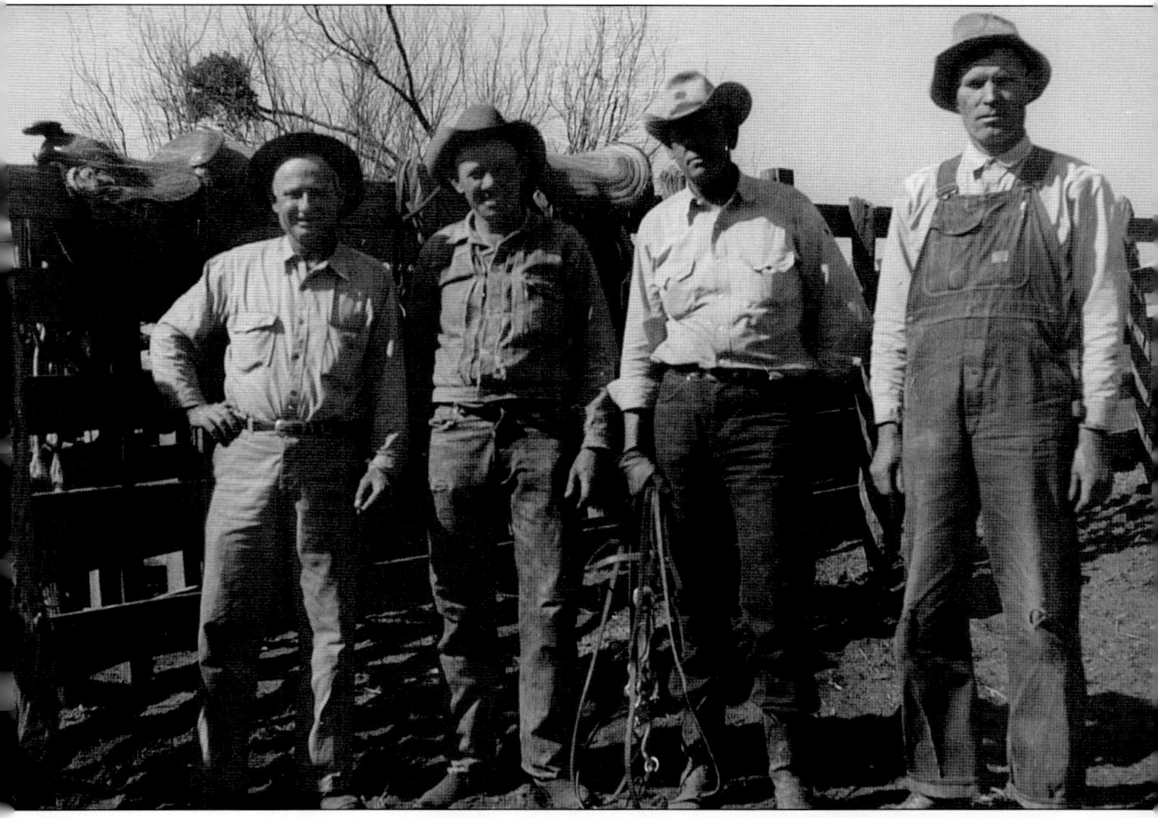

Three Cowboys and a Farmer. In this photograph, taken by Mrs. Charles Moorhouse, four men have just finished running cattle through the chutes seen in the background. Then, as today, neighbors often helped each other with work, especially during shipping and branding, when extra manpower was needed. From left to right are Frank Studer, L.D. Burnett, Deaton Moorhouse, and Oliver Henyan. (Courtesy of Larry Burnett.)

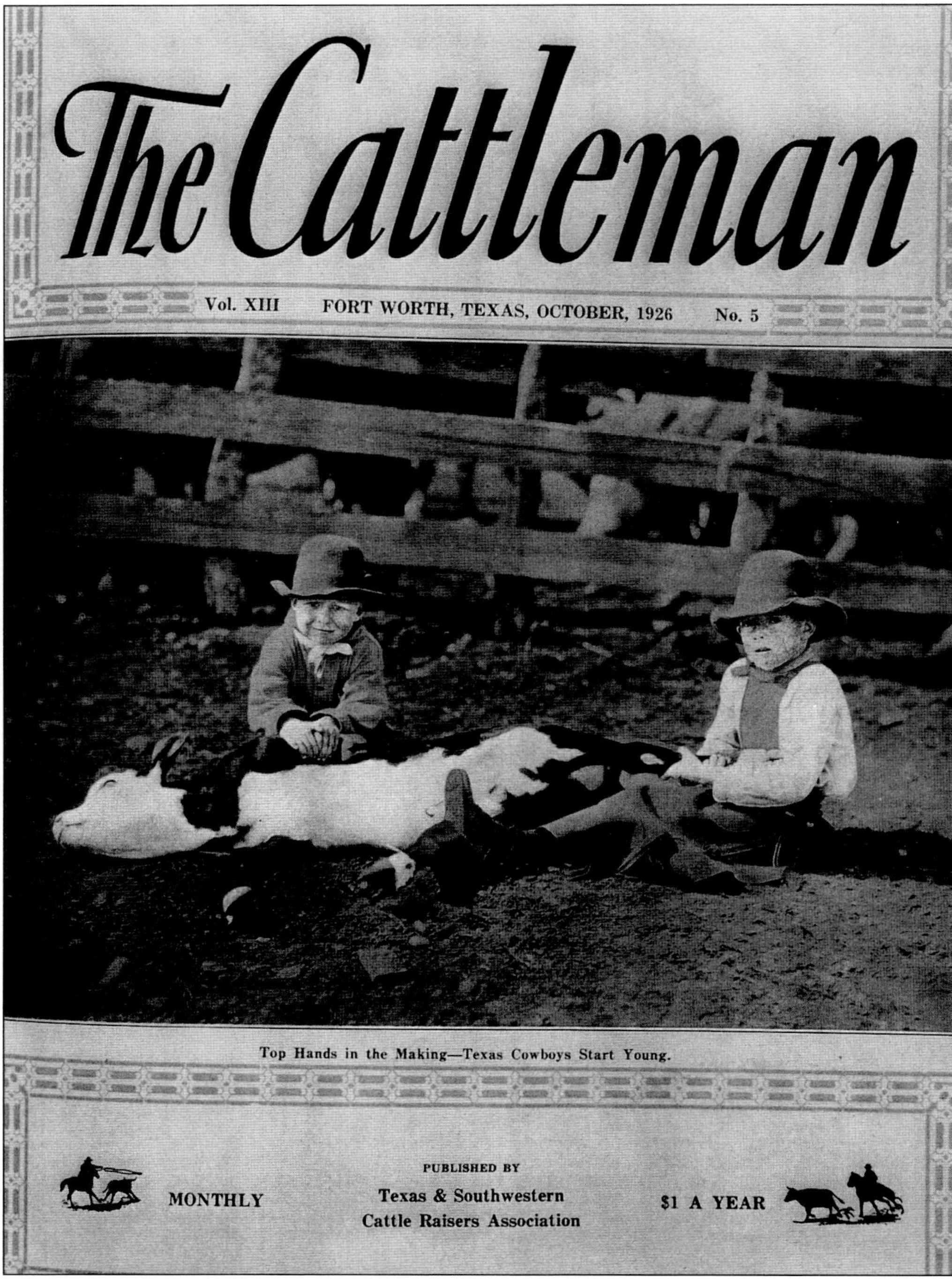

Cover of 1926 *The Cattleman* Magazine. This cover features Stevens cousins Elmer Jr. and John Vance, son of Roy Stevens, helping with branding on the Stevens Ranch. The caption reads, "Top Hands in the Making—Texas Cowboys Start Young." Branding is still the best means of identifying cattle. *The Cattleman* magazine is a publication of the Texas and Southwestern Cattle Raisers Association (TSCRA). (Courtesy of Eta Mae Stevens Moore.)

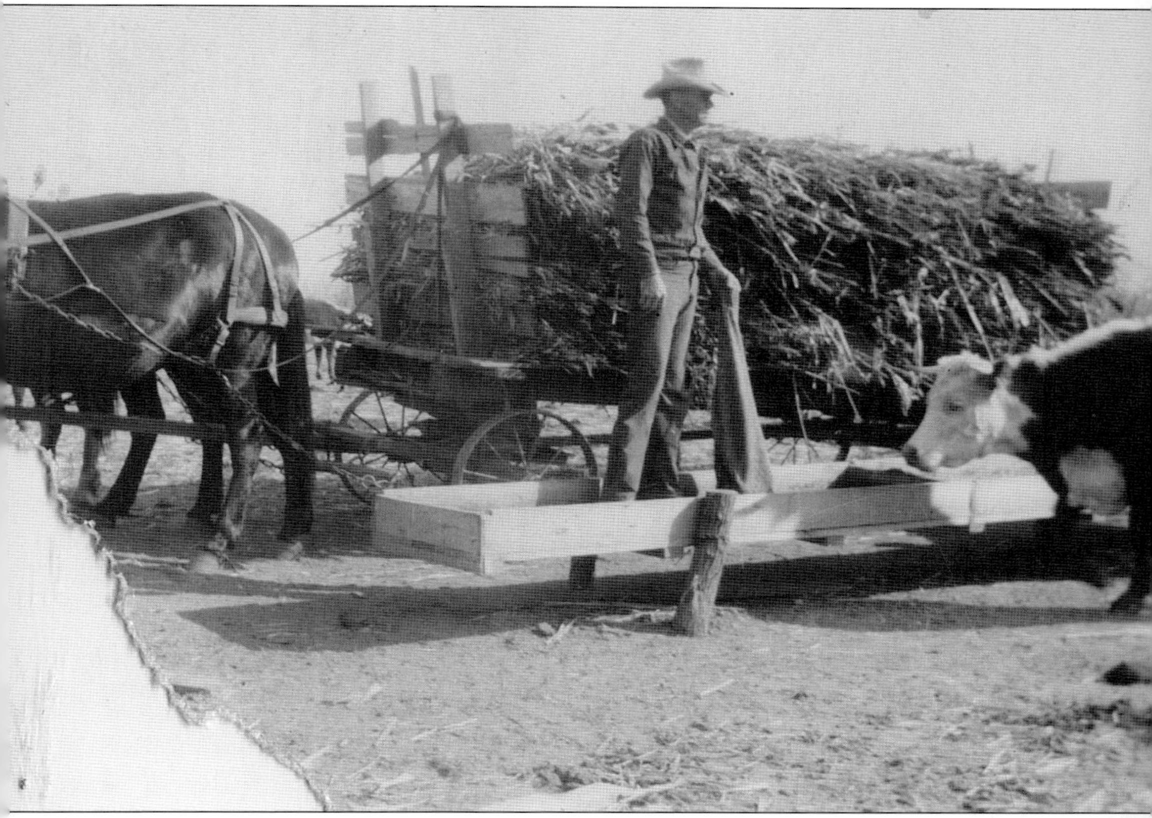

Wayne Sims Feeding Cake and Cane. Sims has just finished pouring cottonseed cake into a cattle feeder. Cake is a by-product of cotton production. Cottonseeds and hulls are ground up, milled, and compressed into pellets. The feed wagon behind Sims is piled with a type of sorghum cane, possibly red top, which was used as forage for cattle. (Courtesy of Margaret Higgins Johnson.)

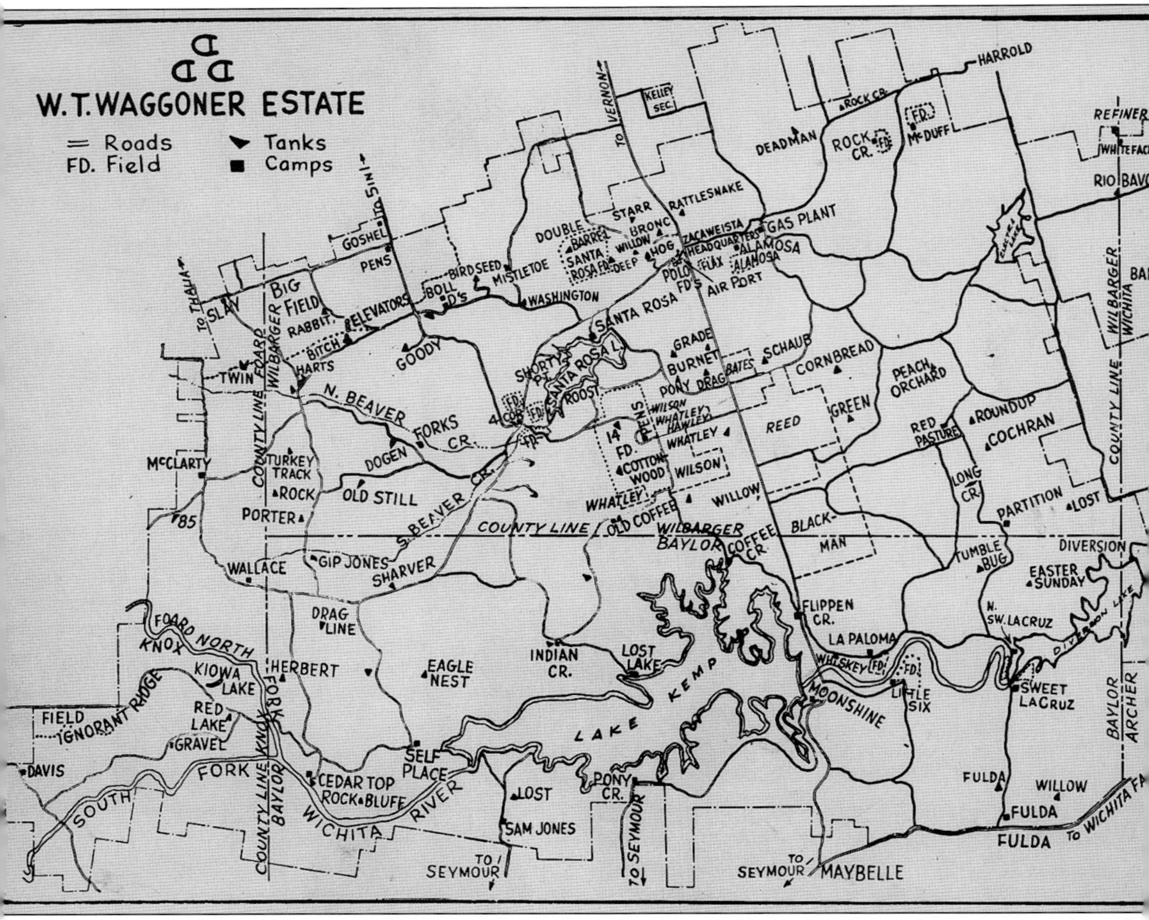

Waggoner Estate Map. The Waggoner Ranch was established by Daniel Waggoner. Though its headquarters are in Wilbarger County, the ranch holds nearly 200,000 acres and Lake Kemp in Baylor County. The ranch's famous 3Ds-in-reverse brand came into usage about 1866. Merrick Davis and Tom Irby sold their ranches on the Big Wichita River to Waggoner in 1900, but they retained 21 sections of land in Baylor County. (Courtesy of Baylor County Museum.)

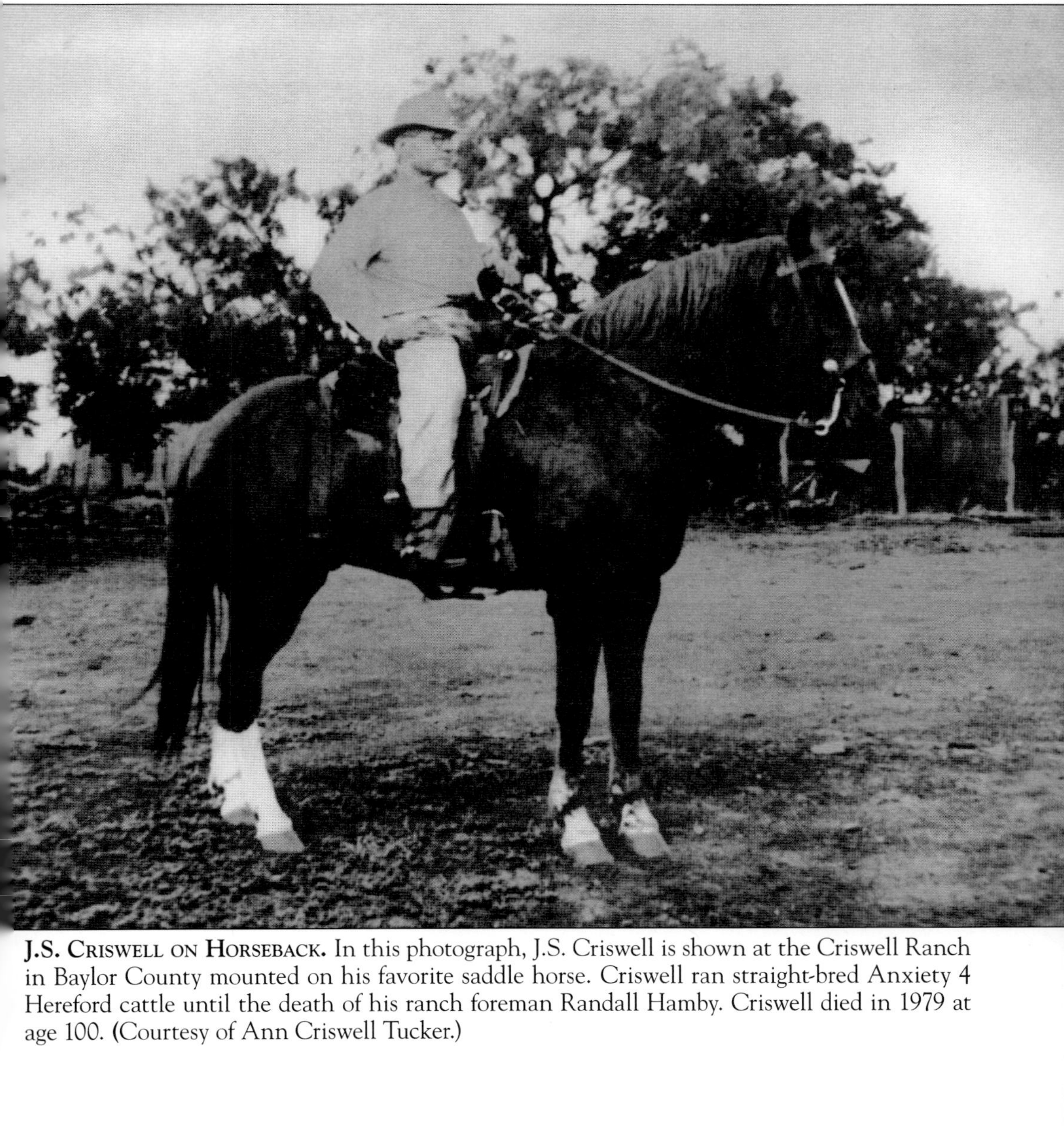

J.S. CRISWELL ON HORSEBACK. In this photograph, J.S. Criswell is shown at the Criswell Ranch in Baylor County mounted on his favorite saddle horse. Criswell ran straight-bred Anxiety 4 Hereford cattle until the death of his ranch foreman Randall Hamby. Criswell died in 1979 at age 100. (Courtesy of Ann Criswell Tucker.)

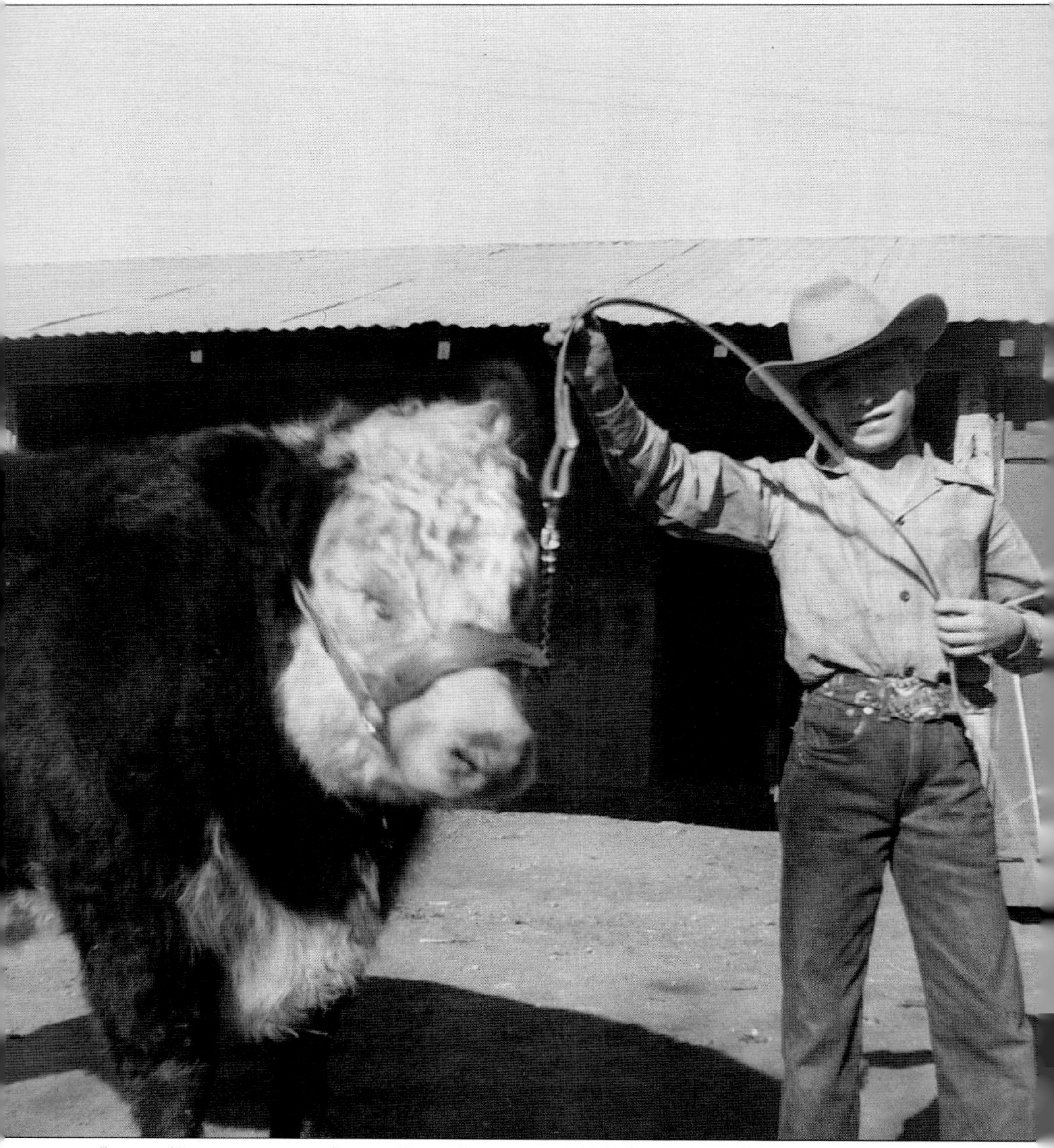

Larry Burnett with Steer. Larry Burnett, age 10, prepares to show one of the Carter Taylor Ranch steers at the Baylor County Steer Show in 1954. The show later evolved into the Baylor County Junior Livestock Show, which today has added many more livestock divisions, including hogs, poultry, and rabbits. Several years ago, heifers (unbred females) were also added as a category. (Courtesy of Larry Burnett.)

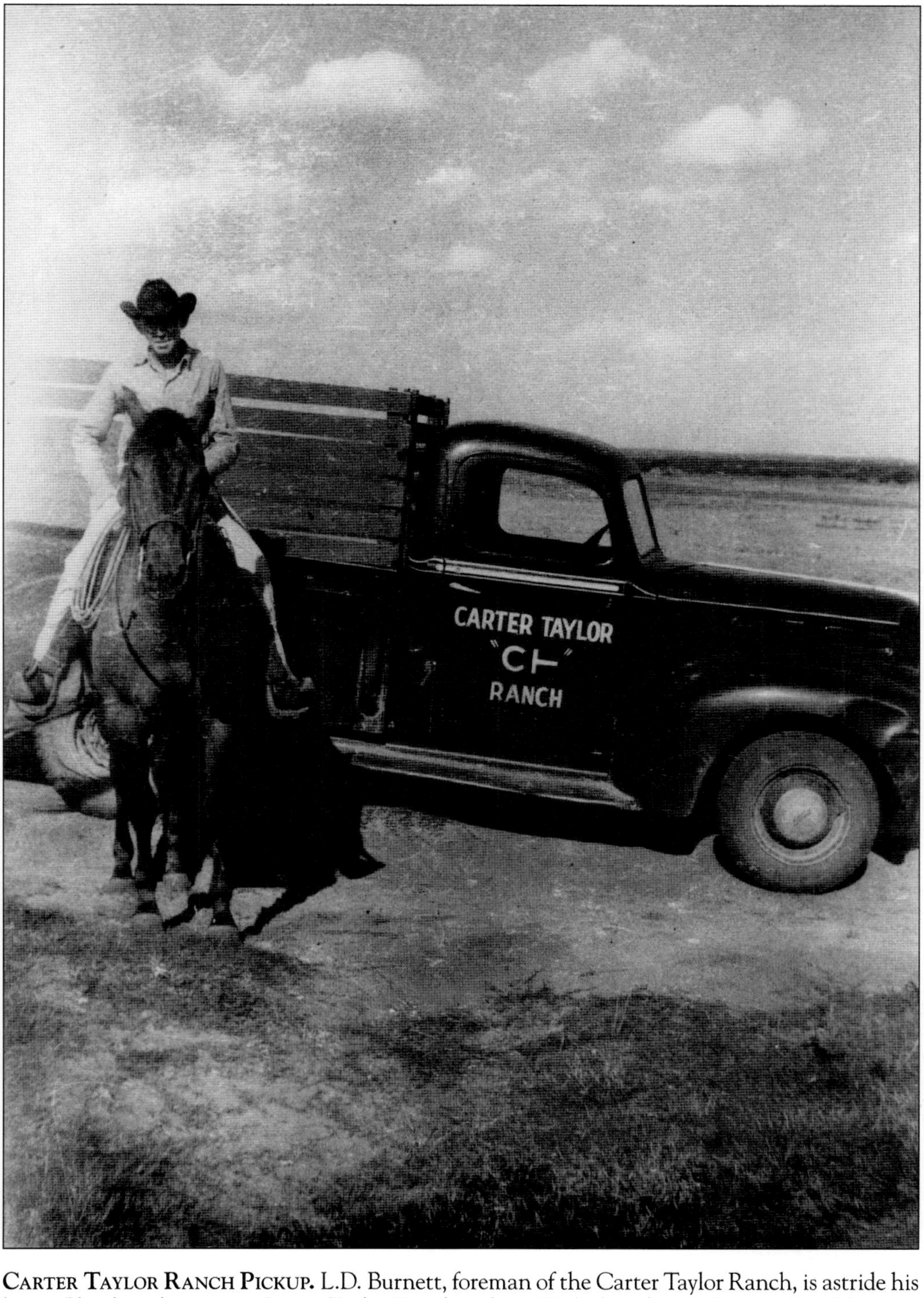

CARTER TAYLOR RANCH PICKUP. L.D. Burnett, foreman of the Carter Taylor Ranch, is astride his horse Chuck and next to a Carter Taylor Ranch pickup. With the advent of mechanized farming came use of these trucks. Pickups and horses are still indispensable on today's working ranches. The Carter Taylor Ranch was founded by judge Carter Taylor, and the brand was first registered in 1882. (Courtesy of L.D. Burnett.)

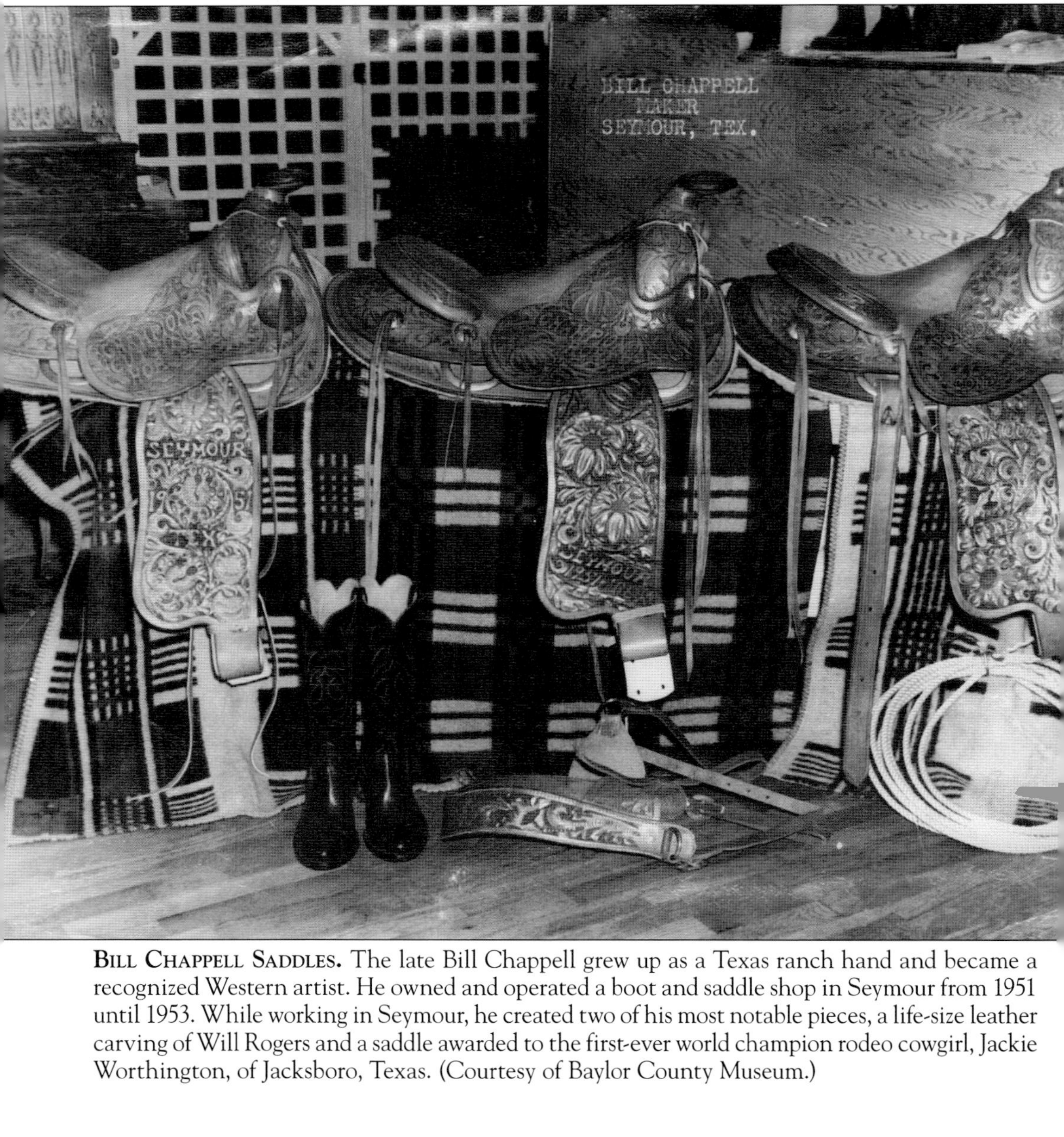

Bill Chappell Saddles. The late Bill Chappell grew up as a Texas ranch hand and became a recognized Western artist. He owned and operated a boot and saddle shop in Seymour from 1951 until 1953. While working in Seymour, he created two of his most notable pieces, a life-size leather carving of Will Rogers and a saddle awarded to the first-ever world champion rodeo cowgirl, Jackie Worthington, of Jacksboro, Texas. (Courtesy of Baylor County Museum.)

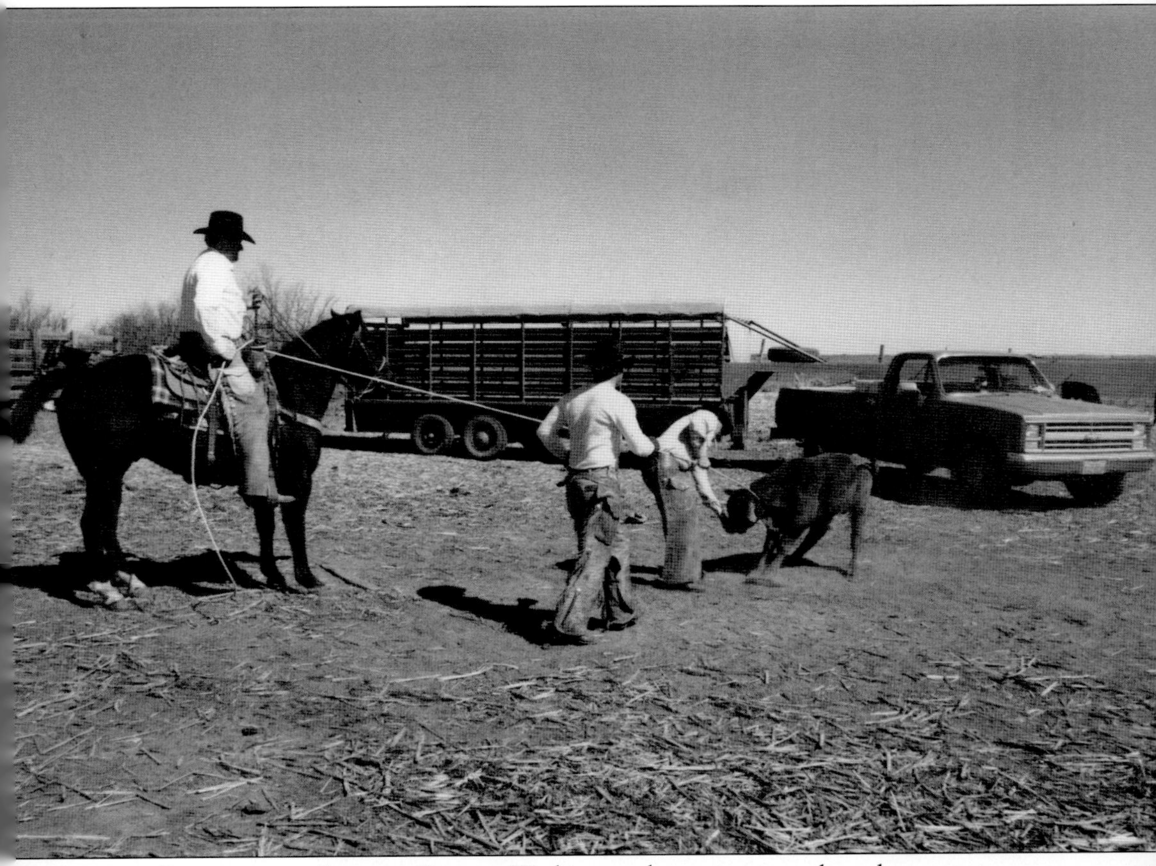

Working Cattle at the Peacock Ranch. Working cattle requires a good cow horse, strong men, and teamwork. In this photograph, Ronnie Sagle (mounted) has roped a calf for doctoring. The other two men are unidentified. The Peacock Ranch is located in the northwest part of the county where the elevation varies from mesquite flats to cedar breaks. (Courtesy of Dixie Peacock.)

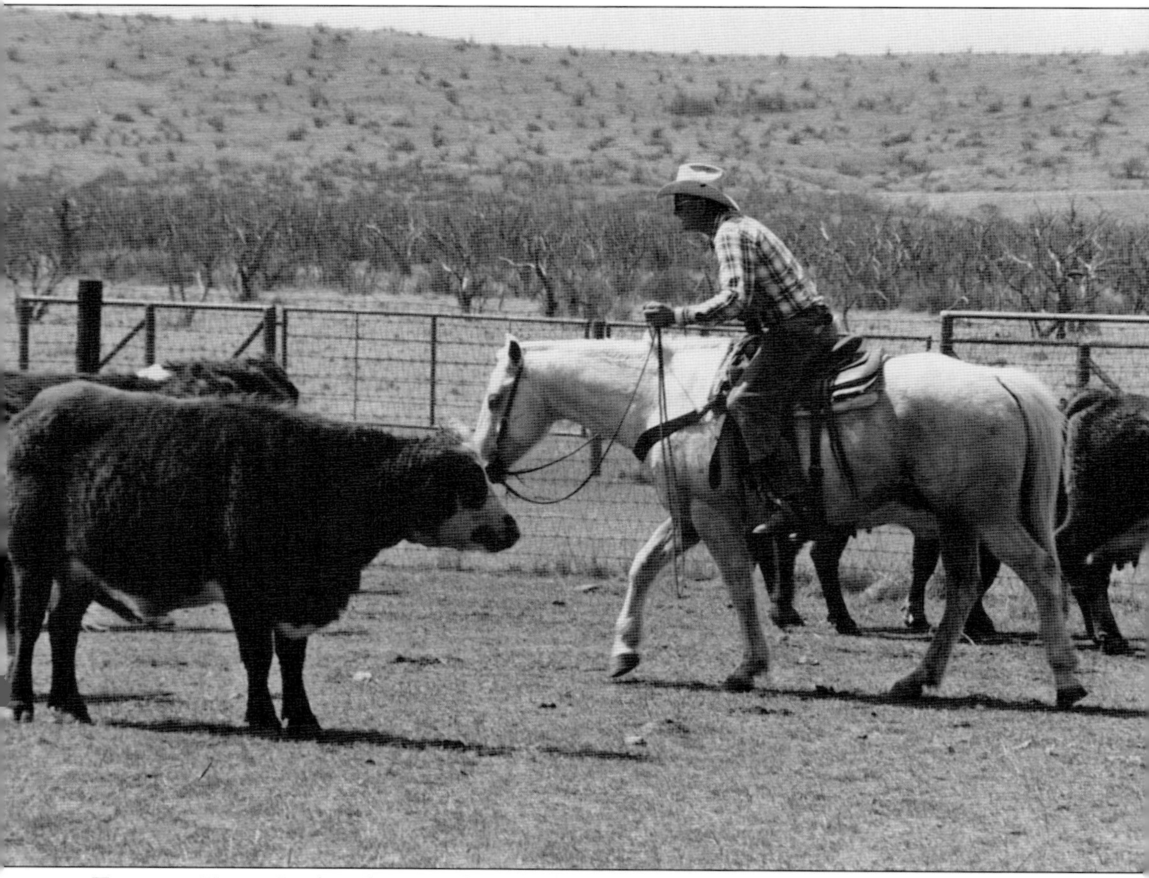

Taking a Tally. In this photograph, an unidentified rider is attempting to get an accurate count of the number of cattle in a pen. His horse is moving slowly and quietly, and the man is standing slightly in the saddle trying to make sure he has a good view of all the cattle. Keeping accurate counts of cattle is part of the daily check. Missing cattle could mean that a thief is at work or that cattle are lost, sick, lame, or in some way not able to move with the herd. (Courtesy of Baylor County Office of the USDA.)

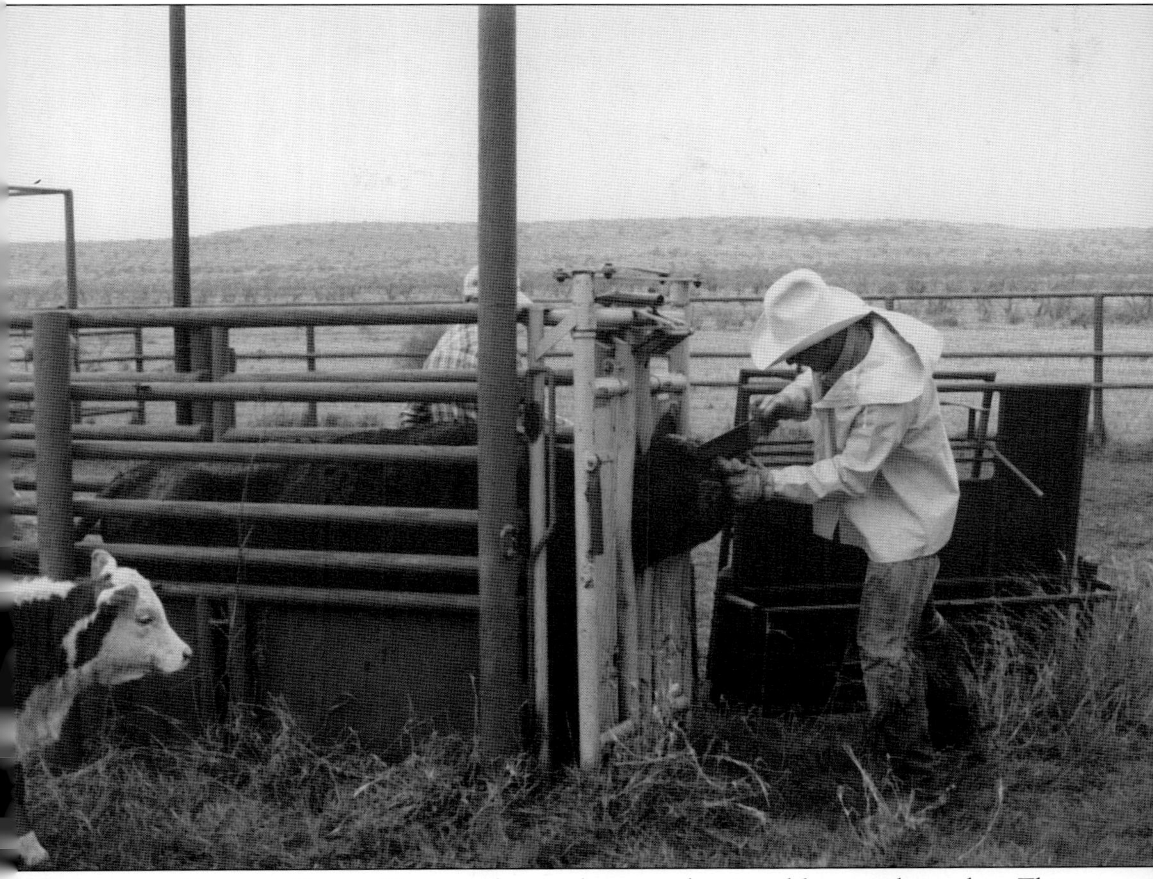

DEHORNING CALVES IN CHUTE. Horns are frequently removed or tipped from yearling calves. This is done for both safety and economic reasons. Chutes were one of the first laborsaving devices developed after the closing of the open range. They also provide a safe method of restraining cattle for treatment of injury or vaccinations. (Courtesy of Dixie Peacock.)

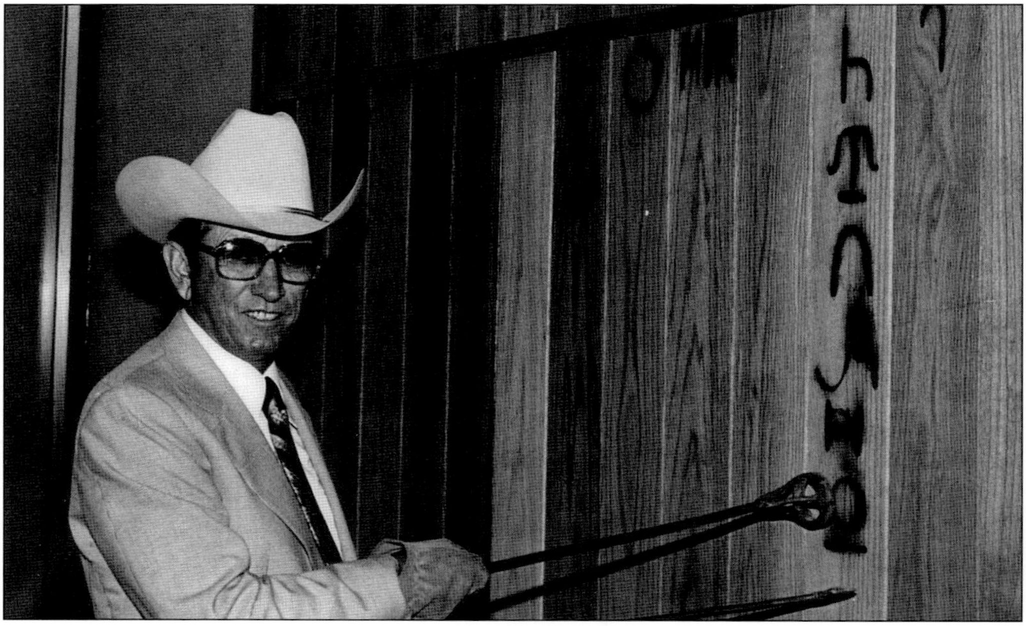

Wall of Brands at Texas A&M. In the 1970s, Texas A&M University honored the state's ranching heritage by asking 10 ranchers from each county to place their brands on a wall. In this photograph, Claude Cowan Jr. is placing his brand on the paneling. The other Baylor County brands shown, from top to bottom, belong to Lawrence Harmel, brand first registered in 1944; the Hashknife, 1881; the Arledge Ranch, 1934; John A. Young Ranch, 1935; George Higgins, 1916; and Claude Cowan Ranch, 1915. (Courtesy of Baylor County Museum.)

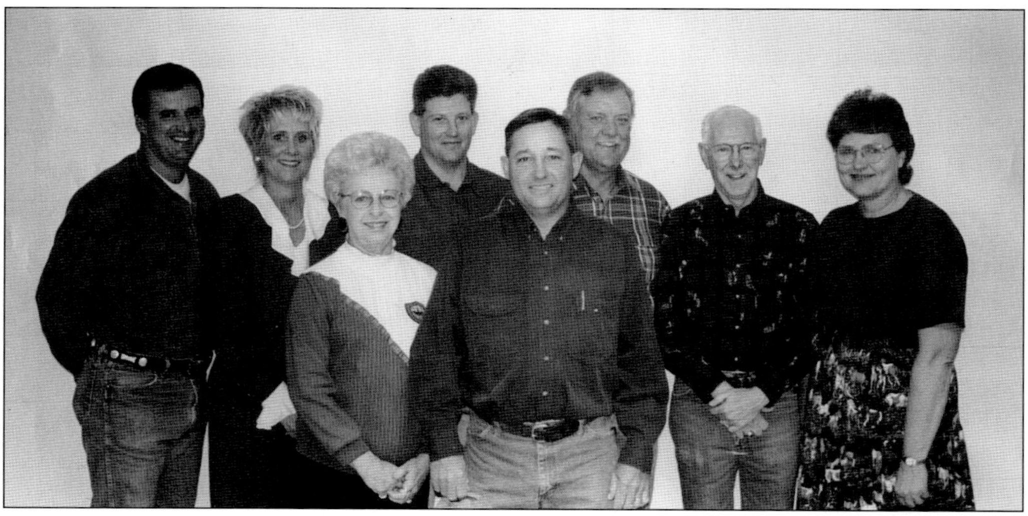

Baylor County Agriculture Day Committee. In 1991, Seymour began to recognize the importance of agriculture to the county with Ag Day. Ag Day is held the second or third Tuesday in April at the Cliff Styles Activity Center. There are agricultural-related booths, door prizes, a catered lunch, and speakers. Noted speakers have included Pres. George W. Bush and Susan Combs and Todd Staples, both Texas agriculture commissioners. Committee members from the mid-1990s pose for a photograph. From left to right are (first row) Joyce Green and John Studer; (second row) Brad Goble, Treva McNeil, Nathan Cockrell, Larry Miller, Cyril Keith, and Billie McMorris. (Courtesy of Baylor County office of the USDA.)

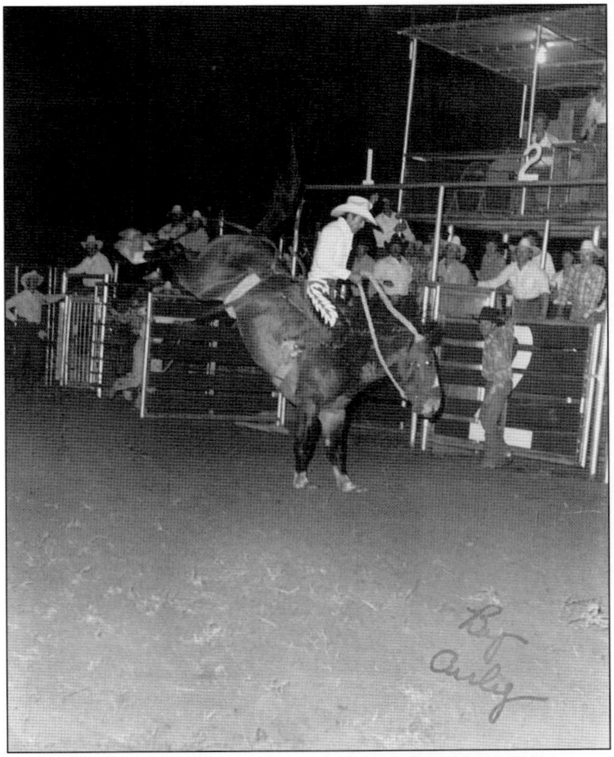

BENNY ARCHER RIDING RATTLER. This photograph of Seymour resident Benny Archer was taken during the last rodeo held at the old arena in 1982. Rattler was a 1,400-pound stud owned by Wall Rodeo Company, of Stephenville, Texas. He had not been successfully ridden for two years prior to Benny's eight-second ride. (Photograph by Seymour Rodeo photographer Curly Loving; courtesy of Benny Archer.)

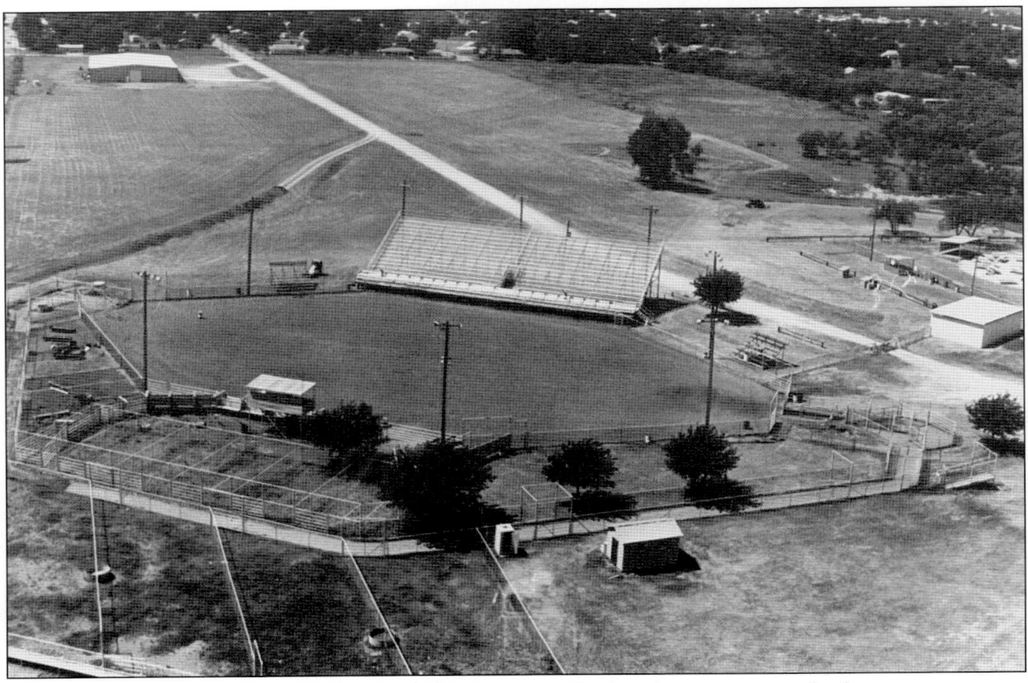

SEYMOUR RODEO ARENA. In July 1983, the Seymour Rodeo Association staked out a new arena near Seymour Creek, site of the 1896 Cowboy Reunion. With donations of money, time, and labor from the community, the arena was completed. The first rodeo in the new facility was held in July 1984. (Courtesy of Baylor County Banner.)

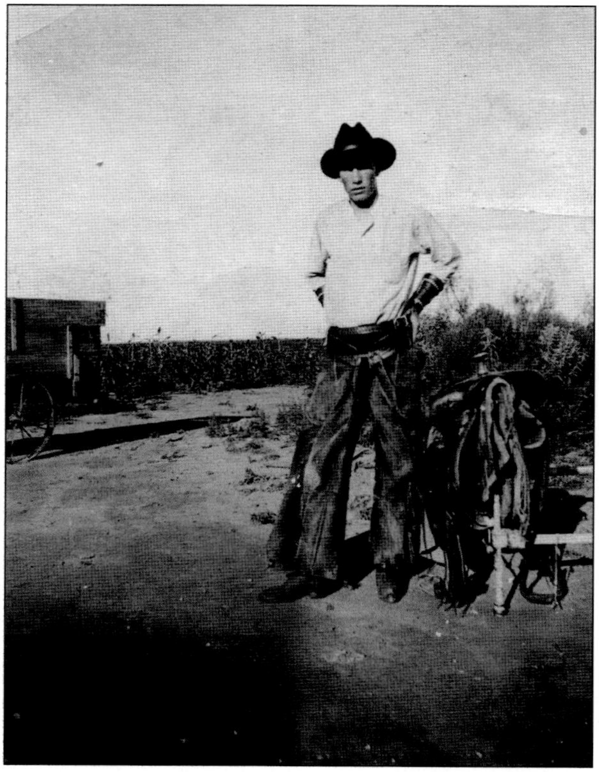

Ben Johnston with his Saddle. This photograph taken in the late 1930s illustrates the timeless and functional nature of cowboy gear and attire. Johnston is wearing Western boots with spurs, worn leather chaps, wrist cuffs, and a good felt Western hat. Though the wrist cuffs are rarely seen on the county's working cowboys today, the rest of the gear, with a few minor variations, has not changed significantly. Ben Johnston cowboyed in the Round Timber community. (Courtesy of Betty and Donald Welch.)

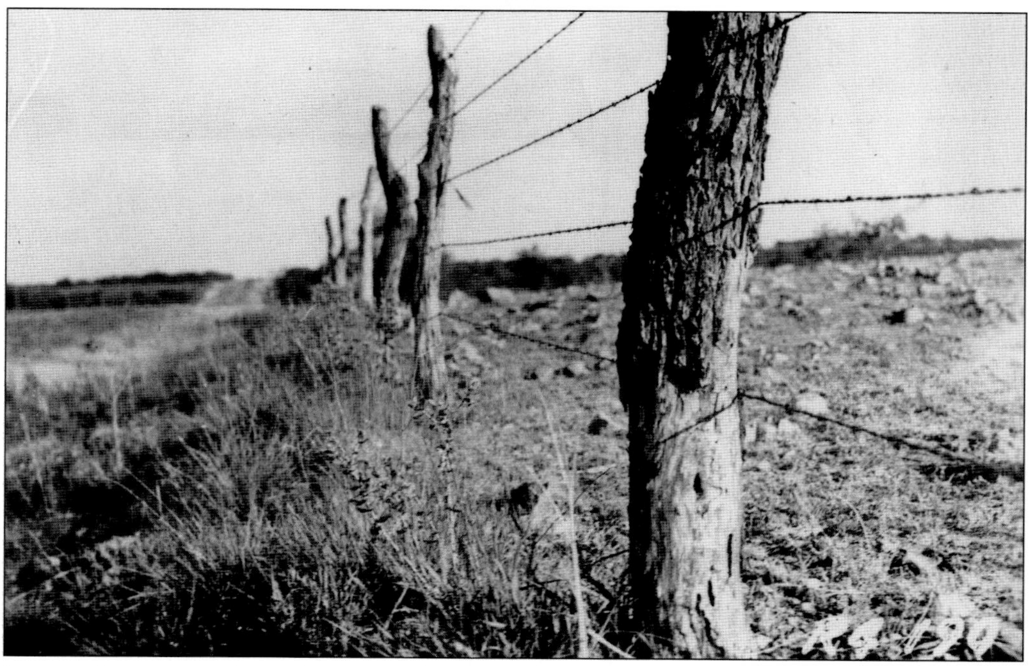

Barbed-Wire Fence. Barbwire was developed to prevent free-range cattle from destroying farmers' crops. Its development signaled the end of the open range, the decline of Texas Longhorn cattle, and the rise of European shorthorns. Fenced land meant new approaches to raising beef. (Courtesy of Baylor County Office of the USDA.)

Three

BUSINESSES

The first businesses in most small West Texas towns were generally the blacksmiths. They were often quickly followed by saddle and harness makers and masons. Seymour was no exception, and J.W. Davenport had the first business in town, a blacksmith shop. Blacksmiths were vital to the growth of the community. They made horseshoes, plowshares, bolts, rings, hooks, and all iron needed for a well-finished wagon or farm implement. Among the first smiths were J.W. Davenport, P.A. Tackitt, W.H. Francis, Sam Killion, and Allen Durham. Charles Hall started a harness and saddle shop in 1880 and sold it to A.R. Benge in 1884. In 1890, W.R. Trawick bought the business, and he sold it to the Baker brothers six years later. The Bakers continued to run it as long as they lived. Ingram and Perrin had the first dry goods shop. It operated in a building located on the northeast corner of the square. This structure also served as a temporary courthouse.

Grocery, hardware, and dry goods stores and hotels soon followed, and, finally, the professional classes arrived. By 1890, Seymour supported all the necessary businesses for a prosperous 19th-century town and was entering a boom period.

The economic upswing began with the Fort Worth and Denver Railway's announcement that it intended to build an extension from the Wichita Falls line into the sparsely settled area southeast of Wichita Falls as a feeder line that could bring cattle and hogs into Fort Worth. At the time, Fort Worth had a packing plant that could handle about 800 head of cattle and 1,200 hogs a day. Seymour boosters went into action and raised $50,000 to offer as an incentive. Regrettably, in 1891, the Texas Legislature passed the Jim Hogg Alien Land Law. This legislation was designed to prevent land speculation by foreign-controlled corporations and stipulated that foreign landholders must become Texas citizens or surrender their land in six years. Panic ensued, the banks cancelled financing and withdrew their loans, and the boom collapsed. Seymour was destined to remain a small West Texas town.

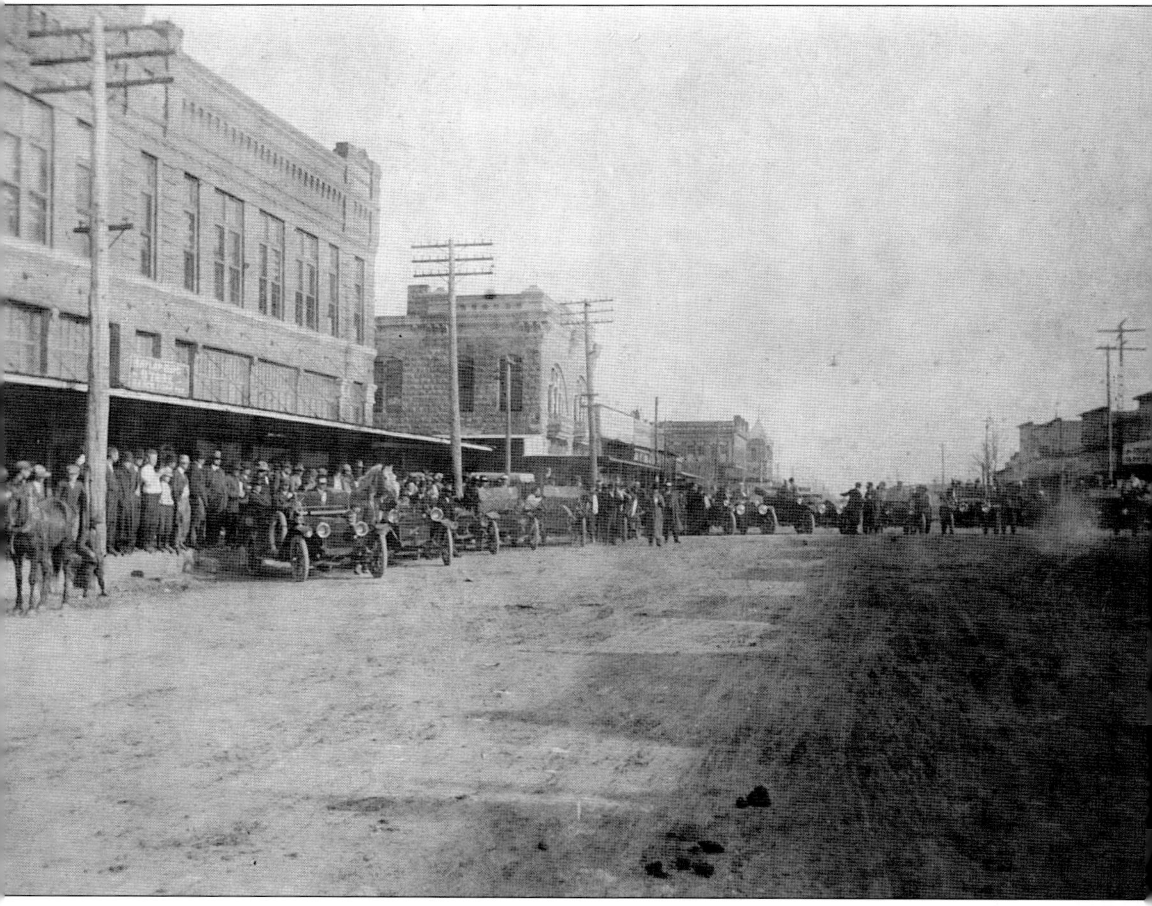

SEYMOUR STREET SCENE, C. 1910. Barely visible on the left side of the photograph is a sign for the Baylor Drug Store, one of the oldest drugstores in West Texas. It was started in 1882 by J.G. Kennan. It went through a series of owners, and in 1955 was owned by Mr. and Mrs. Jett Burnett. The business closed in late 1994 or early 1995. The first drugstore in Seymour was owned by Dr. L.T. Williams. (Courtesy of Baylor County Museum.)

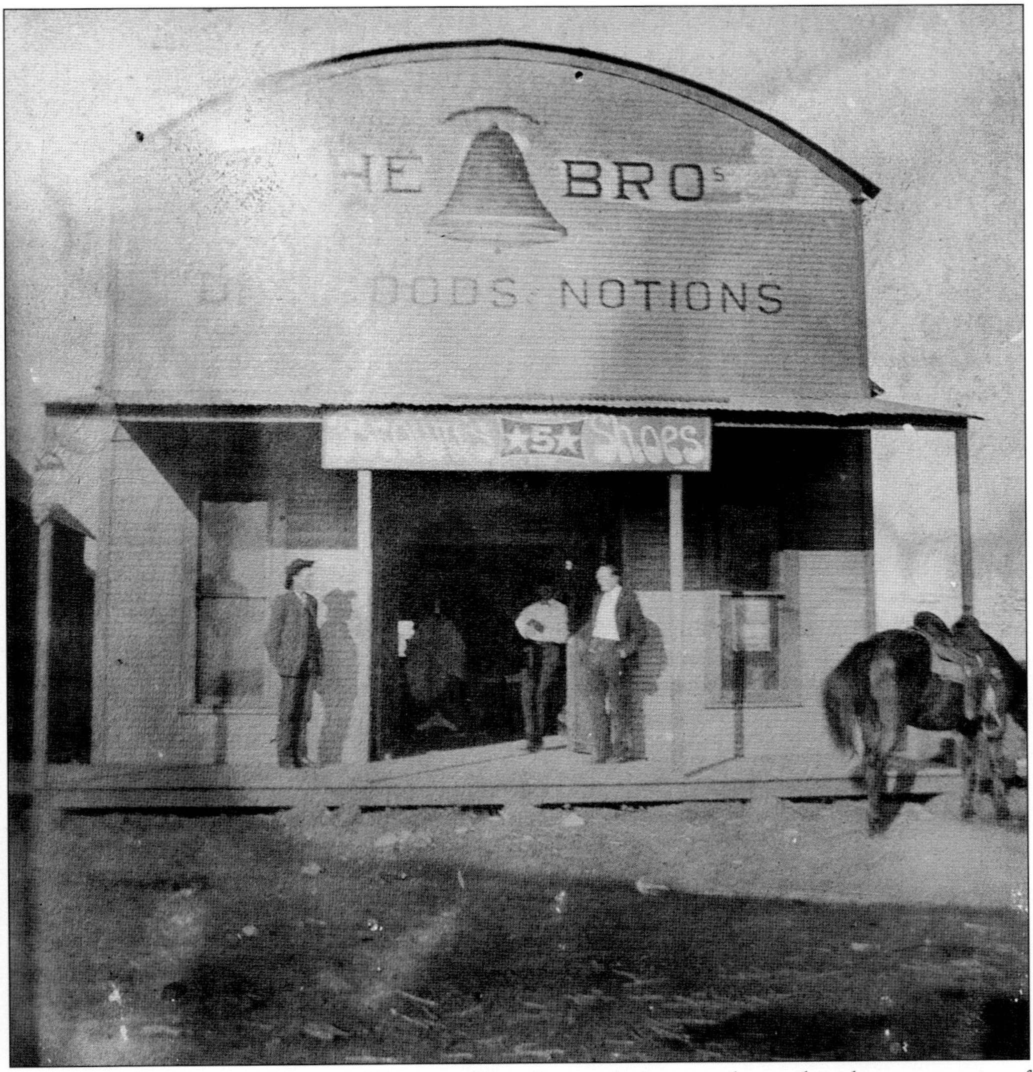

Bell Brothers Dry Goods and Notions. This dry goods shop was located in the community of Bomarton. Bomarton and many of its businesses sprang up overnight in 1906 with the extension of the Wichita Valley Railway from Wichita Falls. This store was owned by Cash Bell. The store had one employee, Bill Brawner. This photograph was taken in 1909. (Courtesy of Baylor County Museum.)

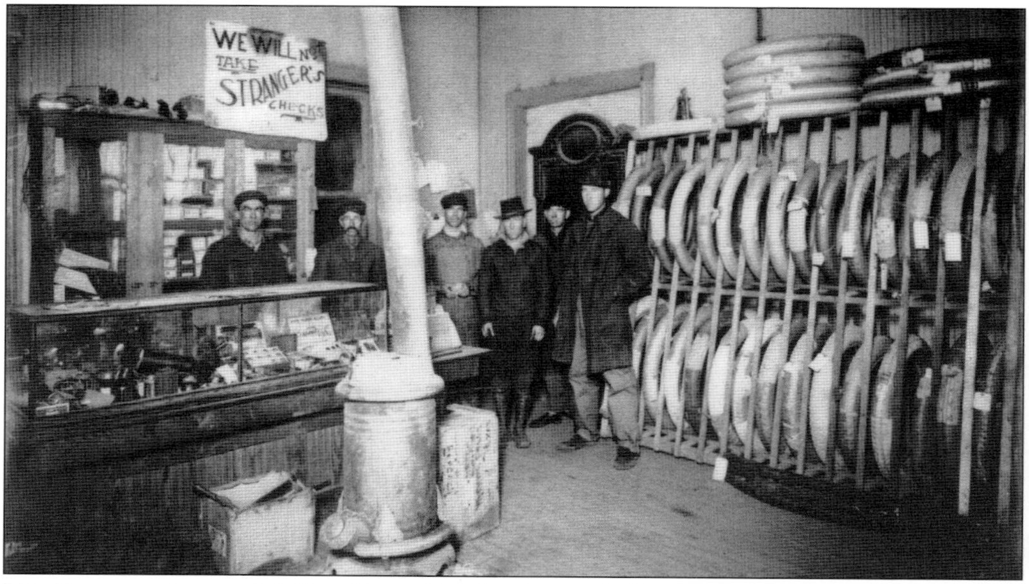

J.D. Fonville Office. J.D. Fonville and his family traveled by covered wagon to Baylor County from Montague County in 1912. They settled initially in the England community and began to farm. By 1919, however, Fonville and his sons had entered the automobile business and opened Seymour's second automobile and vulcanizing shop. The sons were excellent mechanics. They also had the Ford and Buick agencies. Their garage was located at the corner of East Nevada and Main Streets in a rock building. The Breedlove brothers had the first automobile agency (Ford) in Seymour in 1917.(Courtesy of Baylor County Museum.)

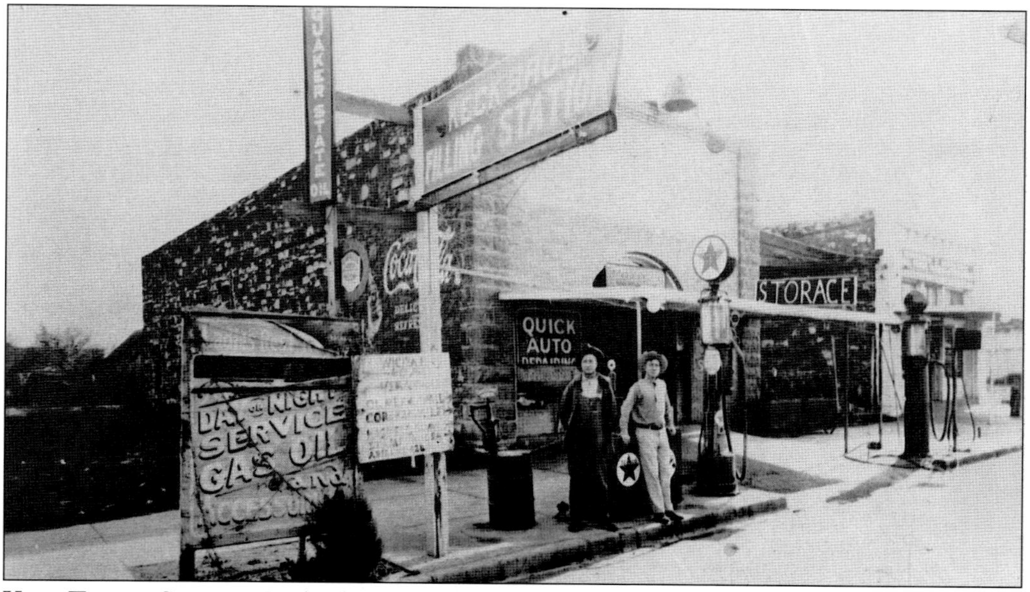

Keck Texaco Station. In this late 1920s photograph, Frank Keck and his brother Walter stand in front of their Texaco station at 200 North Main. Frank was the Texaco consignee for Seymour and the county. The pumps are located curbside, and the gas was dispensed by first pumping gas into the glass cylinder and then pumping the amount required into the vehicle. The rock building where this station was located was torn down, and the site is now the parking lot of Lawrence Brothers Grocery. (Courtesy of Charles T. Sessions.)

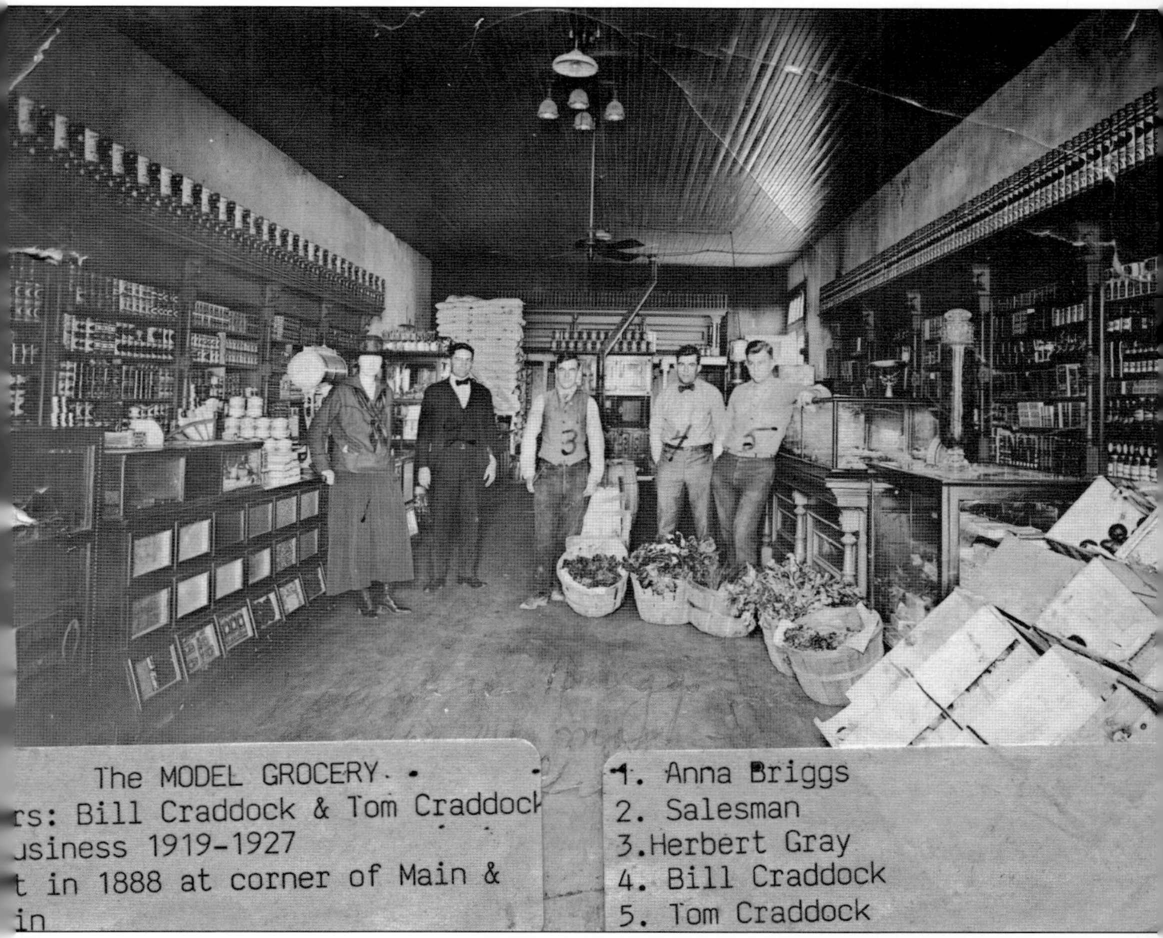

MODEL GROCERY STORE. The Model Grocery was owned by T.L. (Tom) Head. In 1899, Head came to Seymour and started to work in J.E. Murrie's grocery store. He bought the store in 1914 and operated it under the name Model Grocery. He sold the business in 1919 or 1920 to Tom and Bill Craddock. From left to right are Anna Biggs, unidentified, Herbert Gray, Bill Craddock, and Tom Craddock. (Courtesy of Baylor County Museum.)

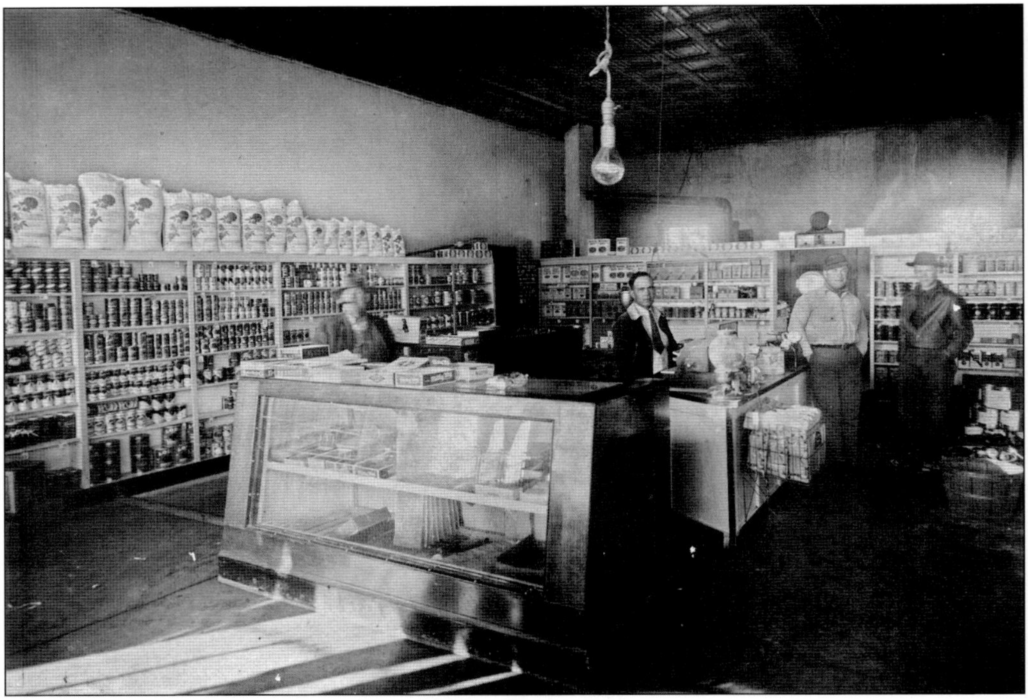

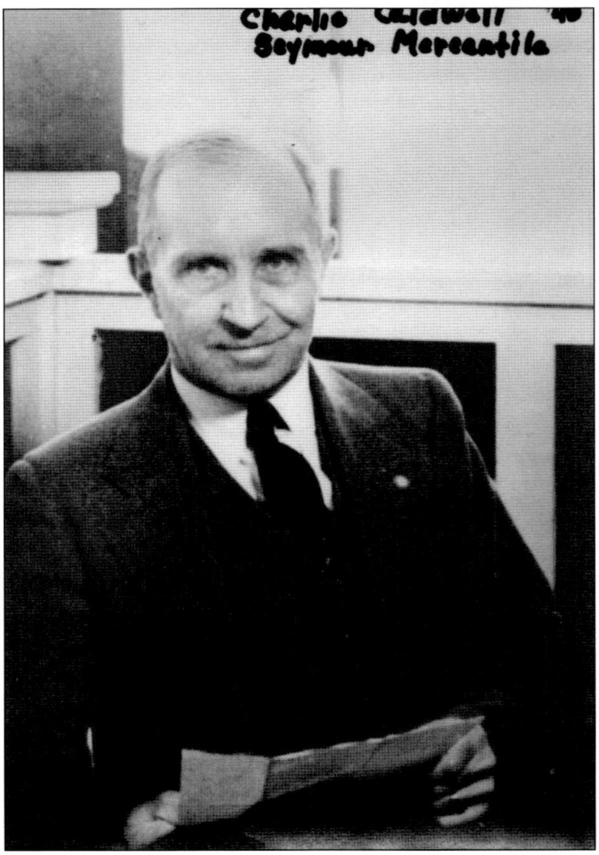

UNIDENTIFIED GROCERY STORE. This small market is well stocked with canned goods, including Campbell's soup, Red Rose flour, and cigars. It is estimated that between 1879 and 1930, at least eight grocery stores were operating in Seymour. Meat markets were often separate enterprises. (Courtesy of Baylor County Museum.)

CHARLIE CALDWELL OF SEYMOUR MERCANTILE. In 1916, West Texas Supply Company reorganized into the Seymour Mercantile Company. Under the executive leadership of Charlie Caldwell, the company expanded into farm machinery with the McCormick franchise and organized a funeral home. Seymour Mercantile was for many years the most prominent business in the county. It ceased operations in the late 1930s. (Courtesy of Sammie Portwood Morris.)

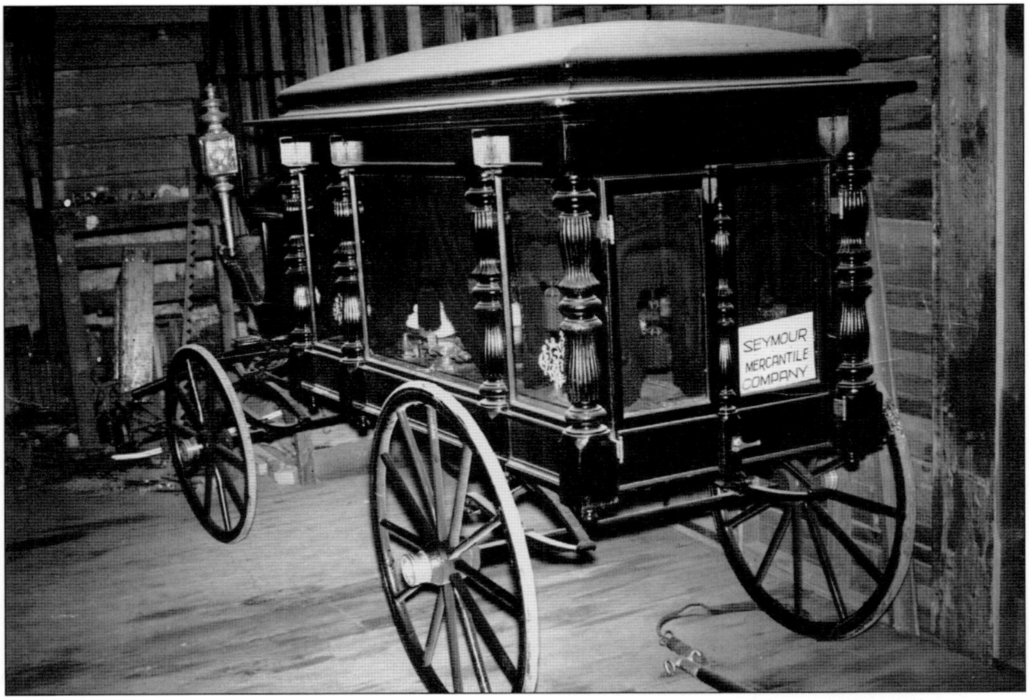

SEYMOUR MERCANTILE HEARSE. Seymour Mercantile operated from 1916 until the late 1930s. Headquarters were housed at the corner of North Washington and Morris Streets, where Dollar General is now located. Goods and services offered included hardware, furniture, guns, ammunition, jewelry, radios, farm machinery, and a funeral parlor. This hearse burned in a fire that destroyed the mercantile warehouse. (Courtesy of Baylor County Museum.)

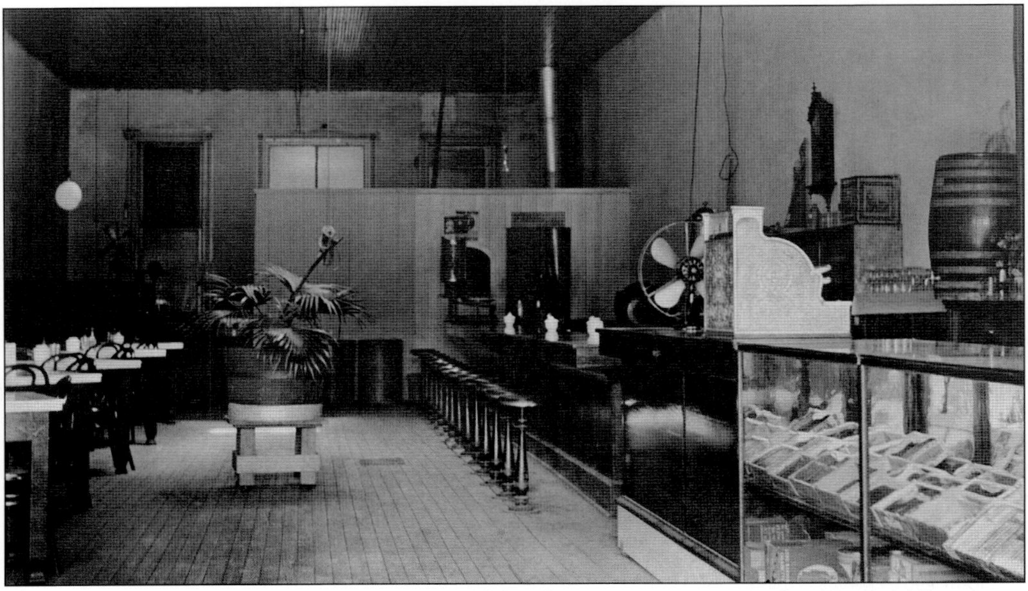

BOMARTON DRUG STORE. Robert Seydler and family came to Bomarton from Lavaca County in 1908. He bought the Patton Drug Store and operated it until 1920, when he sold to Dr. Gaines, one of Bomarton's medical doctors. This photograph was taken after 1910. (Courtesy of Baylor County Museum.)

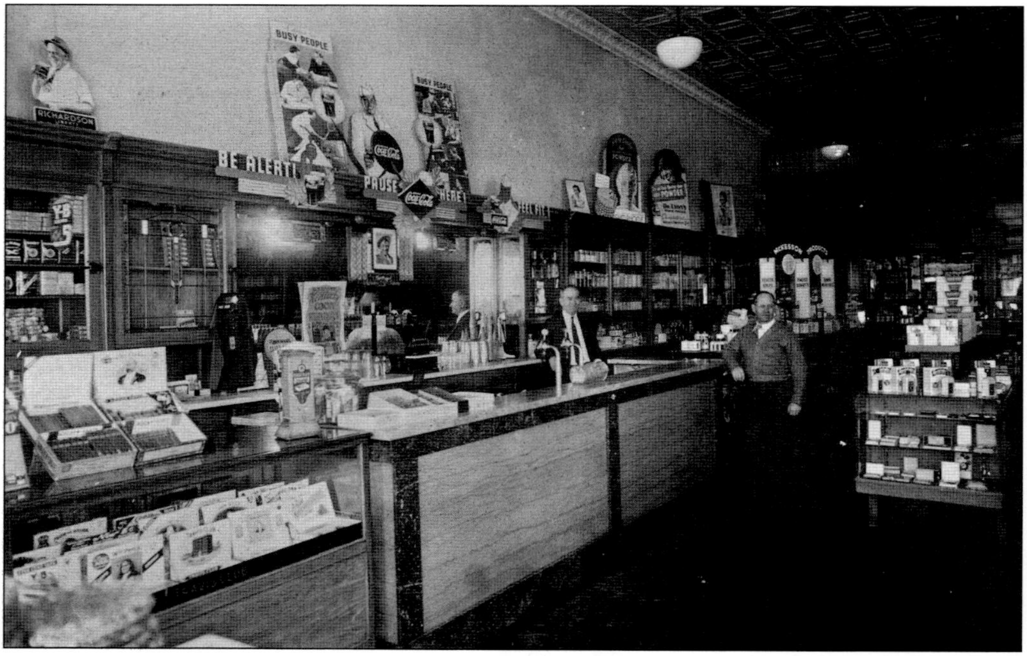

Bill Clough Drugstore. There were many drugstores in Baylor County. Clough's Drugstore was located on Main Street. Today, the location is a parking lot. This undated photograph gives a good view of the store's interior, including its fountain and cigar case. Many drugstores had fountains, and they were popular gathering places. The Clough family also had a jewelry business in the early part of the 20th century. (Courtesy of Baylor County Museum.)

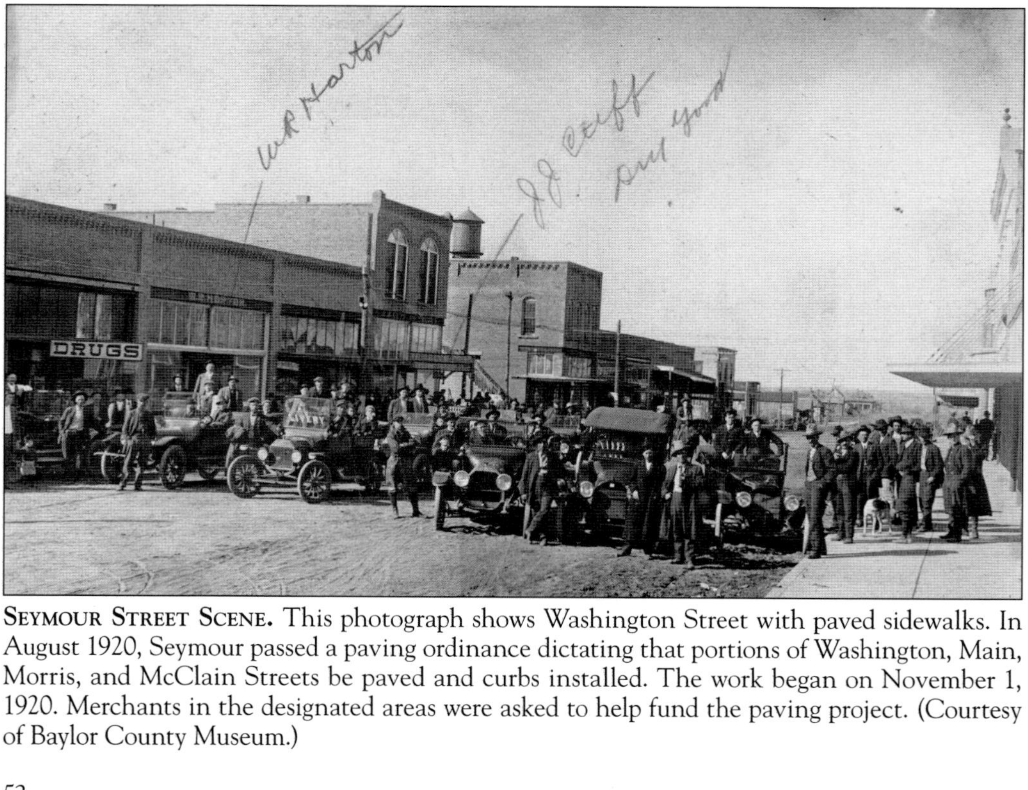

Seymour Street Scene. This photograph shows Washington Street with paved sidewalks. In August 1920, Seymour passed a paving ordinance dictating that portions of Washington, Main, Morris, and McClain Streets be paved and curbs installed. The work began on November 1, 1920. Merchants in the designated areas were asked to help fund the paving project. (Courtesy of Baylor County Museum.)

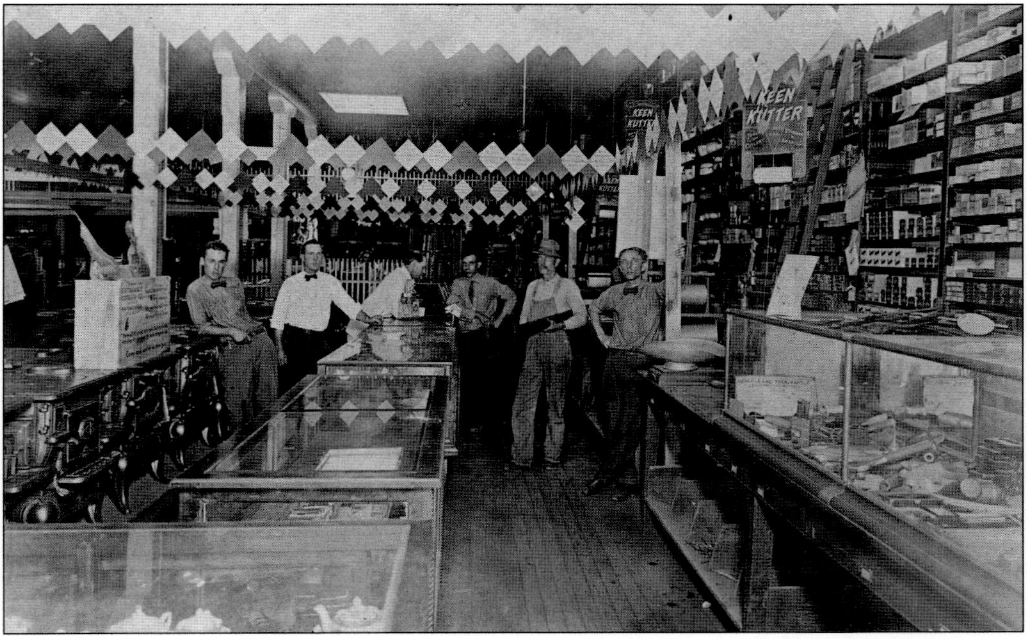

HILLIARD HARDWARE STORE. Seymour had many furniture, dry goods, and hardware stores. W.R. Hilliard operated one of the early hardware stores. He sold the business to Wesley Harrison, who was a merchant for 56 years in Seymour. Careful inspection of the photograph reveals the eclectic collection of merchandise handled by merchants. (Courtesy of Baylor County Museum.)

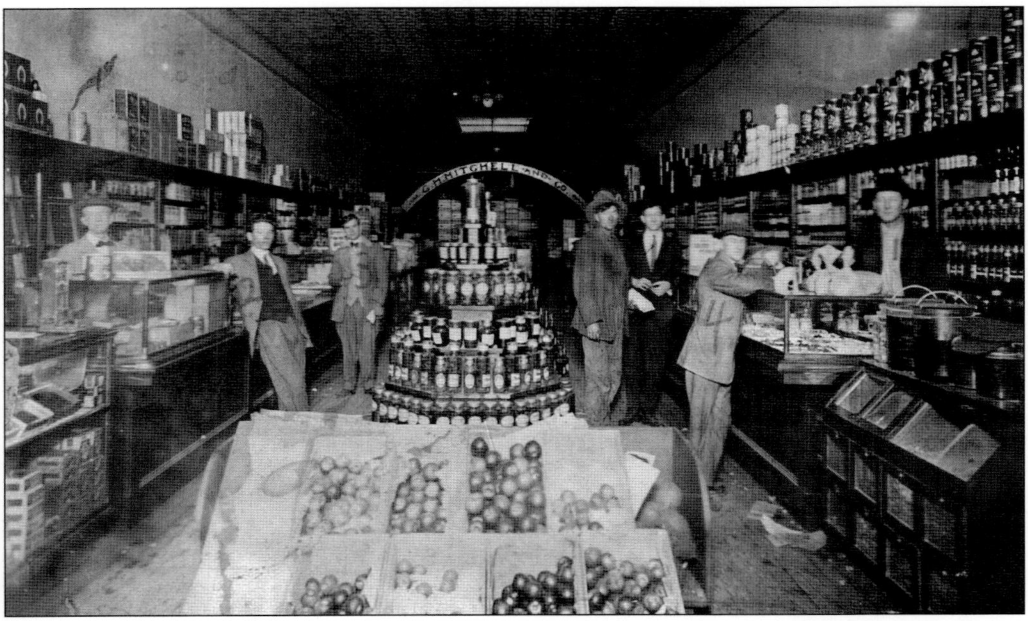

MITCHELL'S GROCERY STORE. By 1890, Seymour had all the businesses of a prosperous 19th-century Western town. *Salt Pork to Sirloin* lists Seymour as having at least nine grocers between1879 and the 1930s. The grocery in this photograph originated as the Luck and Taylor grocery, became the Taylor Mitchell grocery, and finally the C.H. Mitchell grocery. From its inception, it was located in the block were Bayco now operates at 205 East McClain Street. (Courtesy of Baylor County Museum.)

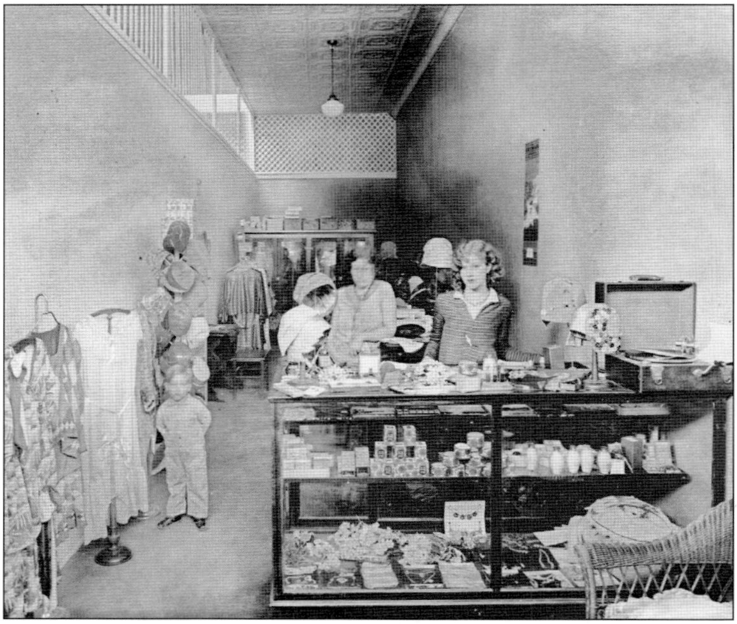

Ladies' Dress Shop. This photograph taken in 1927 is of a ladies' dress shop housed in the basement of the Farmer's National Bank. In the photograph are Alta Cockerell (center), her two-and-half-year-old son Charles, and her sister Laura Prichard. This image demonstrates the long, narrow nature of early building architecture in Baylor County as well as the use of decorative tin ceilings. (Courtesy of Baylor County Museum.)

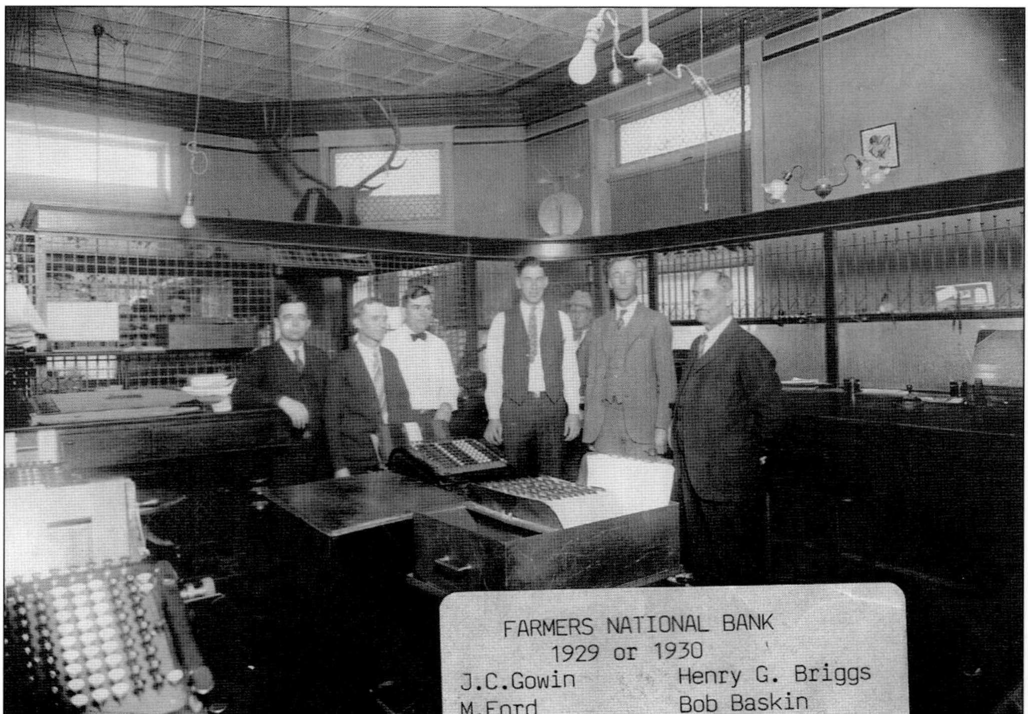

Farmers National Bank, 1929. This photograph shows the interior of the Farmers National Bank in 1929 or 1930. Pictured are, from left to right, J.C. Gowin, M. Ford, Bill Craddock, Henry G. Briggs, and Charles Randall. Randall moved to Baylor County in 1898 and bought a small ranch near the Ogden community. He was a director of the Farmer's National Bank until his death on June 4, 1941. An unidentified customer stands in back. (Courtesy of Baylor County Museum.)

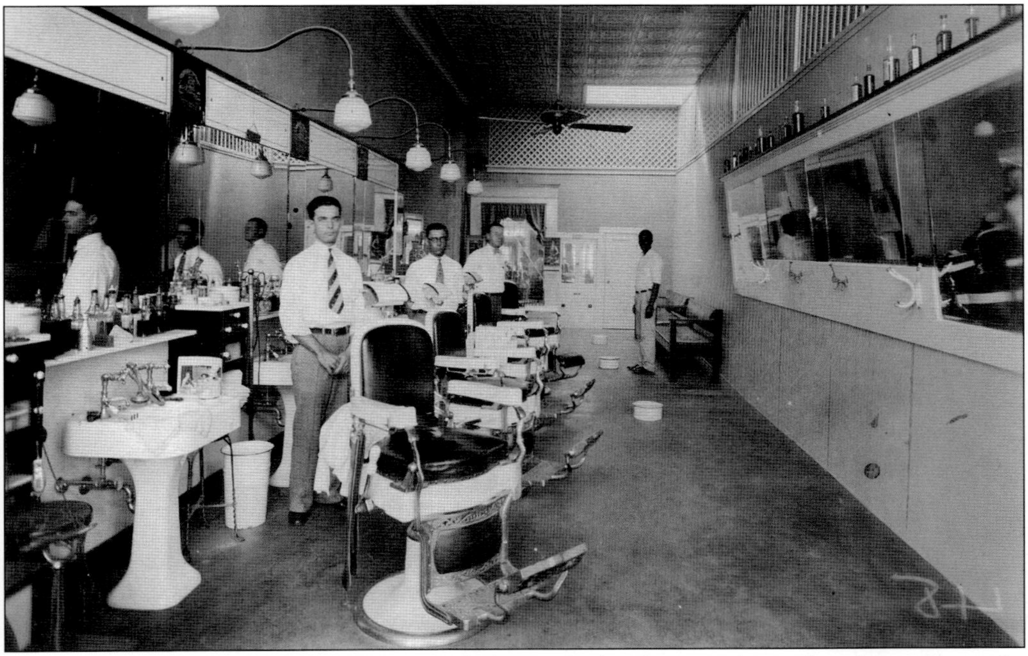

LON BLACKBURN BARBERSHOP. The Lon Blackburn barbershop was located on Main Street. In this c. 1940 image are, from back to front, Lon Blackburn, Frank Kotulek, Ben Stocking, and "Shoe Shine" Herbert Dunn. Listed as working in 1887, Wayne Cryer, I.P. Metcalf, and Henry Suster were the early barbers in town. (Courtesy of Baylor County Museum.)

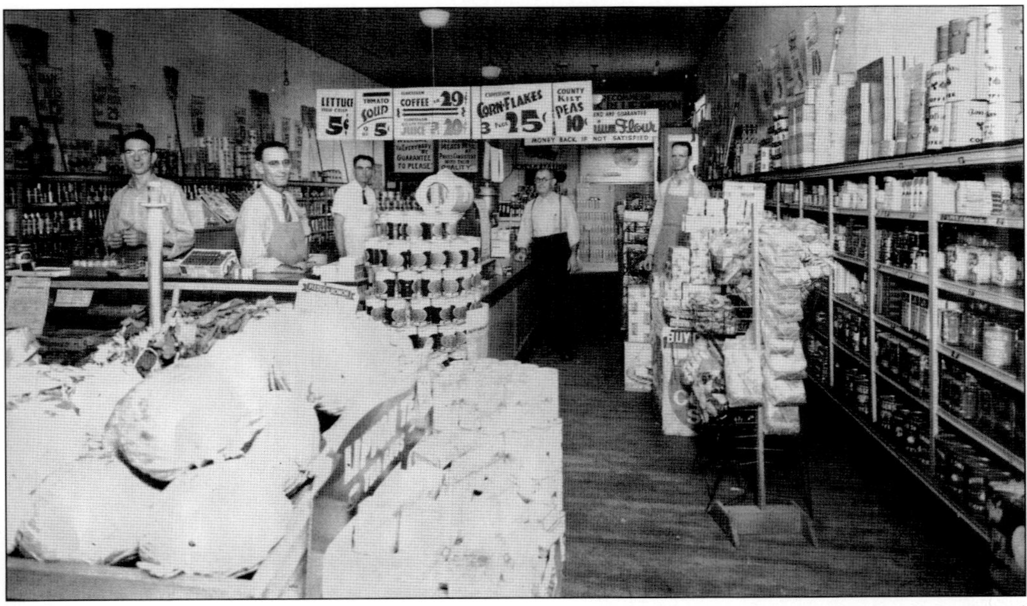

SIMS GROCERY STORE. The Sims grocery store was located on the northwest corner of Main and McClain Streets. While frozen and convenience foods were not available, home delivery was. A customer could call for a grocery delivery, Sims would fill the food order, and he was not averse to picking up a spool of thread or running other errands for a valued customer. From left to right are Travis Warren, George Sims Sr., Raymond Warren, Joe Macha, and Morris Perkins. (Courtesy of Baylor County Museum.)

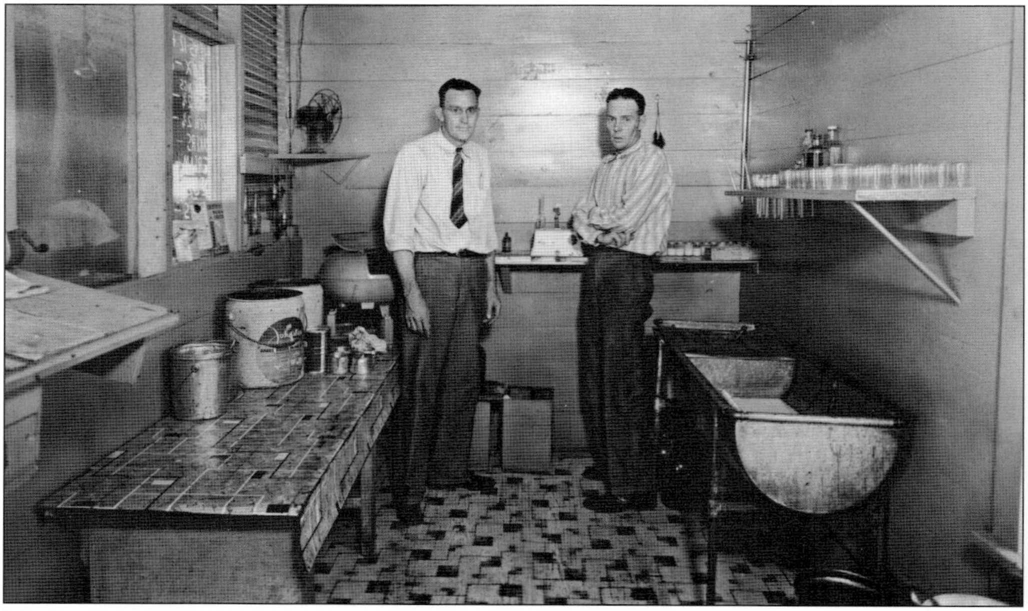

MEADS CREAM-TESTING ROOM. For the first half of the 20th century, nearly every farm had a dairy cow that produced milk, butter, and cream. Fresh cream was taken into Seymour, where the amount of butterfat was tested. Customers were paid based on the fat content. There was more than one cream-testing room in Seymour, and the practice continued until sometime in the mid-1950s. Cream-testing rooms also examined eggs for freshness. The money received from fresh cream supplemented the income of many farmwives. (Courtesy of Baylor County Museum.)

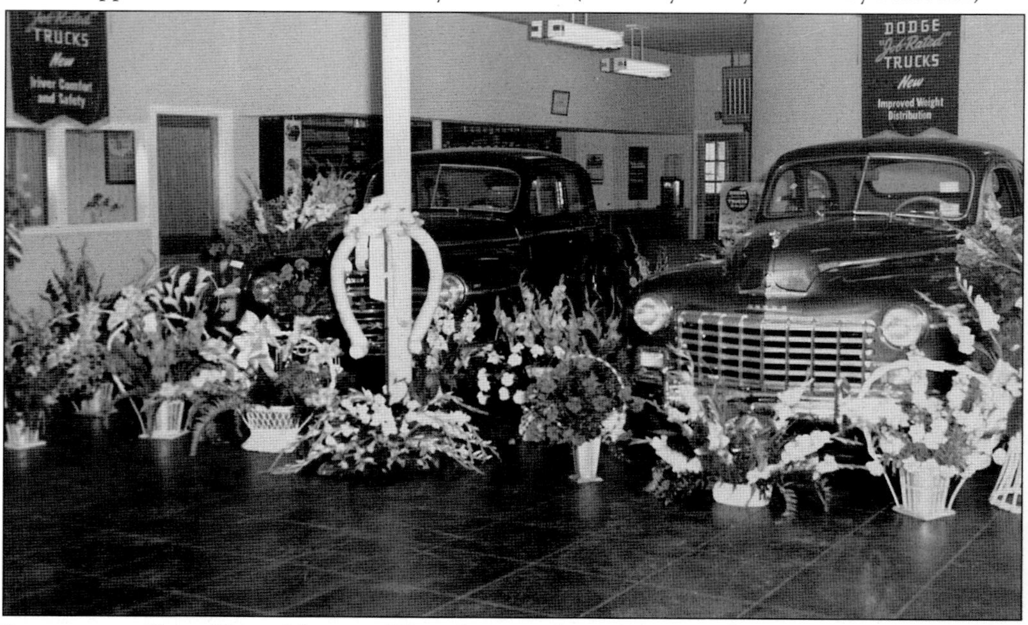

INTERIOR OF CARL HASH MOTORS. This photograph is of the grand opening of the Carl Hash Dodge dealership in 1941. He sold Dodge automobiles for 14 years, Buicks for 21 years, both Buicks and Fords for 5 years, and when the dealership closed in June 1981, he had been a Ford dealer for 10 years. Hash also owned a flying school located on the Olney Highway. (Courtesy of Charles T. Sessions.)

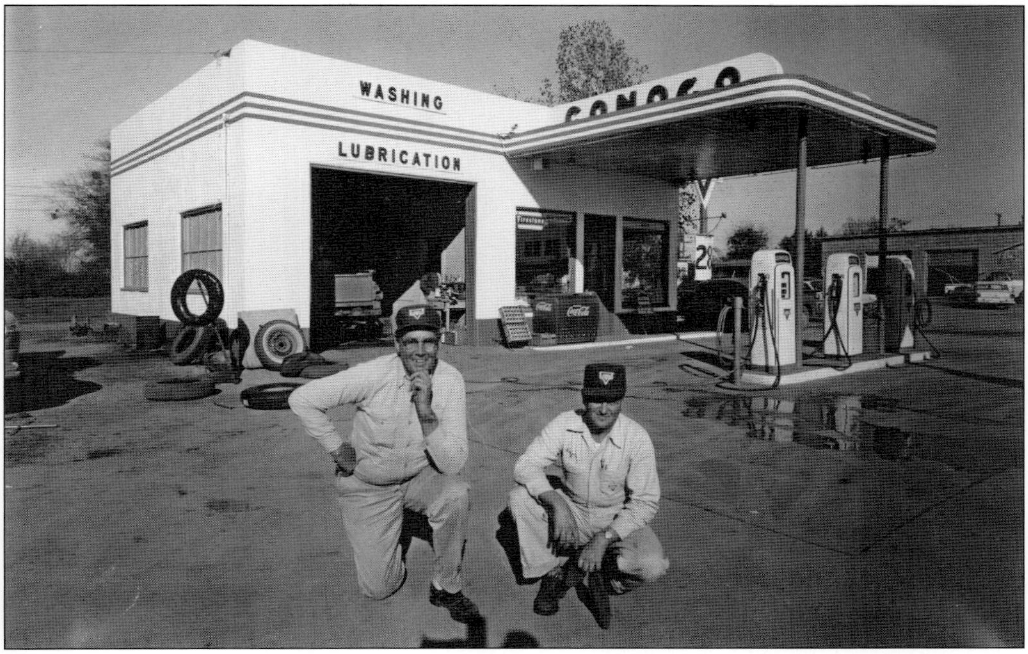

STANDLEE SERVICE STATION. Baylor County once boasted 50 service stations. This Conoco station was owned by Royce Standlee and was located at the corner of California and Washington Streets. Royce Standlee (right) is shown with employee Curtis Thurman. (Courtesy of Irma Standlee.)

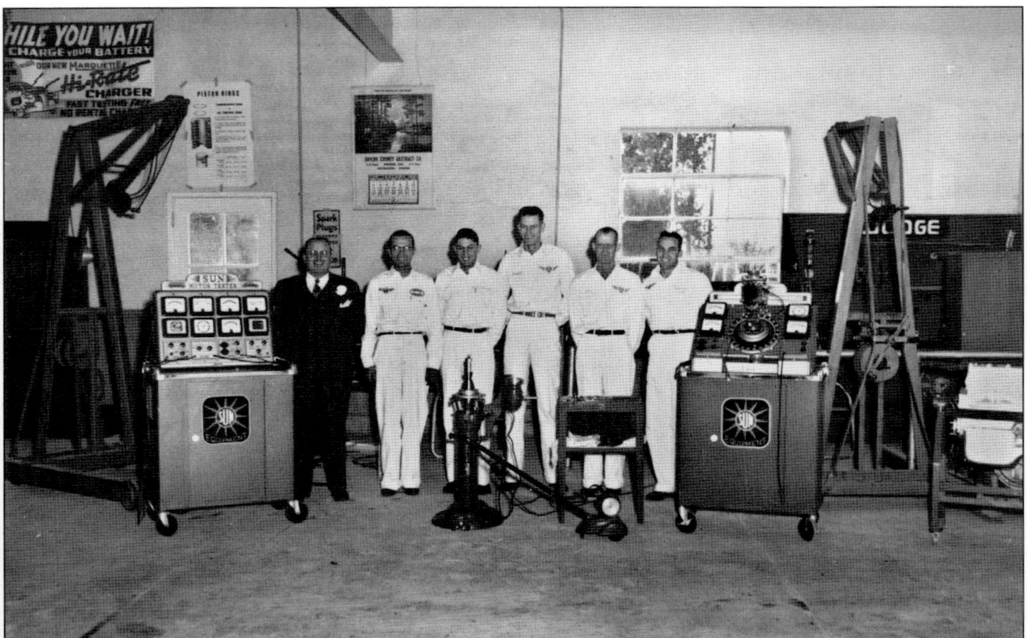

CARL HASH MECHANICS. Carl Hash is shown with his five mechanics in a technologically current shop. Besides the garage, the dealership had parts and service departments. Carl's wife, Oma, served the dealership in many capacities, including, secretary, bookkeeper, and overall manager. She also drove the taxi during the period the Hashes operated a taxi service. (Courtesy of Carolene Hash Stovall.)

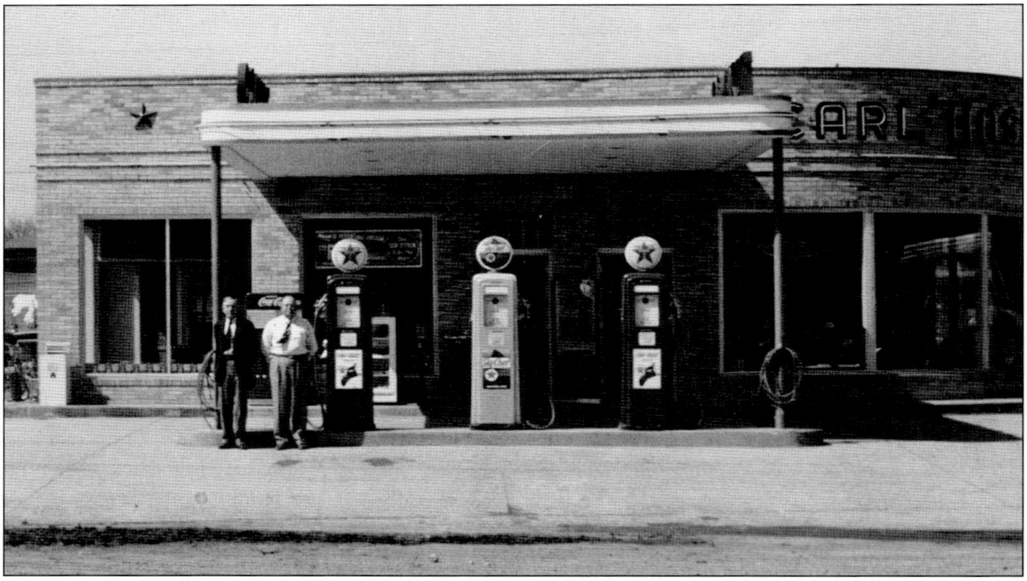

Carl Hash and Frank Keck. Carl Hash (right), owner of the dealership, and Fran Keck, owner of the building, are pictured in front of the filling station at Carl Hash Motors. He opened his dealership in 1941, selling Dodge passenger cars and Dodge work trucks. The number of local automobile retailers peaked in the mid-1950s, when there were at least six dealerships. (Courtesy of Charles T. Sessions.)

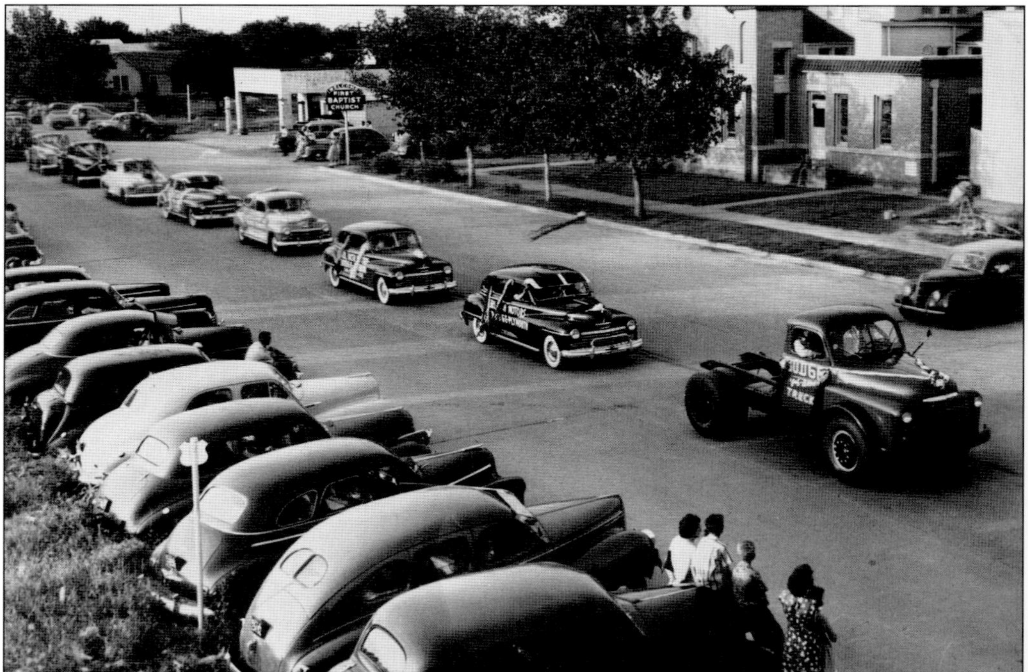

Carl Hash Cars in Rodeo Parade. A Dodge tow truck from Carl Hash Motors leads a long line of decorated automobiles down Washington Street in a rodeo parade. Spectators line the street across from the First Baptist Church. This building was constructed in 1915, torn down in 1959, and replaced with the current modern sanctuary. (Courtesy of Carolene Hash Stovall.)

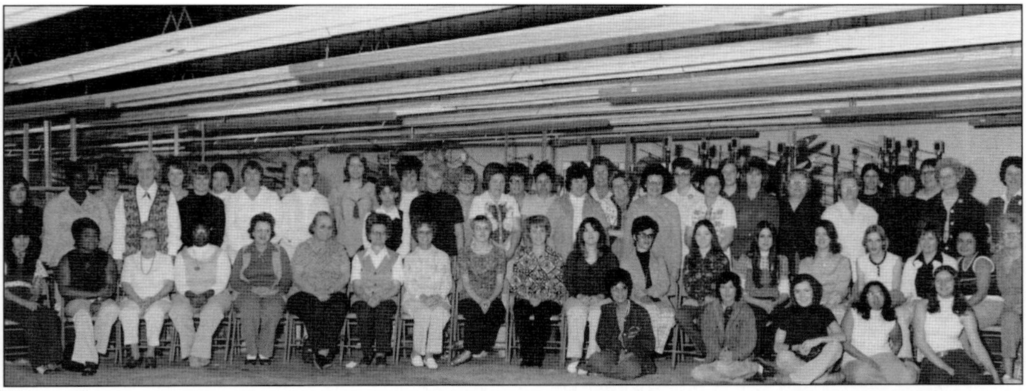

Russell Newman Employees, Photograph One. Russell Newman was a small manufacturing company located in Baylor County in the 1970s. It manufactured women's apparel. In 1974, it had 73 employees, the majority of them women. It was a boon to the economy of the town because for the first time, women had discretionary income to spend locally. In this photograph are, from left to right, (first row) Louisa Vasquez, Nora Young, Christy Bickley, Frances Alvarado, and Debbie Matus; (second row) Janie Romo, Hazle Degeade, Nina Brown, Norma Spell, Marie Knezek, Elizabeth Watson, Ethel Bierkenfield, Nell Russell, Jean Harvey, Reta Blakely, Vicky Floyd, Margaret Urbanczyk, Judy Alexander, Carmen Figueroa, May Ann Mitchell, Pam McCauley, Dessie Otts, Ofelia Garcia, and Grace Ward; (third row) Nora Sosa, Ida Jo Stinnet, Rita Young, Irene Rainwater, Charlotte Neskorik, Kay Lindsey, Joan Sims, Betty Coker, Louise Hall, Mary Marak, Carolyn Ferrier, Linda Rogers, Evelyn Ragland, Sandy Carpenter, Annie Copeland, Pat Benson, Nancy Robertson, Cynthia Sturgeon, Lara Warren, Linda Robertson, Jo Rozell, Juanice Copeland, Jane Dormire, Vickie Jackson, Glenda Decker, Winnie Howry, Gladys Teague, Theda Myers, Pat Stone, Dolores Kasparek, Fay Hobbs, and Jean Weaver.

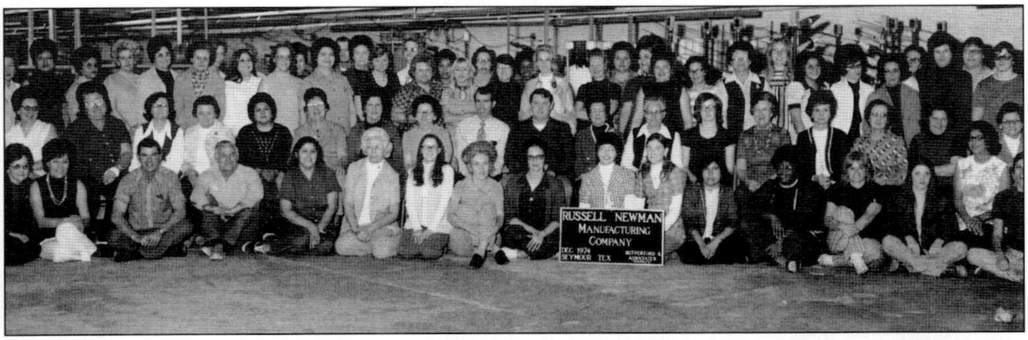

Russell Newman Employees, Photograph Two. Here, from left to right, are (first row) Leo McWhorter, Katie Lunsford, Mike Blakely, Paul Davis, Julia Alvarado, Bernice Ragland, Sue Bruce, Anita Boland, Jane Bridges, Mary Hutchens, Jeanette Blake, Modesta Costilla, Audery Porter, Saundra Orsak, Sue Bufkin, Maria Sandoval, and Theda Myers; (second row) Adeline Covington, Johnnie Henner, Jeanette Jacobs, Jean Alexander, Janie Garcia, Lanna Mae Lowrence, Zula Conners, Vlasta Macik, Bob Ford, Gayland Howell, Ann Lain, Ida Vaden, Nancy Royston, Gladys Lambeth, Delphine Carrington, Lillian Royston, Virginia Hitch, and Mary Natus; (third row) Naomi Ussery, Eva Flores, Kathy Casillas, Joyce Goss, Erlene Meinzer, Maureen Birkenfield, Evelyn Herring, Brenda Wright, Emmalee Crowell, June Warner, Grace Schumacher, Sylvia Myers, Darryl Otts, Leona Colgan, Francis Betts, Mozelle Moore, Linda Miles, Connie Saens, Shirley Howeth, Barbara Hardin, Polly Hutchens, Gaye Thomas, Maribeth Ford, Mildred Wacker, Billie Goodwin, Fiona Hostas, Beverly Brown, Oma Rice, Jerrie Hiller, Connie Royston, Vera Garcia, Burly Richardson, Norma Harper, Wanda Daft, Barbara Haynes, Dolores Kasparek, Carolyn Howery, and Marilyn Devrow.(Both, courtesy of Delores Kasparek.)

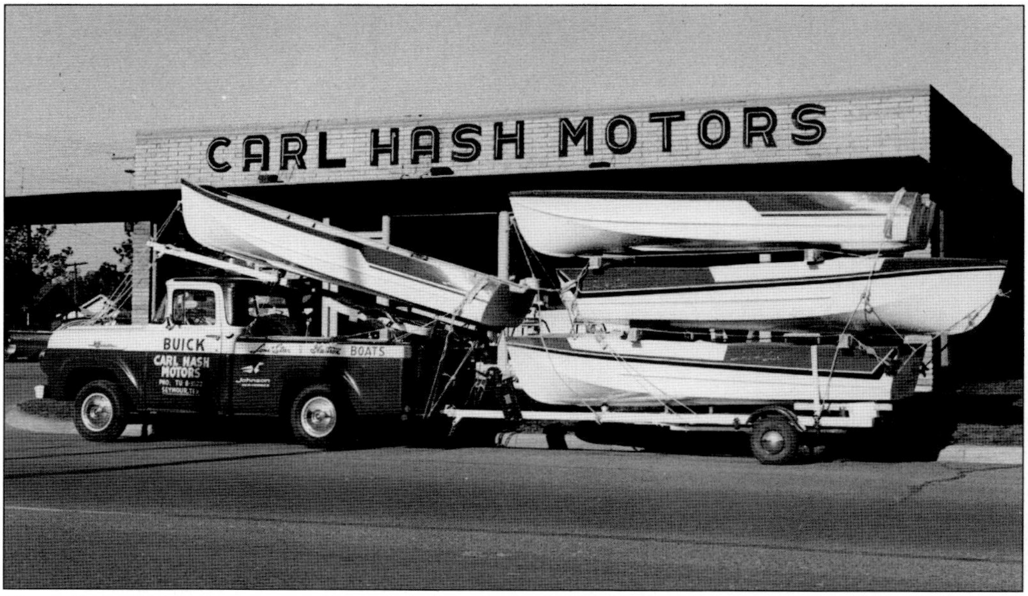

Carl Hash Motorboats. This photograph was taken in front of the Carl Hash Building, located at 210 South Washington Street, and shows the dealership's expansion into motorboats. The structure behind the boats was designed and owned by Carl and Oma Hash. The Hashes had many business ventures and enterprises in Seymour, including a taxi service and a flying school on the Olney Highway. Both Carl and Oma were licensed pilots. (Courtesy of Baylor County Museum.)

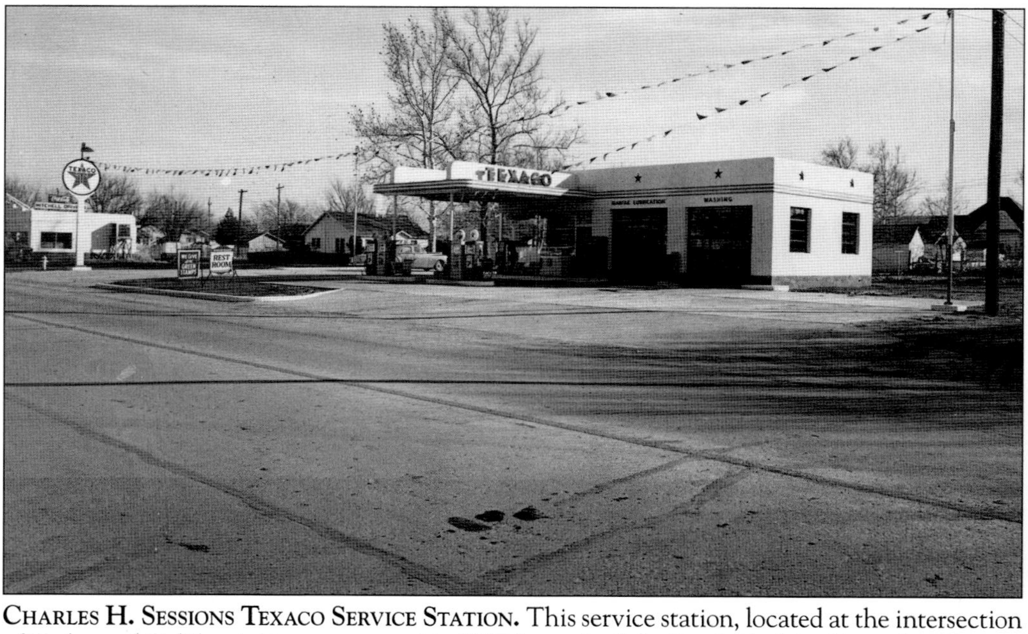

Charles H. Sessions Texaco Service Station. This service station, located at the intersection of Cedar and California Streets, opened in 1955. It was built by Frank Keck and leased to Texaco, which in turn leased it to Charles H. Sessions. The station was open 24 hours a day, seven days a week. Besides selling gas, employees repaired flat tires, washed cars, and changed oil. Sessions ran the station until 1977 when it was purchased by his son Charles T. Sessions. Charles T. stopped selling gas in December 1989. (Courtesy of Charles T. Sessions.)

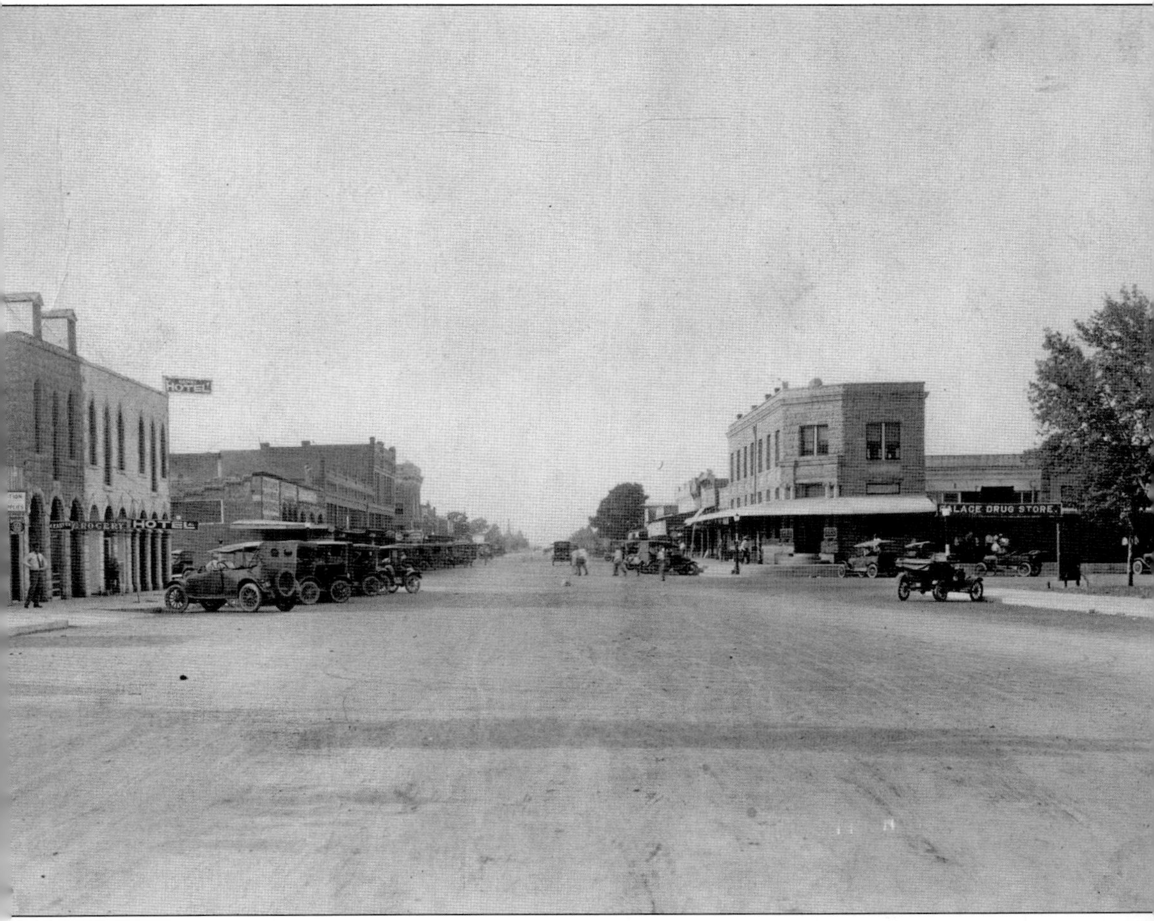

View of Washington Street. This street scene is undated but was most likely taken in the late 1920s. The view is looking north, and the street is lined with Model T cars. The rock building in the near left has been torn down and replaced with modern architecture. The structure on the corner on the right is the Farmer's National Bank. A new building was erected in 1964 in the same location. Though the structures have changed, the street design remains the same. A paving ordinance passed by the city in the early 1920s resulted in the streets being paved with bricks. (Courtesy of Baylor County Museum.)

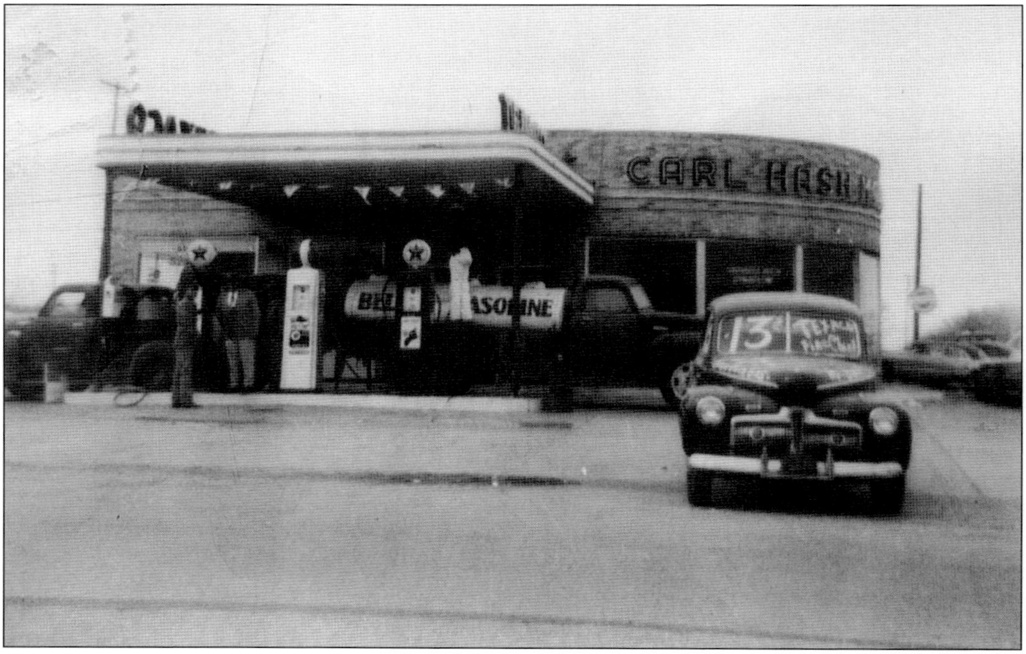

Gasoline Wars on Washington Street. The caption on the back of this photograph reads, " 'Gas War' 13.9 cents a gallon. Dealers Welcome." At this Carl Hash gas station, so many tankers came to fill up that the fire department stood by in case fire should break out on all the spilled gasoline. (Courtesy of Baylor County Museum.)

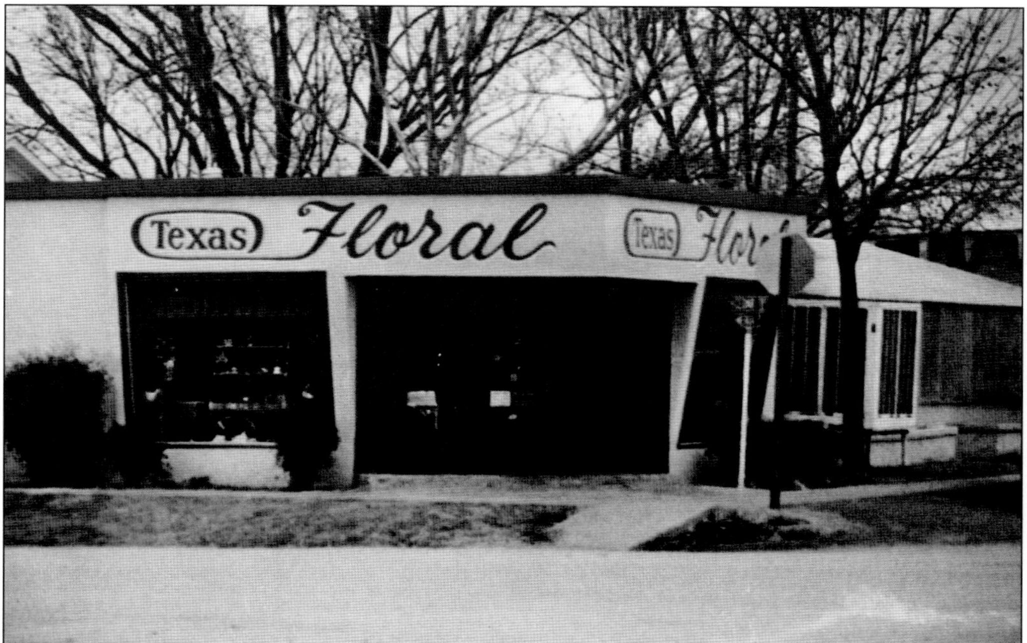

Texas Floral Shop. Glen Ray Howell started Texas Floral Shop was in the 1950s. It has provided flowers for funerals and special occasions since its inception. When he retired, his son purchased the business and ran it until he in turn retired. The shop is still in business today and owned by Pam Jackson. (Courtesy of Baylor County Museum.)

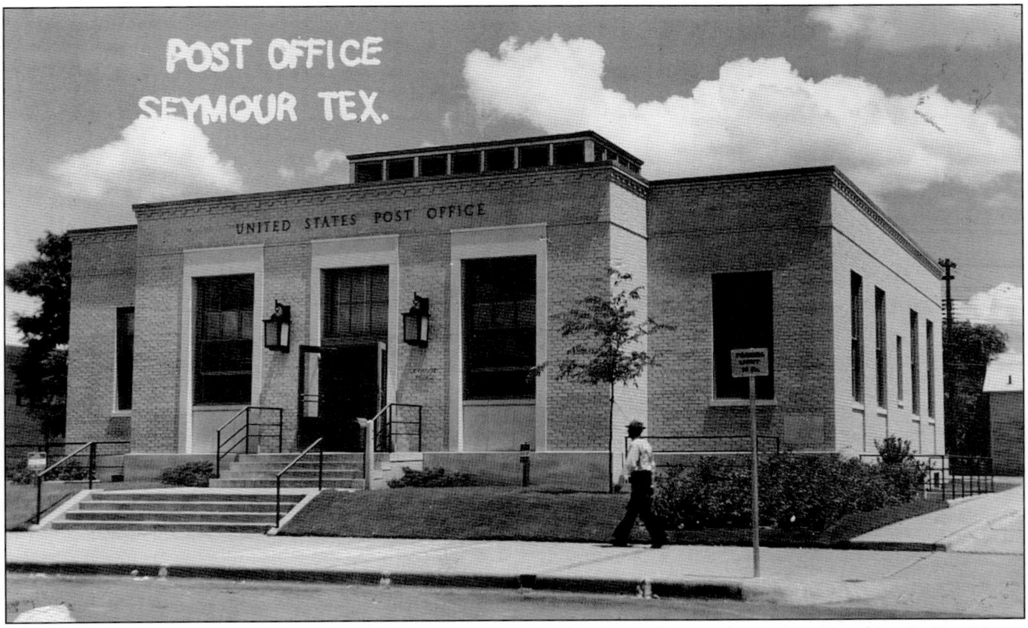

UNITED STATES POST OFFICE. In 1930, the post office was housed in the Craddock Building located at the 100 block of North Main Street. A need for a new building arose, and in 1938 it was announced that a new post office was to be constructed. The new building opened in October 1940, and this facility still serves the county. The post office features a mural by Tom Lea entitled *Comanches*. (Courtesy of Baylor County Museum.)

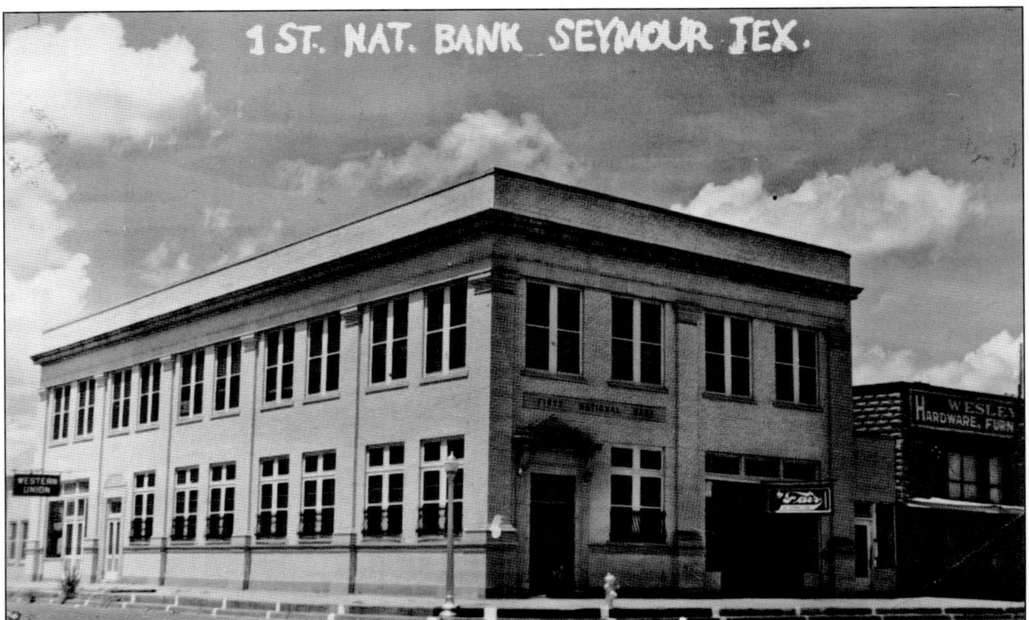

FIRST NATIONAL BANK. The First National Bank was organized by G.S. Plants. Its first day of business was Monday, March 31, 1890. Since its founding, four different buildings have served the bank at the original site. The current structure was remodeled in 1967. This photograph is of the bank in 1929. (Courtesy of Baylor County Museum.)

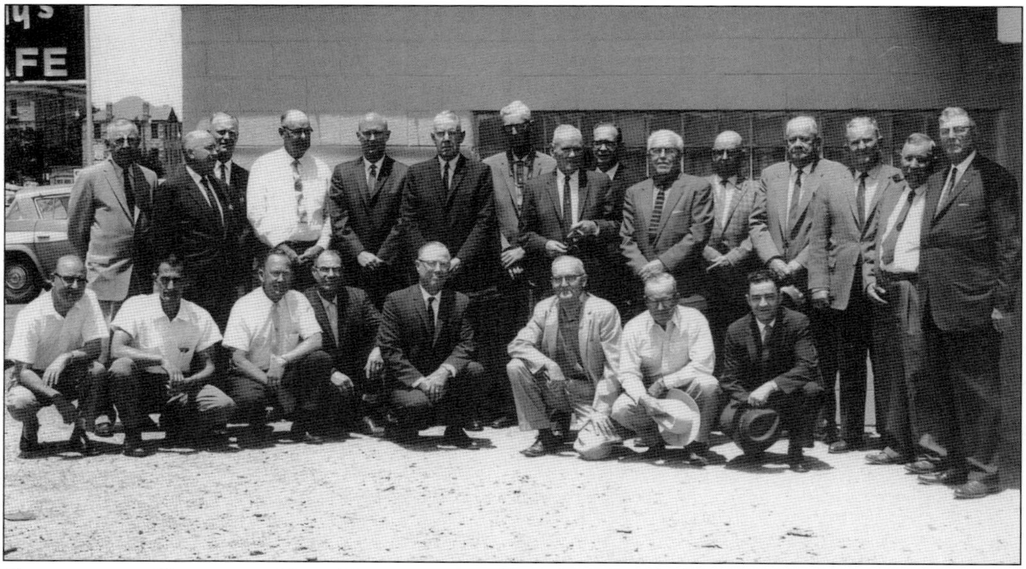

CHAMBER OF COMMERCE PAST PRESIDENTS. This photograph honoring the past presidents of the chamber of commerce was taken in 1960 at Roddy's Café. Past Presidents from 1925 to 1960 were honored at the luncheon. The Seymour Chamber of Commerce was organized on March 11, 1921. R.R. Kellum was unanimously elected as the first president. (Courtesy of Baylor County Museum.)

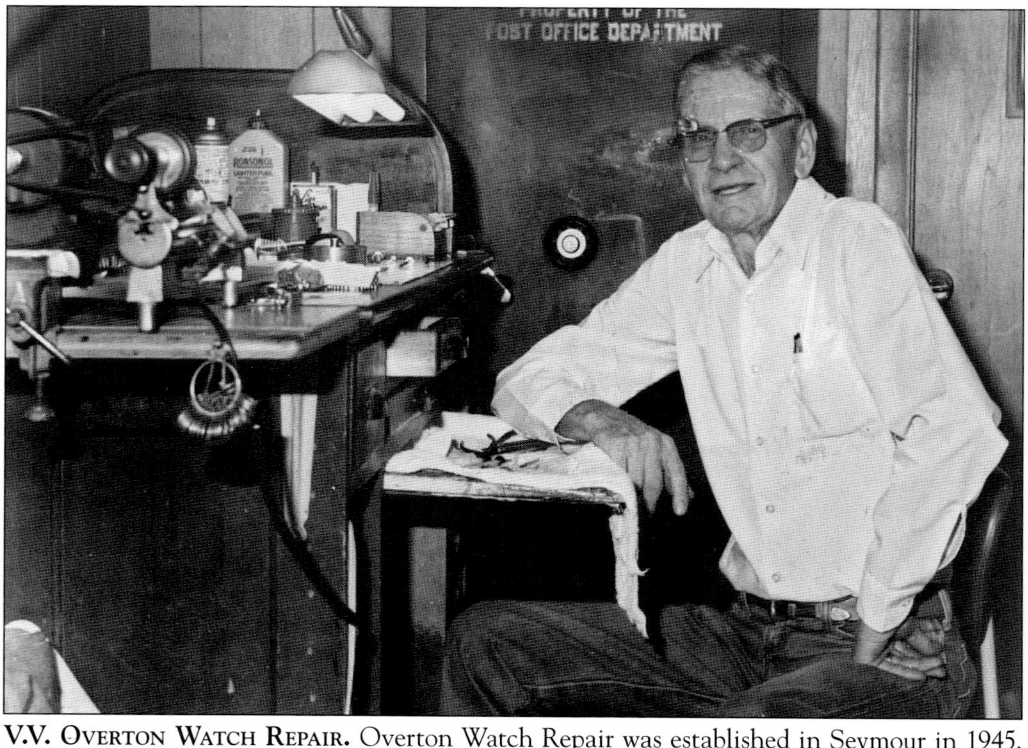

V.V. OVERTON WATCH REPAIR. Overton Watch Repair was established in Seymour in 1945. Overton is at the workbench he used for over 50 years. Early jeweler A.E. Richmond opened a jewelry store in Seymour in 1904 and continued the business until his death. His son James then continued the enterprise until he retired. (Courtesy of Baylor County Museum.)

Four

SODBUSTERS

The nation at the end of the 19th century witnessed an influx of immigrants. Encouraged by the Homestead Act of 1862, many immigrant farmers and their families arrived in Baylor County, swelling the number of people living in the existing small communities and creating new ones. Farming began to assume importance with their arrival, and the first cotton crop was harvested in 1891. Cotton soon stood beside wheat and cattle in economic importance.

Many of the farmers who came to the county between 1900 and 1910 had arrived at the Port of Galveston and spent a few years in South Texas before making the journey north. Joseph Orsack and his family decided to move to Baylor County after reading an advertisement for the county in a Houston newspaper that boasted of fat, white-faced cattle grazing on lush, green pastures and insect-free cotton.

While many of these farmers settled on 160 acres, others were able to purchase more land. Joseph Macha came to the county in 1908 and bought the last 208 acres of George Knight's property in what was known as the open section. It was the last land to be fenced and put into cultivation. By 1910, the county had 1,040 farms.

Farmers had their work cut out for them. Ranchers were reluctant to see the land fenced and the end of the open range. The Great Plains had not been plowed, and it had few suitable trees with which to build homes and barns. The protection of their livestock was paramount, and many of these families built and lived in barns before they constructed homes. These early farmers faced huge obstacles with great determination, succeeded in overcoming them, and prospered. Baylor County is indebted to them for helping to create the foundation of one the best agricultural systems in the world.

Land ownership and usage in the county has continually shifted from its inception. Cattle and wheat production are still substantial, but cotton less so. The large tracts of land utilized by ranchers and cowmen in the open range gave way to the smaller acreages of the Homestead Act of 1862. The Homestead Act delivered land in small parcels to large families. The inheritance problems commensurate with large families resulted in the sale of many of these early family farms after the original owners passed on. During the 1960s, a consolidation process into larger parcels began. Farms and ranches became larger. In the last 20 years, land ownership has again shifted with the sale of many farms and ranches to city dwellers, who acquire the land for recreational purposes.

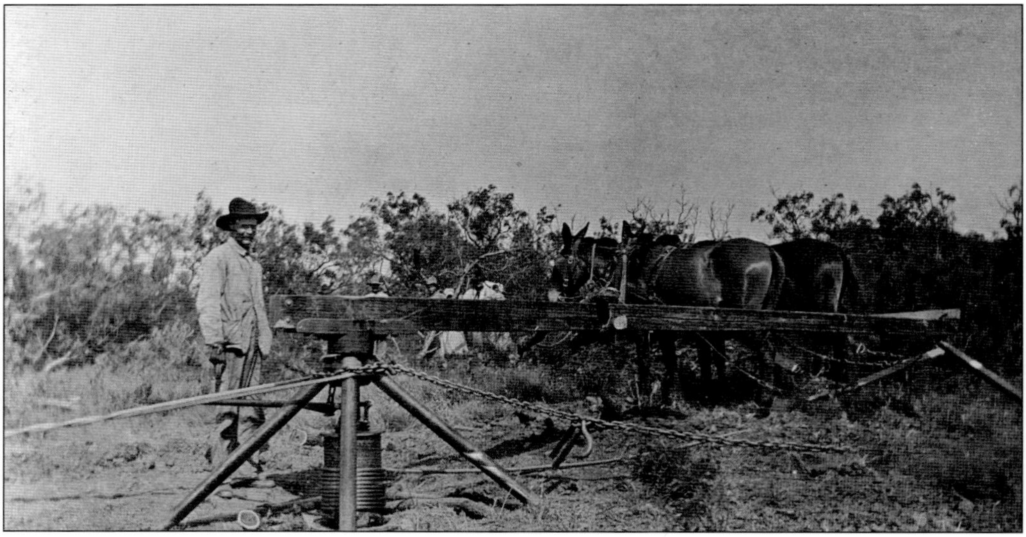

MULE-POWERED STUMP PULLING. In this remarkable early-1900s photograph, Nelson Howe is pulling stumps with a wench, cable, and mule power. Mules and horses made possible the developments in agriculture in the late 19th and early 20th centuries. Clearing land of trees and brush, whether to build a home, create forage for cattle, or ready land to plant crops, was a laborious process for the early farmers and ranchers in the rolling plains of North Central Texas. Today, clearing is often done with a bulldozer. (Courtesy of Betty Welch and Don Welch.)

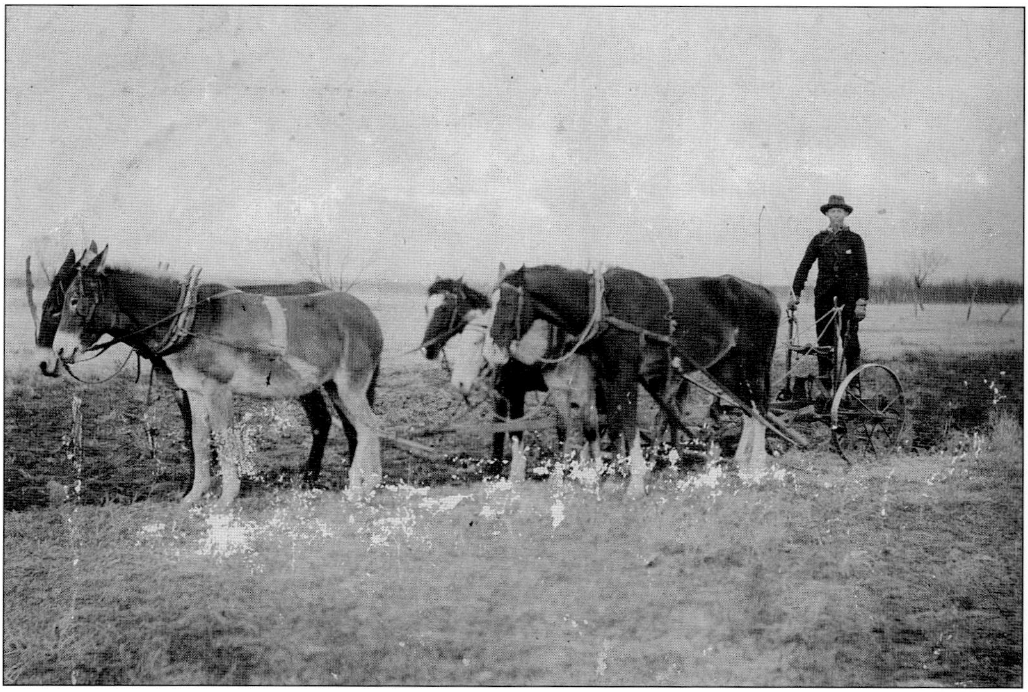

A MIXED TEAM OF HORSES AND MULES. Farmers in the county depended on mules and horses for farming. They plowed, planted, cultivated, and hauled crops and necessary supplies to and from markets. The use of horses and mules persisted through World War I and the Great Depression, but by the late 1930s, they were beginning to be replaced by tractors. (Courtesy of Baylor County Museum.)

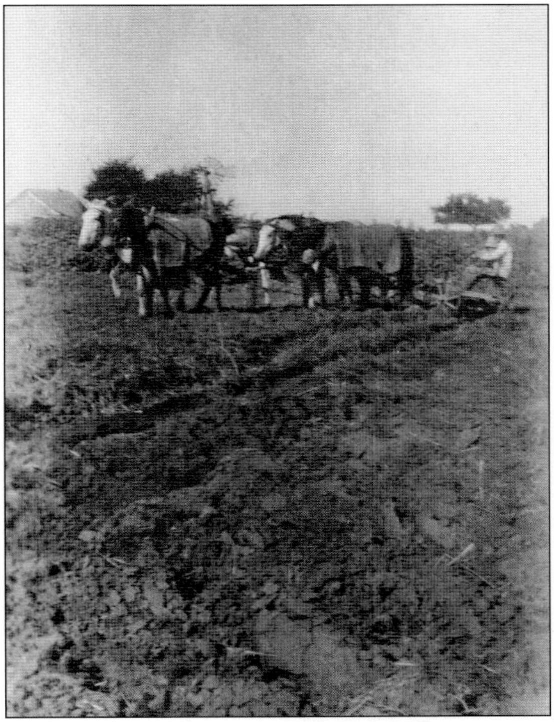

Tow Sack Fly Repellent. Walter Howe is plowing with his son Julian in his lap. The horses and mules have two sacks on their backs to help repel flies. The burlap tow sack is produced from the waste fibers of flax or hemp. It had many usages on farms. (Courtesy of Betty and Don Welch.)

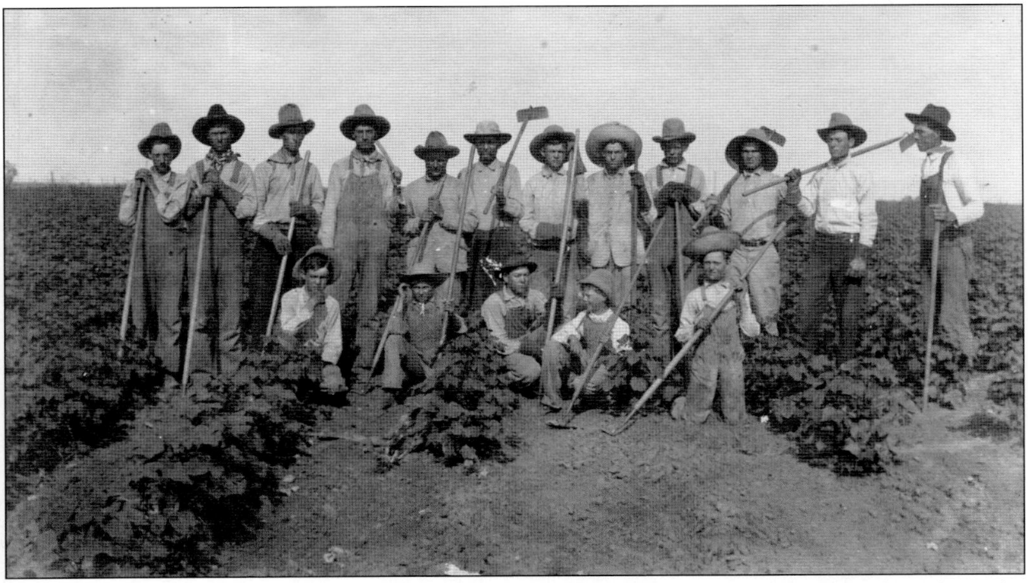

Cleaning W.H. Dodd's Cotton Field. These farmers and hands have gathered to clean the cotton crop of W.H. Dodd, of the Bomarton community. Dodd was ill in 1900 and could not work his crop. Neighbors often joined to help work fields, and they never failed to help a neighbor when illness or tragedy struck. This practice continues today in Baylor County. From left to right are (first row) Lebb Dodd, unidentified, John H. Mills, Bernie Dodd, and Meloy Joiner; (second row) unidentified, unidentified, Edgar Harrison, Clint Joiner, L.D. Miller, unidentified, Claud Dodd, Jack Barb, unidentified, unidentified, Ira Harrison, and Ben Vines. (Courtesy of Baylor County Museum.)

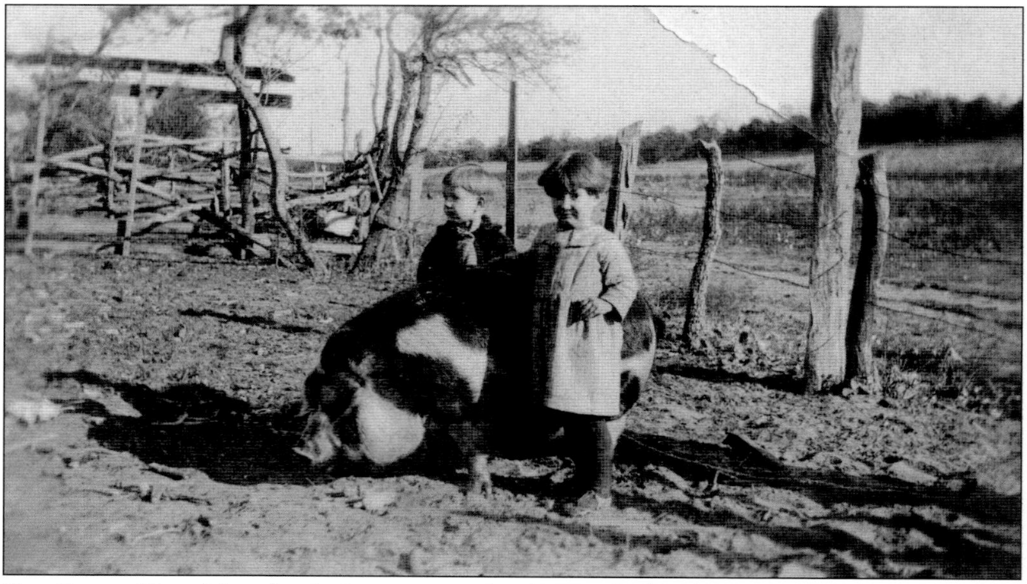

The Family Hog. Most family farms attained a degree of self-sufficiency. Nearly every one had a dairy cow for milk, butter, and cream; chickens for eggs; and a few hogs. Hogs provided the family meat, but they were also raised and sold for cash. These two unidentified children from a farm in Round Timber are shown with a fine specimen of the Spotted Poland China. (Courtesy of Betty and Don Welch.)

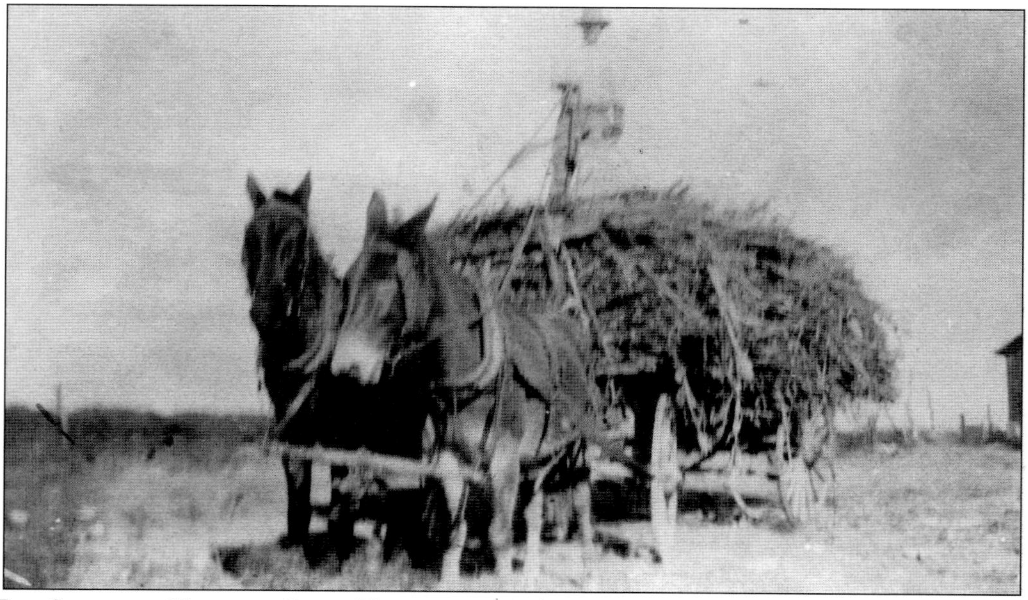

Ben Stennett Hauling Cane. The two types of cane produced locally included sugar cane, which was used to produce molasses for human consumption, and sorghum cane, which was used as feed for cattle. For many people, corn bread or biscuits with molasses syrup was a staple meal during the Depression. This 1913 photograph shows bundled cane used to feed cattle. (Courtesy of Betty and Don Welch.)

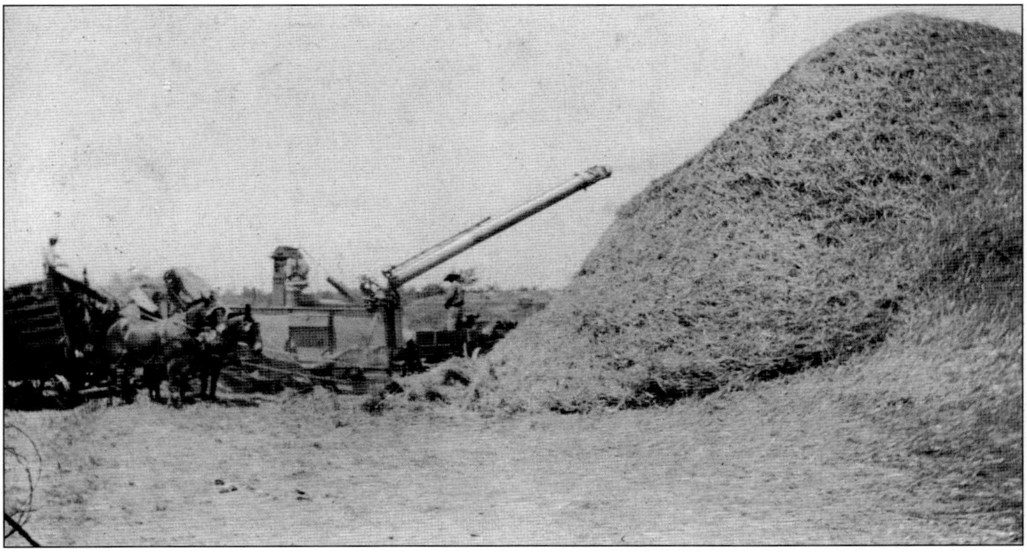

THRESHING WHEAT AT ROUND TIMBER. In this photograph, a large pile of straw is shown; it is the result of separating the grain from the straw, known as threshing. Threshing was one of most labor-intensive activities on any farm until the development of the combine in the mid-1930s. It required the help of most of the neighbors and every family member, including wives and children, who cooked for the large crews and hauled drinking water. (Courtesy of Betty and Don Welch.)

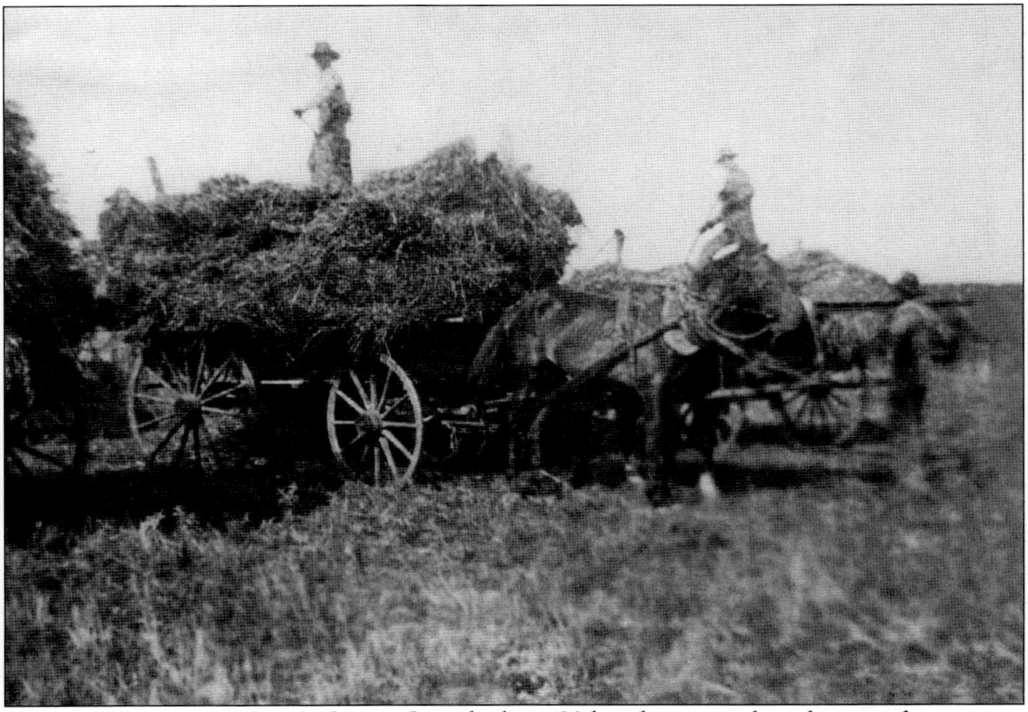

BUNDLE WAGONS AT MARY'S CREEK. It took about 20 hands to complete the crew for a steam-driven thresher in Baylor County. Also needed were 10 to 12 bundle wagons, water wagons, and grain wagons. Threshing crews worked from sunup to sundown and were fed three large meals. (Courtesy of Carolyn Bomberger.)

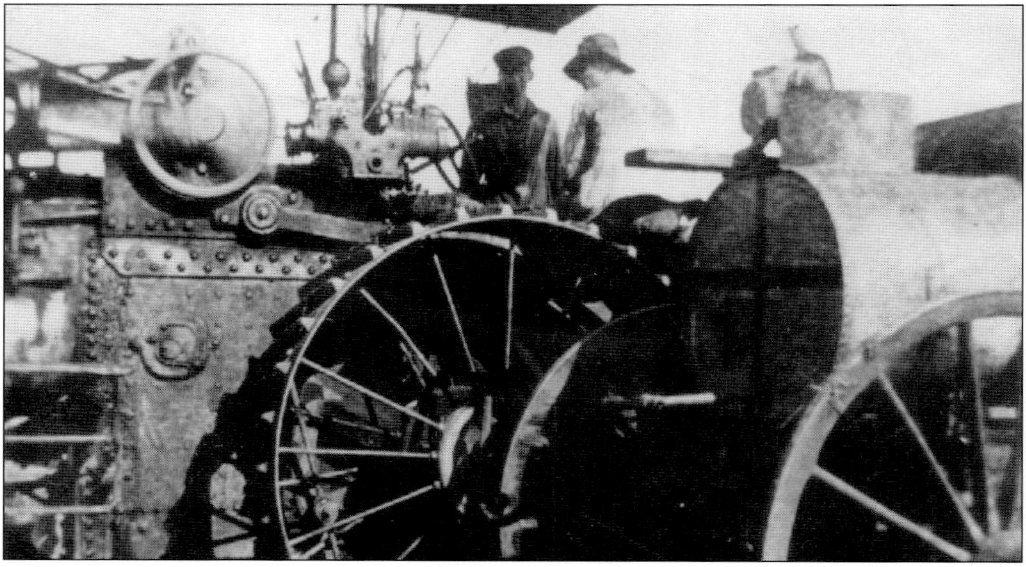

THRESHER AND WATER WAGON. Steam-driven threshers required coal or wood for fuel and a large water supply to create the steam. The water wagon in this photograph gives a good indication of just how much water was needed to operate the engines. Water wagons were usually horse-drawn to facilitate refilling. (Courtesy of Carolyn Bomberger.)

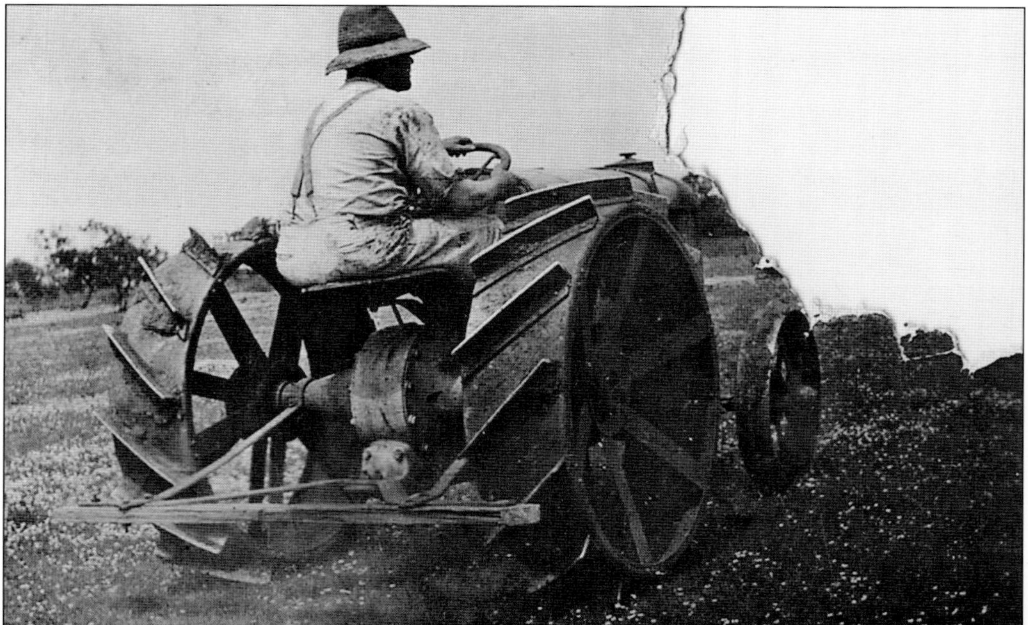

J.H. (HERSHELL) THOMAS ON TRACTOR. Tractors are the main source of power on most of today's farms in the county. The all-purpose tractor was developed in the 1920s. This photograph, taken in the late 1930s, illustrates a few basic differences between the tractors of yesterday and today. The metal wheels have been replaced with rubber tires, modern tractors tend to be much larger (although smaller tractors are still available), and most modern tractors are now equipped with temperature-controlled cabs. Clement Wirz bought his first tractor with rubber wheels in 1939. (Courtesy of the Thomas family.)

Theodore Thurman with Cotton Sack. This photograph shows Theodore Thurman going to work pulling cotton. Workers had a large, canvas cotton sack, which they dragged behind them. When the sack was filled, it was taken to a cotton scale, usually mounted on the back of a truck, and weighed. Cotton sacks when full weighed about 100 pounds. The first cotton crop in Baylor County was produced in 1891. In 1919, a bumper crop in the county produced 25,000 bales of cotton that sold for as high as 44¢ a pound. (Courtesy of Betty and Don Welch.)

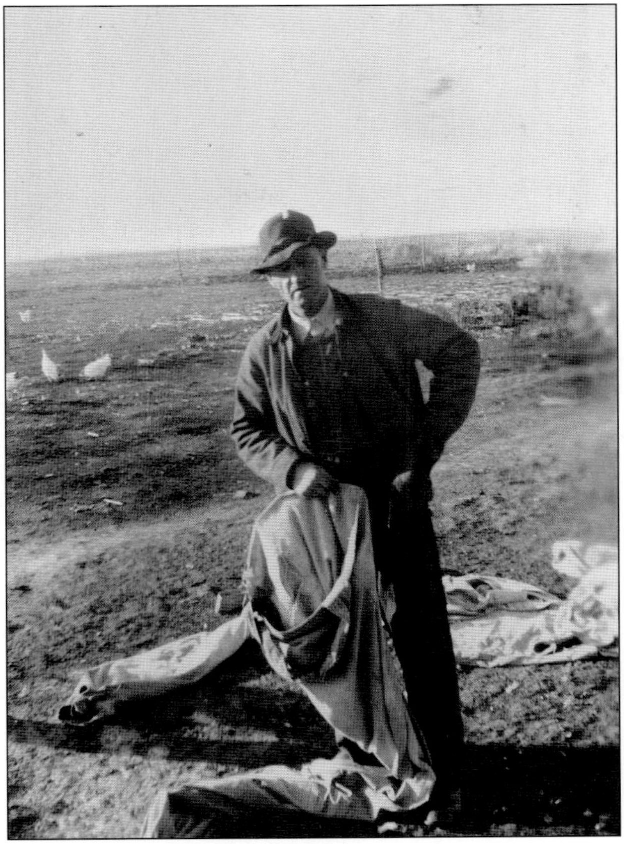

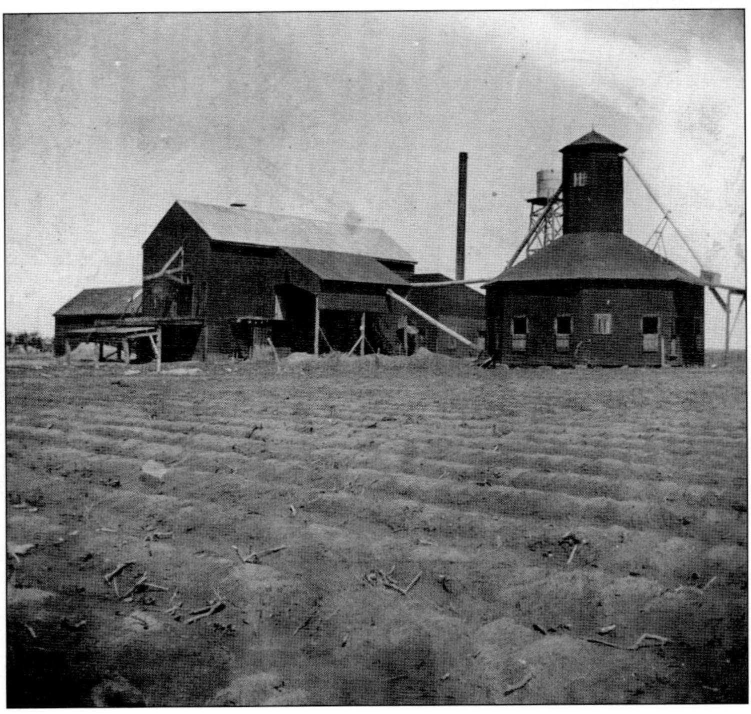

Levelview Cotton Gin. Cotton gins were built in the communities of Bomarton, England, Red Springs, Round Timber, Seymour, Shadyland, and Westover. Gins removed seeds from cotton and baled it for farmers. A by-product of cotton ginning was cottonseed cake, which was fed to cattle. (Courtesy of Betty and Don Welch.)

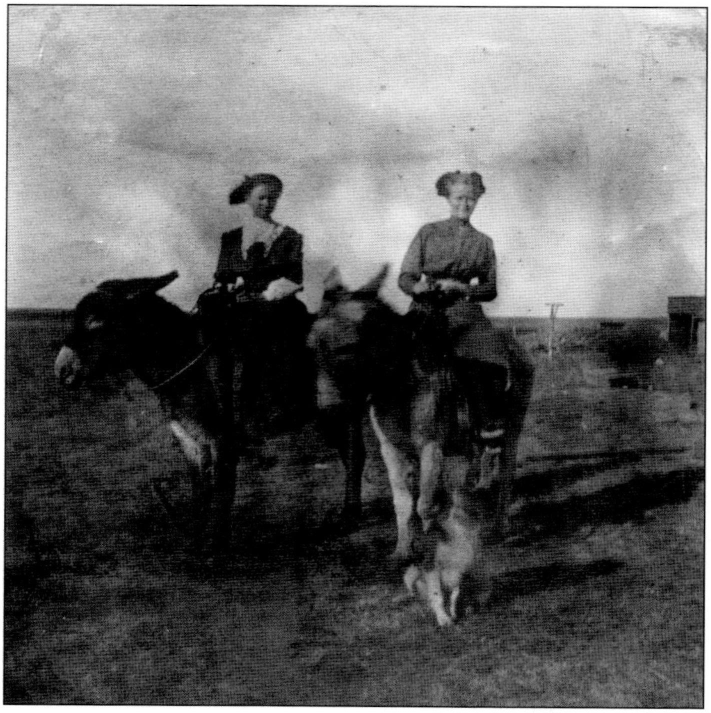

Riding Burros Sidesaddle. Ladies at the turn of the 20th century had several options of transportation when they went visiting: saddle horses, mules, carriages, and walking. Burros were used less often, but they still got residents where they were going. These unidentified ladies are mounted sidesaddle according to social convention. Most ladies did not begin to ride astride until the early years of the 20th century. (Courtesy of Margaret Higgins Johnson.)

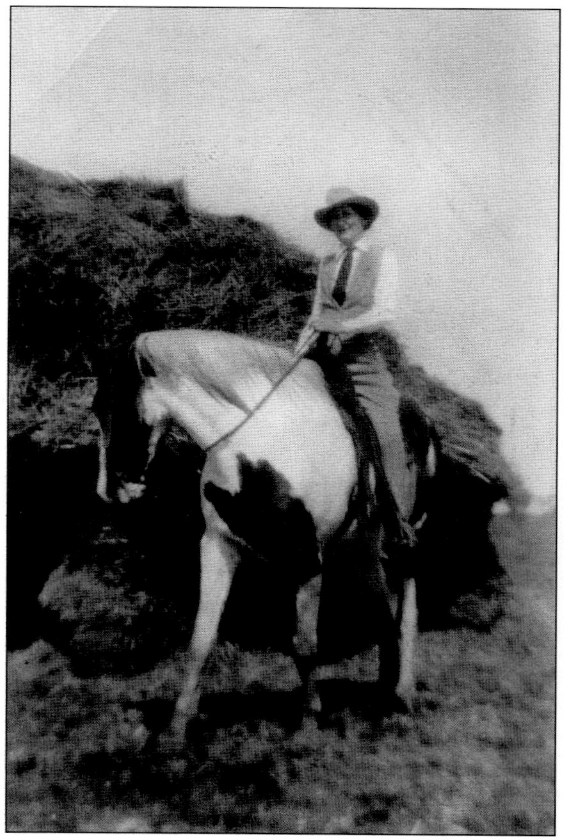

Inspecting a Haystack. In this photograph taken about 1930, Julia Turner Higgins is inspecting a haystack. Hay was first baled with the development of the hay baler. Available in the early 1920s, the first balers secured the hay with wire, and the bales measured about 18 inches by 36 inches. Today, these small bales are given mostly to horses, and cattle are fed with large round bales. The large bales reduce the amount of time spent feeding but waste more hay than the smaller ones. The largest haystack in Baylor County was on the Hershell Thomas farm. It was 250 feet long and about 35 feet tall. (Courtesy of Margaret Higgins Johnson.)

ALEX WARREN ON SADDLE HORSE. The Bill Warren family reached Baylor County on April 23, 1903. The Warrens had moved from Goliad, Texas, and had stopped a year and a half in Burnet before arriving in Baylor County. They settled on land in the southeast part of the county. Bill Warren and his wife had nine children, two of them born in Baylor County. In this photograph, Alex Warren is posed casually on his horse. He is dressed for a special occasion in a suit. (Courtesy of Baylor County Museum.)

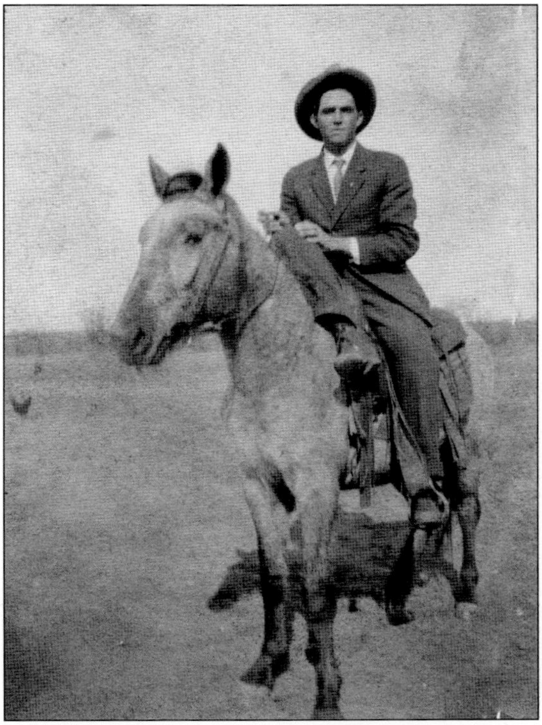

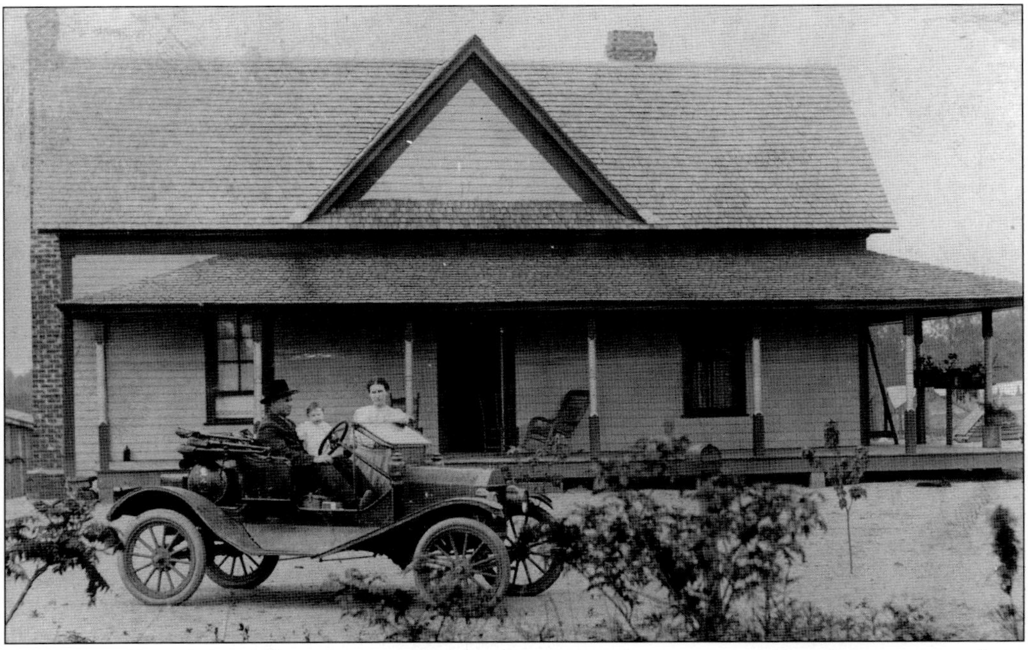

FARMHOUSE, C. 1900. This photograph is an example of a prosperous farmhouse or ranch in the early part of the 20th century. It was probably built between 1890 and 1910. According to the foreword in the publication *Latchstrings*, temporary housing took many forms. Families lived in tents, dugouts, half dugouts, boxcars, and wagons, and one family was even obliged to take rooms above a local saloon. Very few of these early farmhouses remain in the county. (Courtesy of Baylor County Museum.)

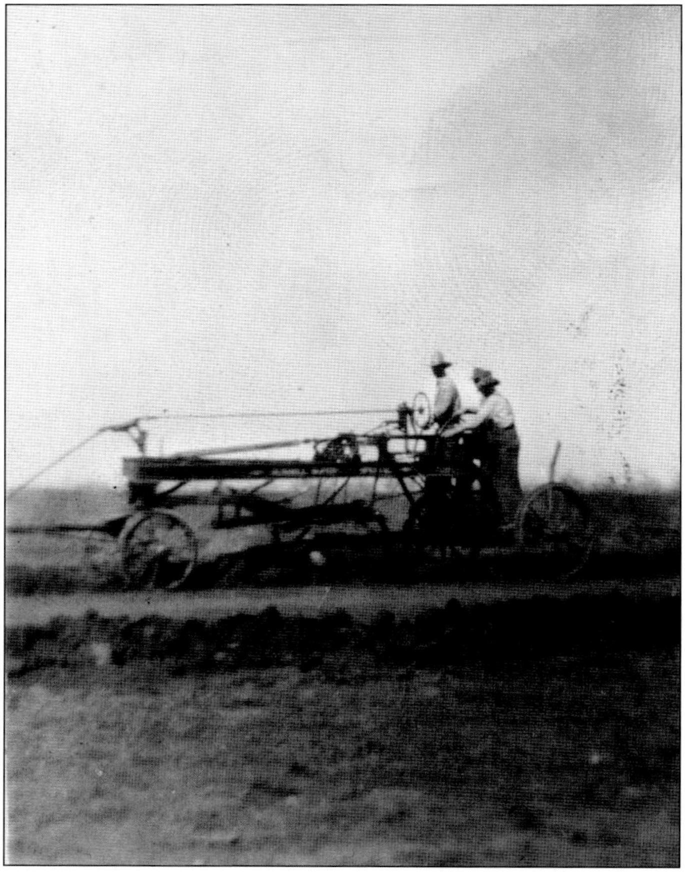

Mule-Drawn Road Grader. Through the 1930s, county roads were maintained by mule- or horse-drawn road graders. It took two men to operate these machines. One drove the grader and the teams; the second man stood on a small platform and operated the blade. Jack Hall and Harvey Thurman are driving this grader on a county road in Round Timber. (Courtesy of Betty Welch.)

Early Bulldozer in Snow. It occasionally snows in Baylor County, and it is especially important to keep the county roads passable. This photograph may have been taken in 1947 when the county received nine inches of snow, and the temperature fell to 14 degrees below zero. (Courtesy of Betty and Don Welch.)

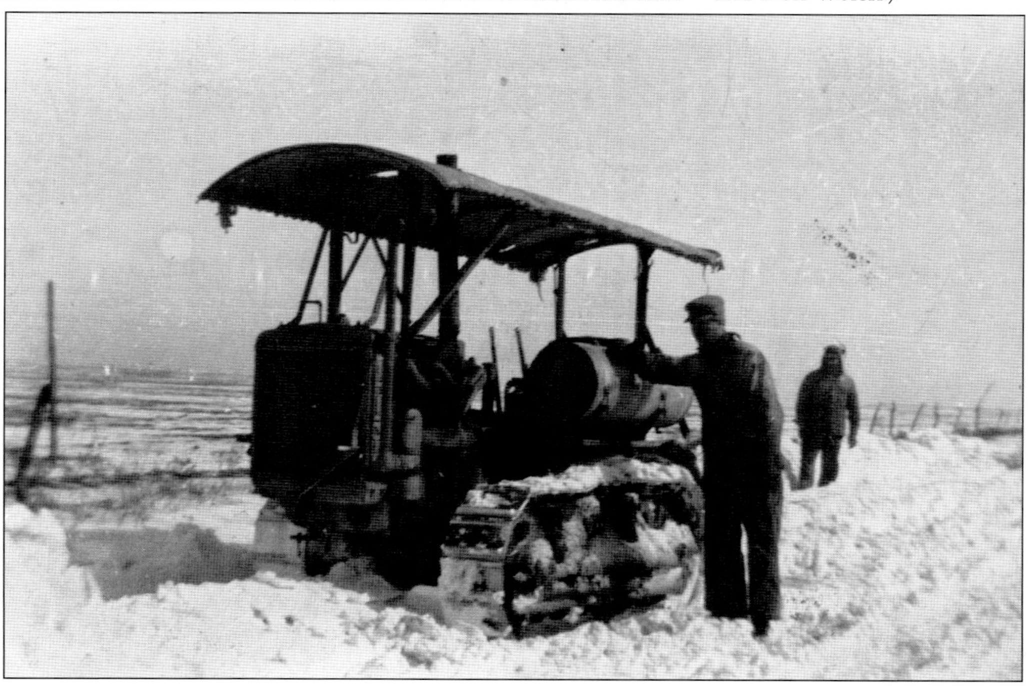

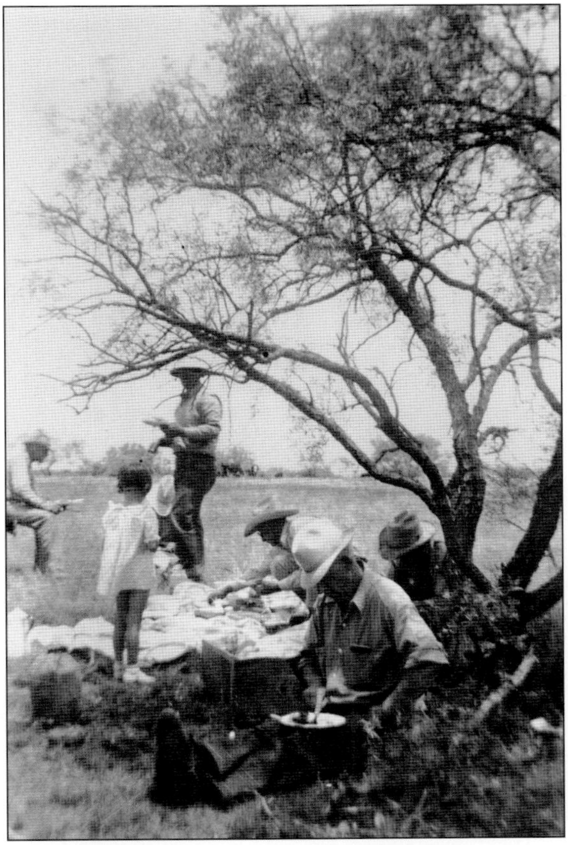

Feeding the Hands Dinner. Hands were often fed in the field. Food could be prepared in a cook shack, chuck wagon, or in the kitchen of the farmhouse and then transported to the field. This photograph from the early 1920s shows a group of hands gathered around a cool shade tree for the noontime meal. (Courtesy of Margaret Higgins Johnson.)

Cotton Wagon. Farmers often need to devise creative solutions to problems with tools at hand. In this photograph, a tractor has been adapted to haul a cotton wagon. Cotton equipment, like other farm equipment, has evolved to be larger and more efficient. Today, large balers compress the cotton before it is hauled to the gin. (Courtesy of Betty and Don Welch.)

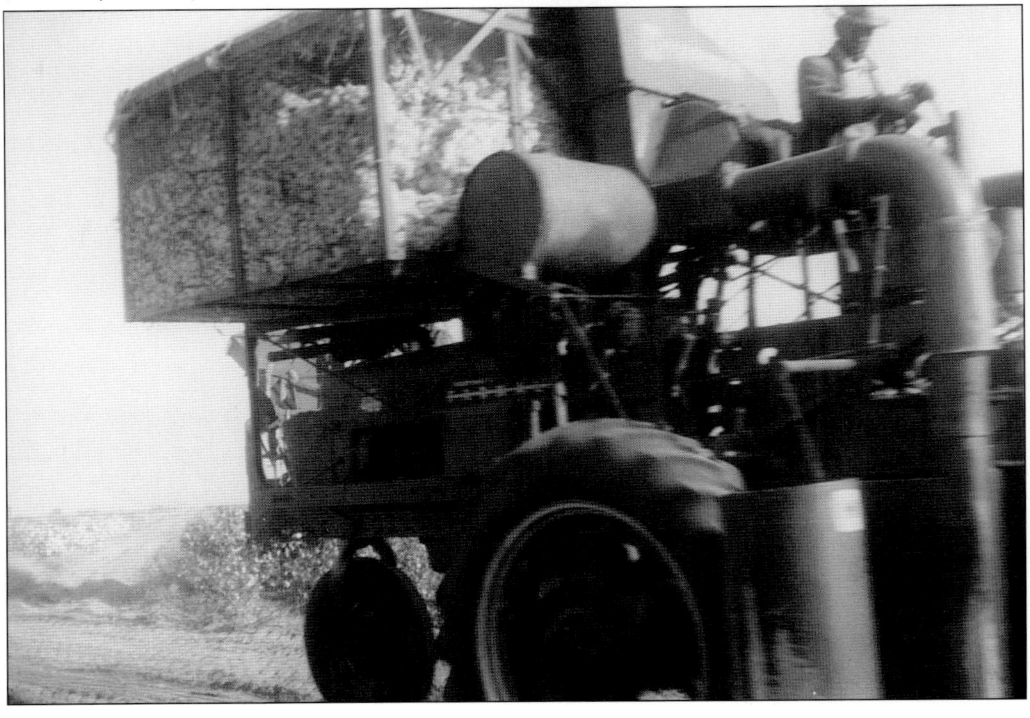

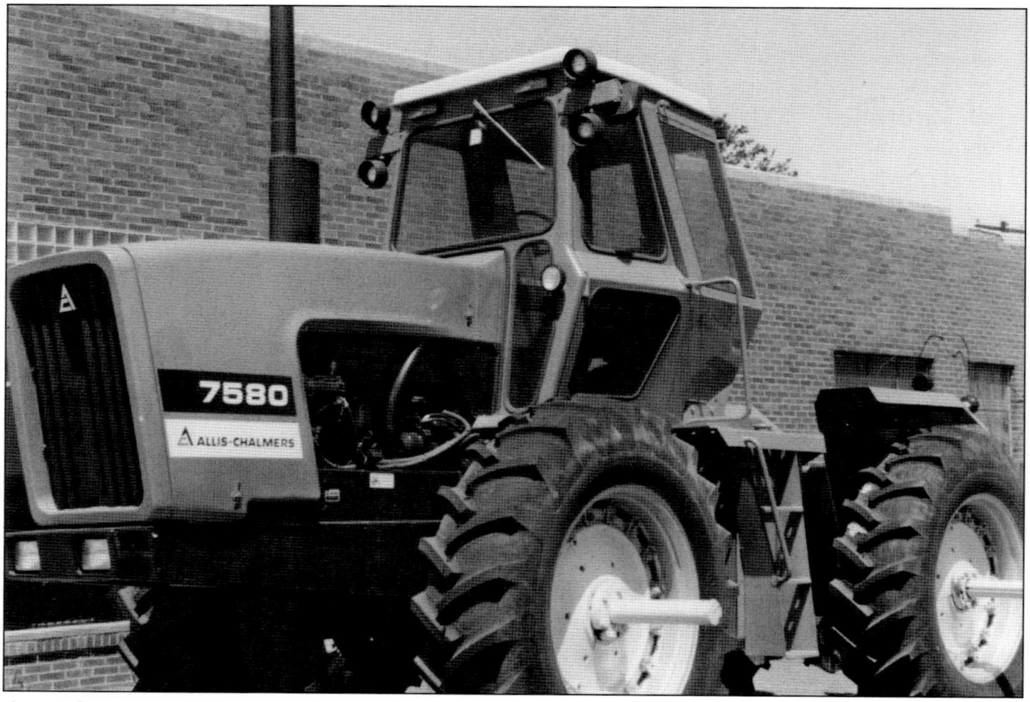

ALLIS CHALMERS TRACTOR. By the 1970s, large tractors such as this Allis Chalmers were in use in the county. The consolidation of the farms that began in the 1960s resulted in a need for tractors that would handle larger tracts of land efficiently. (Courtesy of Baylor County Office of the USDA.)

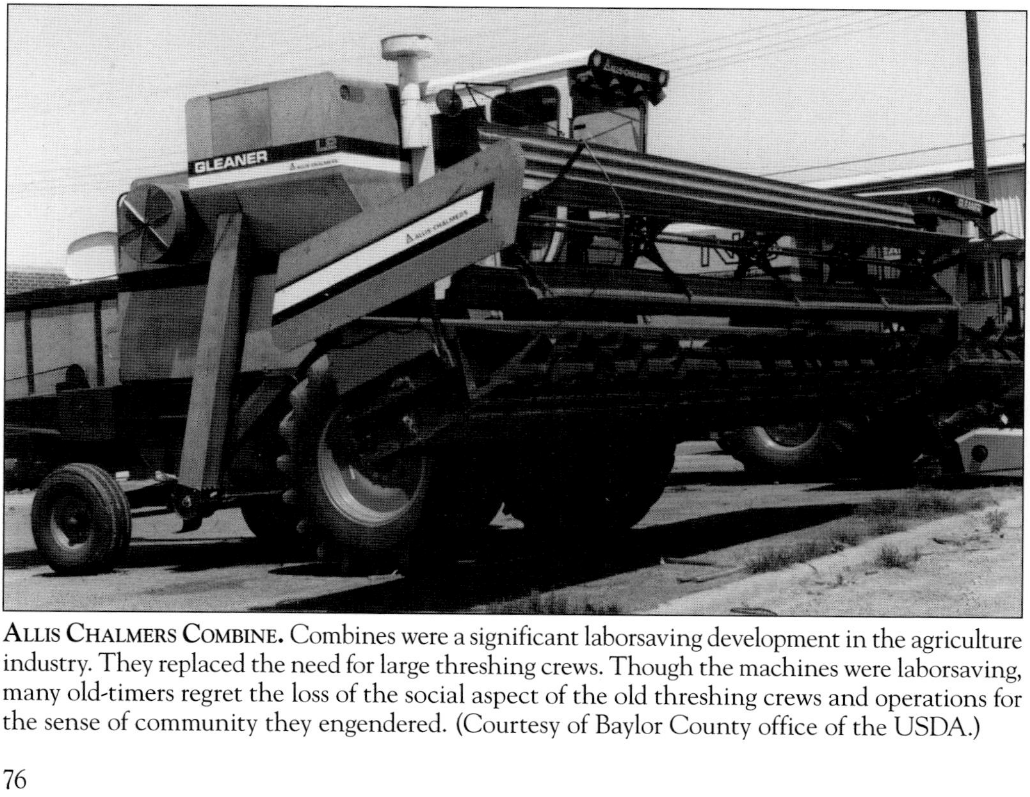

ALLIS CHALMERS COMBINE. Combines were a significant laborsaving development in the agriculture industry. They replaced the need for large threshing crews. Though the machines were laborsaving, many old-timers regret the loss of the social aspect of the old threshing crews and operations for the sense of community they engendered. (Courtesy of Baylor County office of the USDA.)

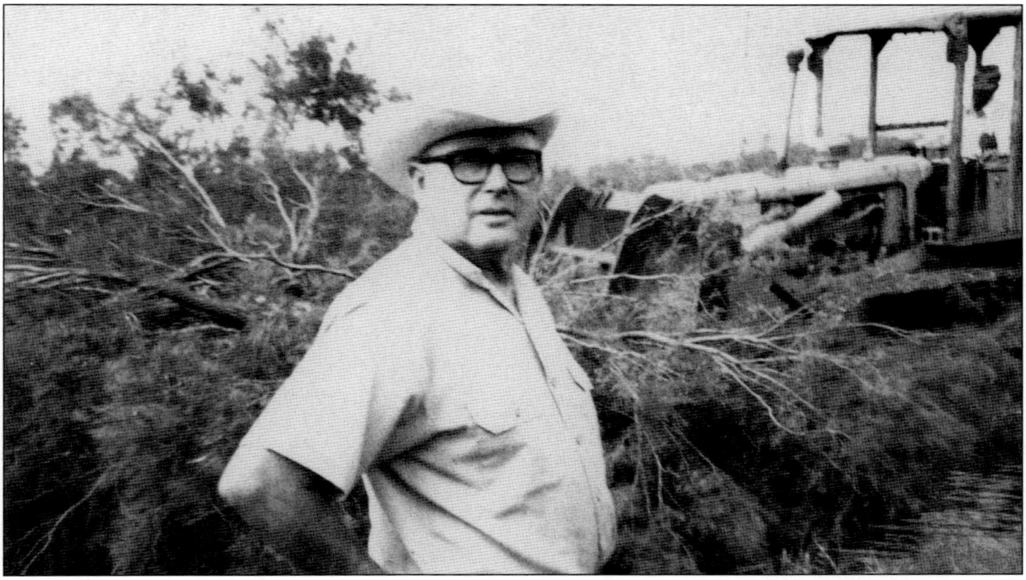

Vern Teague and Bulldozer. Bulldozers are often used to control brush and mesquite trees in pastures. Mesquites have moved steadily north from Mexico. They compete with the grass needed for grazing and use valuable water. When pastures become heavily infested with mesquite trees, they must be removed. Bulldozers effectively clear the brush and trees, but they also disturb the fragile grass. (Courtesy of Baylor County office of the USDA.)

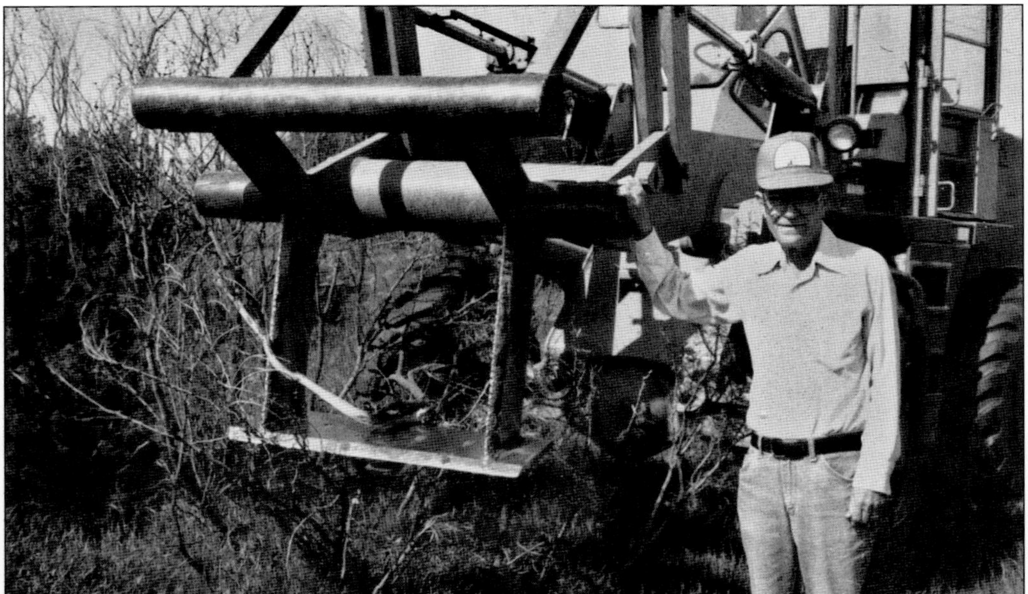

Rufus Whitley and Brush-Control Machine. Brush and weed control is an important element of maintaining pasture and rangeland in the county, and it is accomplished by a variety of means. In this photograph, Rufus Whitley stands beside a low-energy grubber, which was used on the Craddock ranch in a demonstration planned with Baylor County extension agents Lowell Cure and Gary Colthorp in the early 1980s. This machine was designed to specifically target individual trees, and thus eliminate the growth of weeds that resulted after normal root plowing. (Courtesy of Barbara Colthorp.)

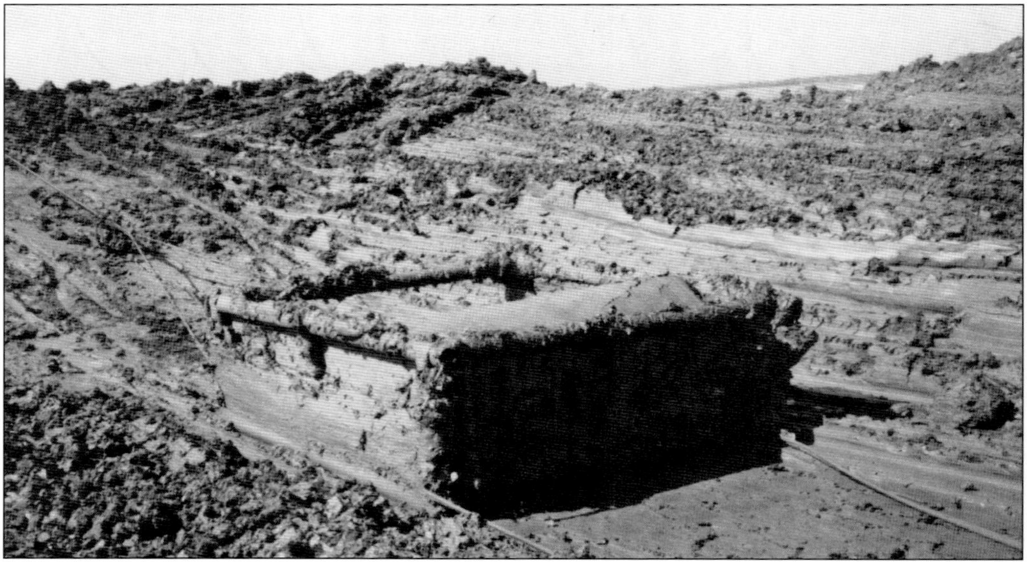

Jack Stout's Mud Bucket. Stock tanks dug into the red clay that proliferates in parts of the county fill with silt over time and must be re-dredged. The equipment used to accomplish this task has varied over the years and was often homemade. A close look at this photograph reveals a large square box in the middle of the tank. Cables were attached to a bulldozer on one end, and a tractor on the other end. When the mud was collected, the box was dragged over the tank dam and dumped on the other side. It removed about two yards of mud in each swipe. This type of box was patented in the 1970s. (Courtesy of Baylor County Office of the USDA.)

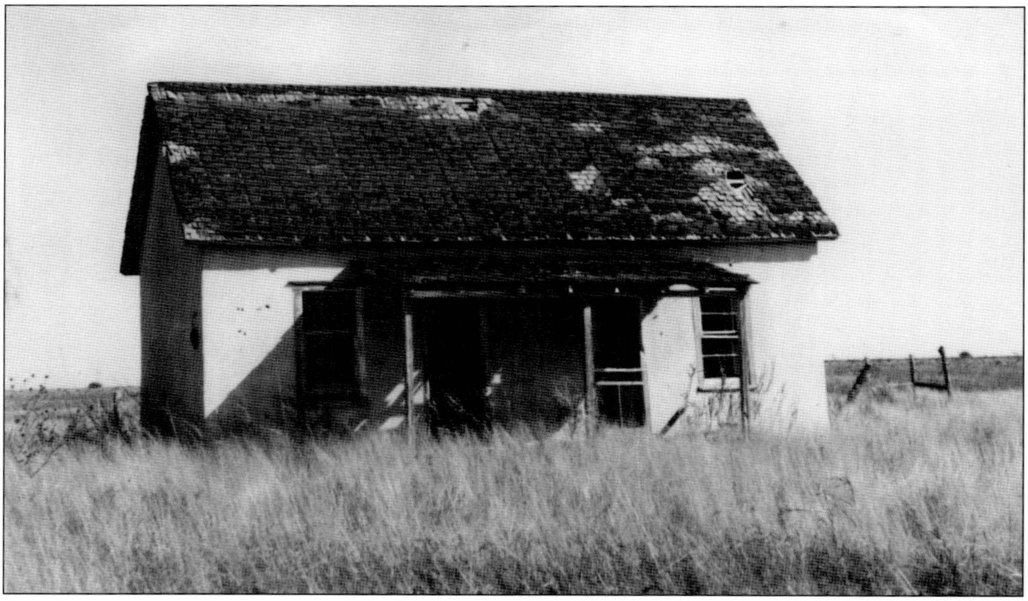

An Abandoned Farmhouse. The countryside in the county used to be dotted with small, abandoned farmhouses. Some of these dwellings fell victim to the Great Depression; others were simply abandoned by families who still farmed but decided to live in town. The numbers of these old farmhouses have dwindled. Some of them were torn down, some fell victim to fires, and others merely deteriorated due to lack of maintenance. (Courtesy of Baylor County Office of the USDA.)

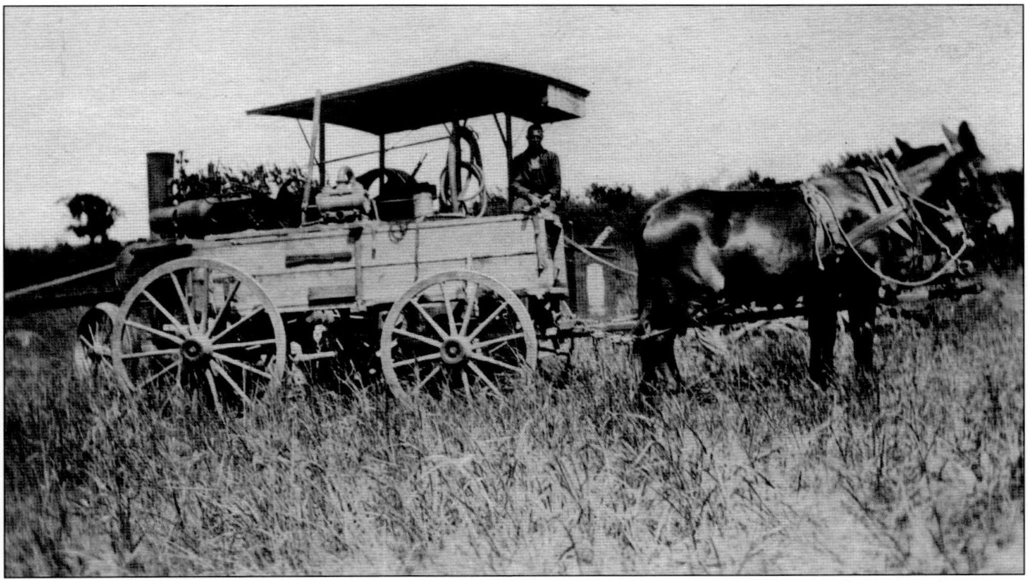

Steam Engine and Water Wagon. Jack Howe poses next to a water wagon for a photograph. Water was pumped from the wagon to tanks on the side of the engine. The water was then piped from the tanks into the engine, which converted it to steam. (Courtesy of Dorothy Morgan Howe.)

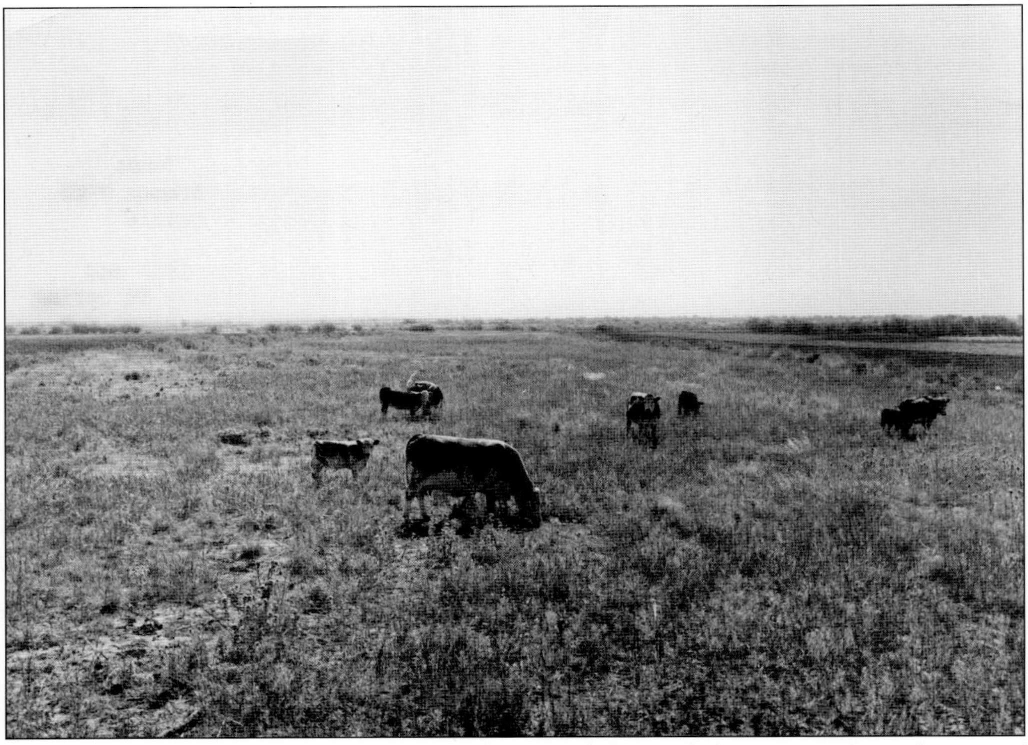

Cow-Calf Operation. Cow-calf operators dominated the cattle business in the early years of the county. This photograph, taken about 1961 on the C.L. Darnell place in Westover, shows cattle grazing on blue panic grass that had been seeded in a waterway. (Courtesy of Baylor County Office of the USDA.)

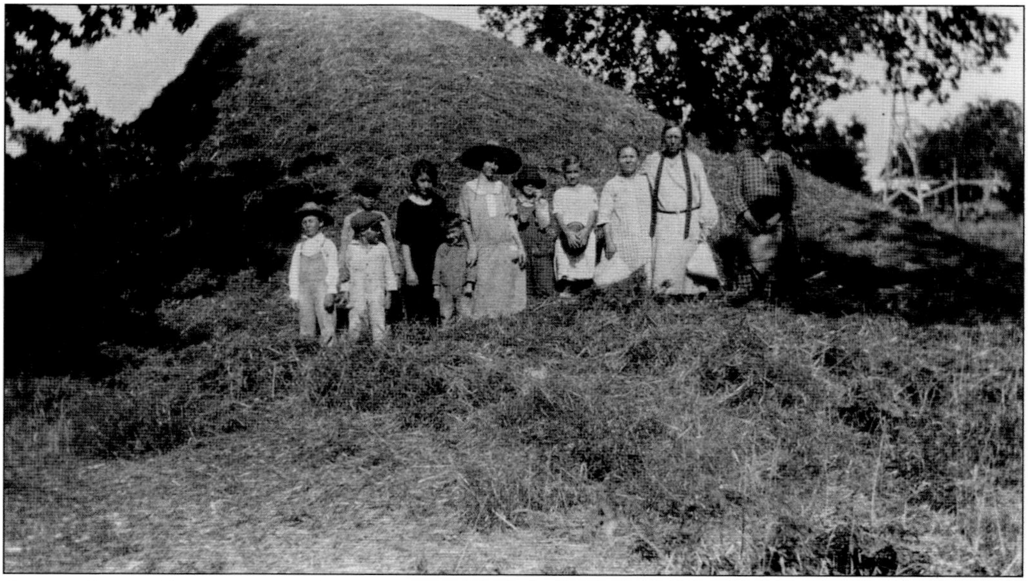

Straw Stack On Stennett Farm. This photograph, taken in 1926, is of a straw stack created from threshing on the Stennett Farm in Round Timber. The individuals pictured most likely helped with the threshing. From left to right are Travis Hulcy, J.T. Howe, Milton Dipprey, Lillie and Tim Coldiron, Allie Devrow, Pete Foley, Bessie and Lucy Bell Stennett, Evie Hulcy, and Bert Dipprey. (Courtesy of Betty and Don Welch.)

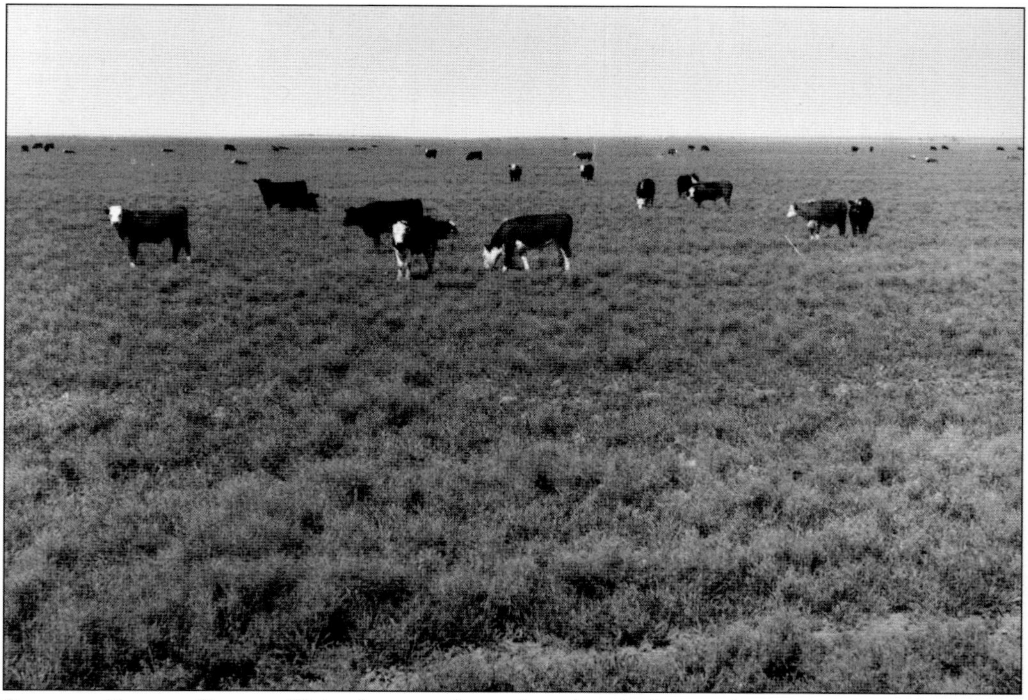

Stocker Feeder Calves. This photograph is of stocker feeder cattle grazing on a wheat field. Market conditions determine whether the wheat is grazed out or harvested. This photograph is also a good example of the landscape in Baylor County, uninterrupted to the horizon. (Courtesy of Baylor County Office of the USDA.)

Five

The One-Room Schoolhouse

Baylor County once had 38 one- and two-room schoolhouses. These schoolhouses were not only educational buildings but also the physical embodiment of the determination of families to create a better life and testimony to community spirit and cooperation. They frequently joined a church and cemetery to become the cornerstones of a community. Once a need for a school was established, trustees were elected, and an individual was found to donate land for the school. If possible, schools were located so that students were not required to walk more than three miles.

Trustees were responsible for paying, hiring, and dismissing teachers. Some schools provided a teacherage for living accommodations, but many teachers had to board with families from the community. Pay was not exorbitant, and teachers were required to be single. They frequently taught multiple grades simultaneously. If there were two rooms, two teachers taught multiple grades simultaneously.

Tradition states that Round Timber had one of the earliest county schools, a log cabin built in 1879. During the 1890s, population growth dictated a new schoolhouse, which was constructed somewhere around 1896 in Round Timber. Both Red Springs and Levelview were built in 1898, and Miller Creek was erected in 1899. School construction continued through the beginning of the 20th century. The last one-room schoolhouse to be built was the Self School in 1925.

For many years, the school term ran from November (after the cotton was harvested) to May. Students were expected to help with the chores. Boys ensured there was a supply of coal or wood for the stoves, and girls dusted the erasers and filled the water jars. Reading, writing, and arithmetic were taught, and if time allowed in the spring, so were geography, history, and science.

Beginning in the late 1940s, these rural schools were consolidated into the Seymour Rural High School District. Bomarton was the last to close in 1955. In spite of scarce resources, these schools provided excellent educations and are fondly remembered by the students who attended them.

These Baylor County one-room schoolhouses represent a unique lifestyle that was the result of conditions in an agricultural era before the development of automobiles and mechanized farming.

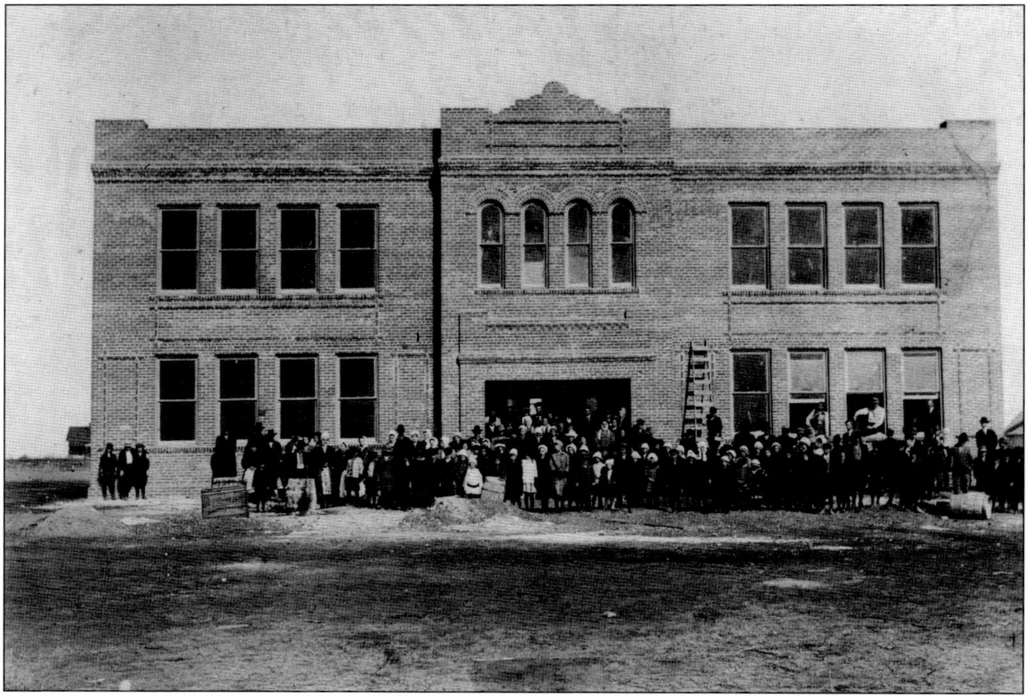

Bomarton School, 1913. Created in 1906, the Bomarton School District was among the last to be consolidated with the Seymour Rural High School District in 1955. In 1913, report cards became mandatory, and in 1926, the school board, in a split vote, approved the wearing of trousers by girls. (Courtesy of Baylor County Museum.)

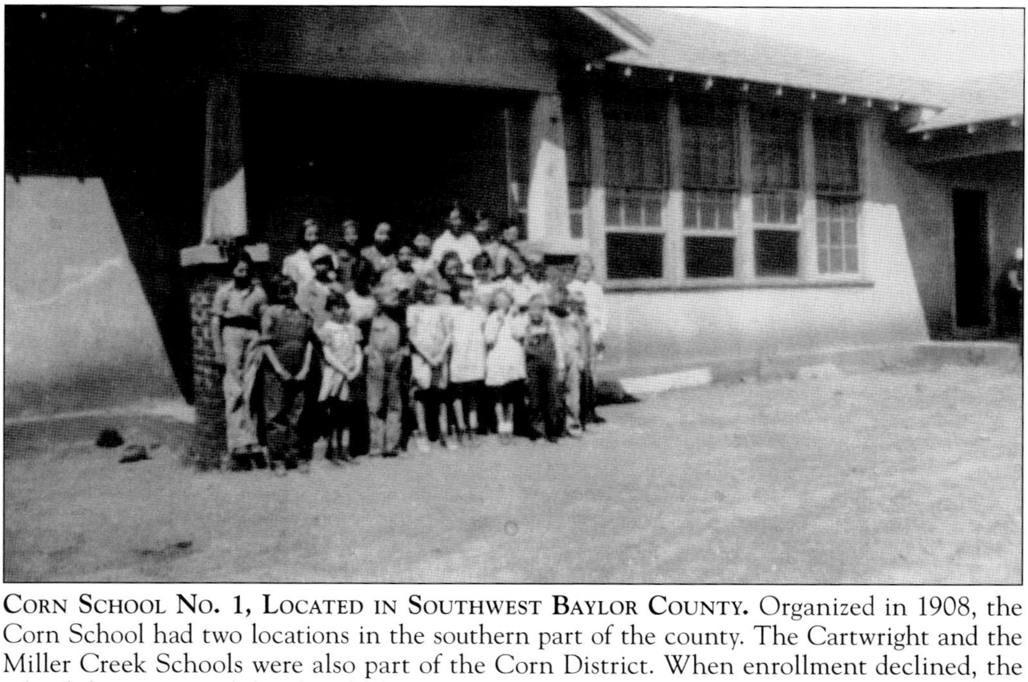

Corn School No. 1, Located in Southwest Baylor County. Organized in 1908, the Corn School had two locations in the southern part of the county. The Cartwright and the Miller Creek Schools were also part of the Corn District. When enrollment declined, the school district consolidated with the Bomarton School District in 1940. (Courtesy of Baylor County Museum.)

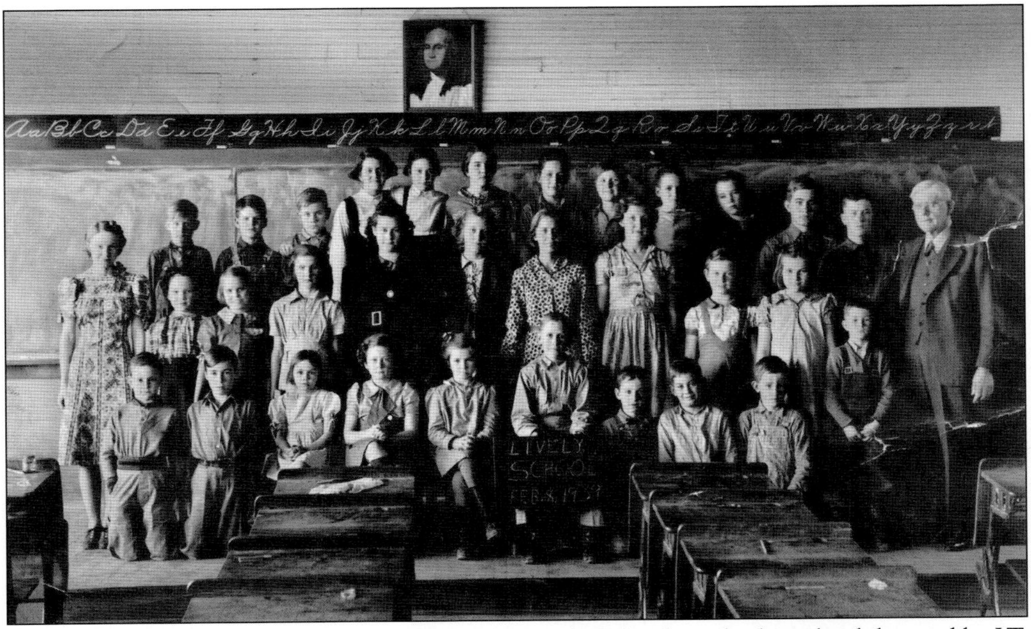

A Typical Schoolhouse Interior, 1939. The Lively School was built on land donated by J.T. Lively. It was not uncommon for schools to be named after the person donating the land. The early schools were usually located approximately three miles apart, within walking distance for the children. Cursive handwriting was a required and desired skill for students to master. (Courtesy of Baylor County Museum.)

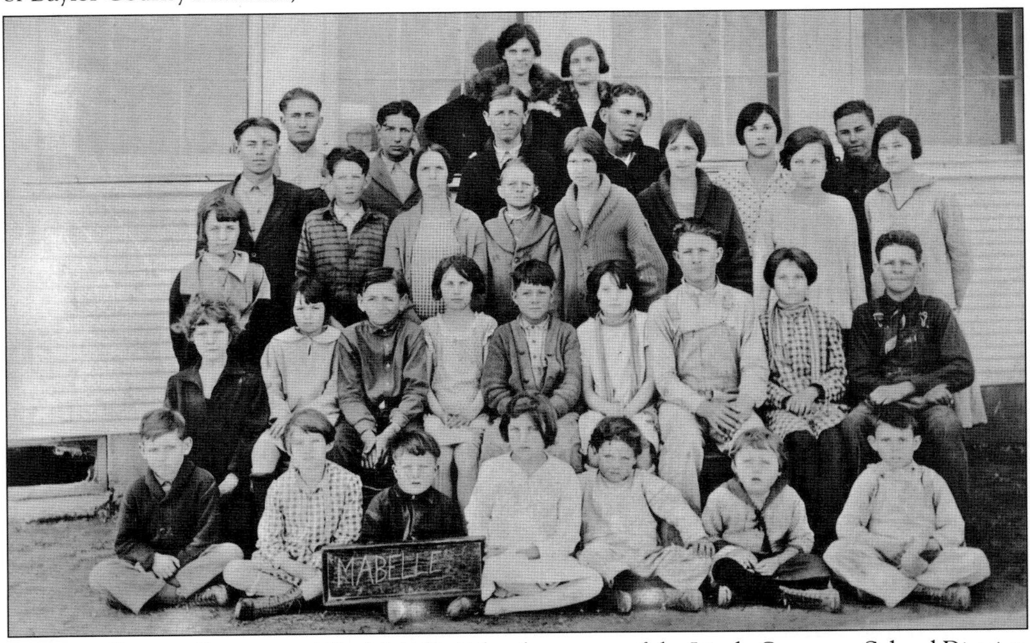

Mabelle School Students. The Mabelle School was part of the Lively Common School District, which was organized in 1900. Other schools in the district were Lively and England, and later on, Fulda, Shawver, Woodrum, and Weims. By 1948, the schools had closed, and students came to Seymour. The Mabelle building was moved to the Seymour Elementary School campus and used for classrooms during the 1950s and 1960s. (Courtesy of Baylor County Museum.)

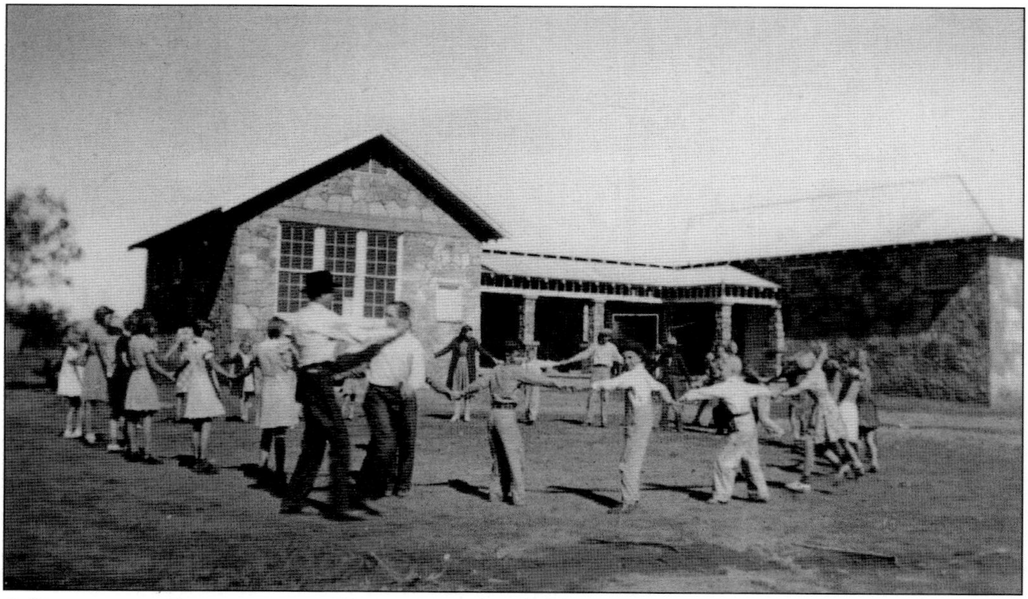

A Break from Learning the Three R's. The children at the Ogden School looked forward to recess in the 1940s as much as children do today. Their school year, however, usually included a break in the fall, not for vacation, but for pulling cotton. (Courtesy of Baylor County Museum.)

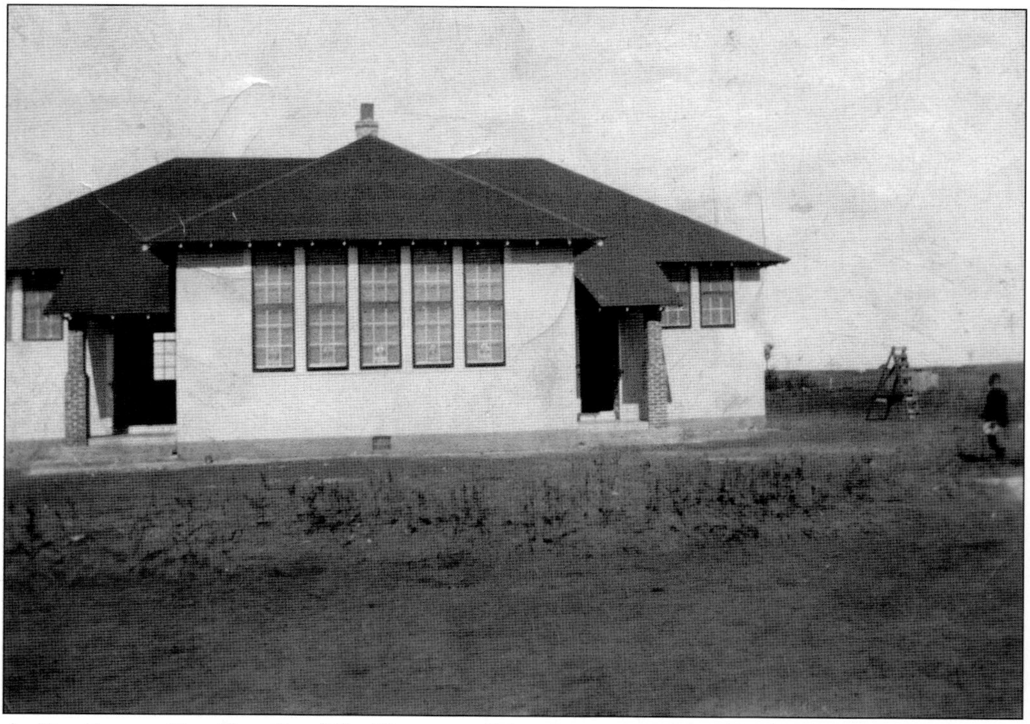

As Far As the Eye Can See. The Plainview School was one of the 38 schools in Baylor County. The school closed in 1943. However, the building would have a second life later as the field house for the Seymour Panther football teams. The athletes would no longer have to dress at the gym and run up the hill. This field house was located at the north end of the football field and would be used until the mid-1980s. (Courtesy of Baylor County Museum.)

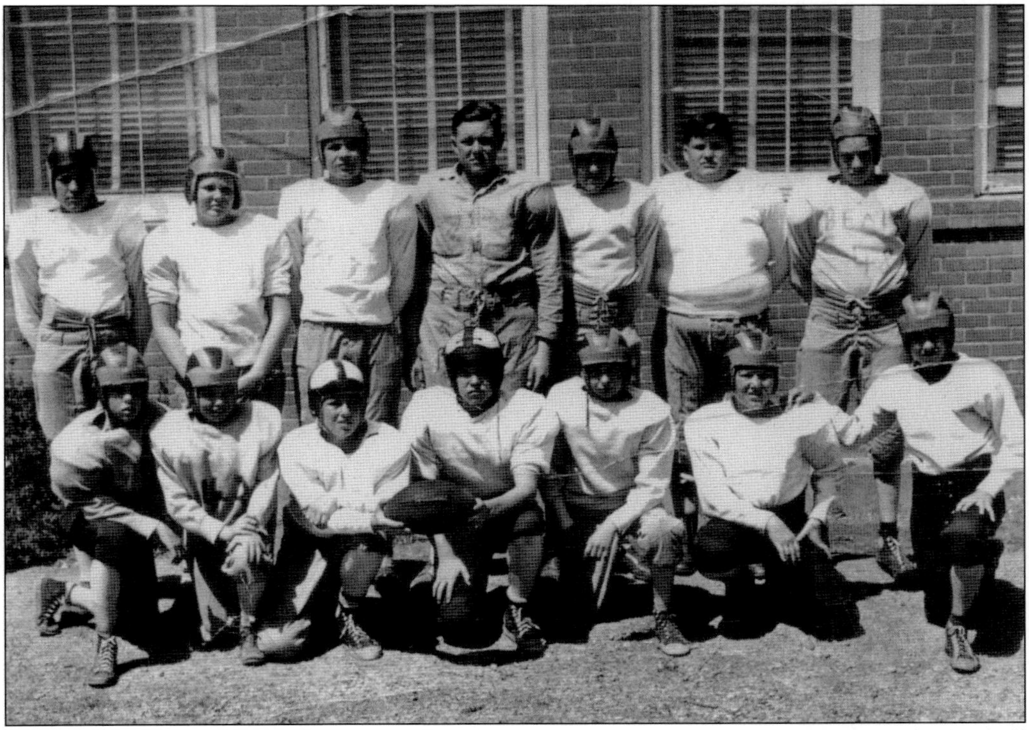

Time for Some Red Springs Football. Red Springs School, formed in 1898, sported a football team in 1948. Members of that Bulldog team are, from left to right, (first row) Buddy Patterson, Ronnie Cline, Jim Baldwin, Joe Crump, JoJo Hrncirik, Charles Baldwin, and Jerry Massey; (second row) Luke Nickerson, Billy W. Powell, Bryan Robertson, Charles Parker, Benny Cowart, Bob Miller, and Bobby Lee Powell. The team played with handed-down equipment from Seymour. School administrators felt a football team might keep some of the older boys interested in school. A.B. Martin coached the team. (Courtesy of A.B. Martin.)

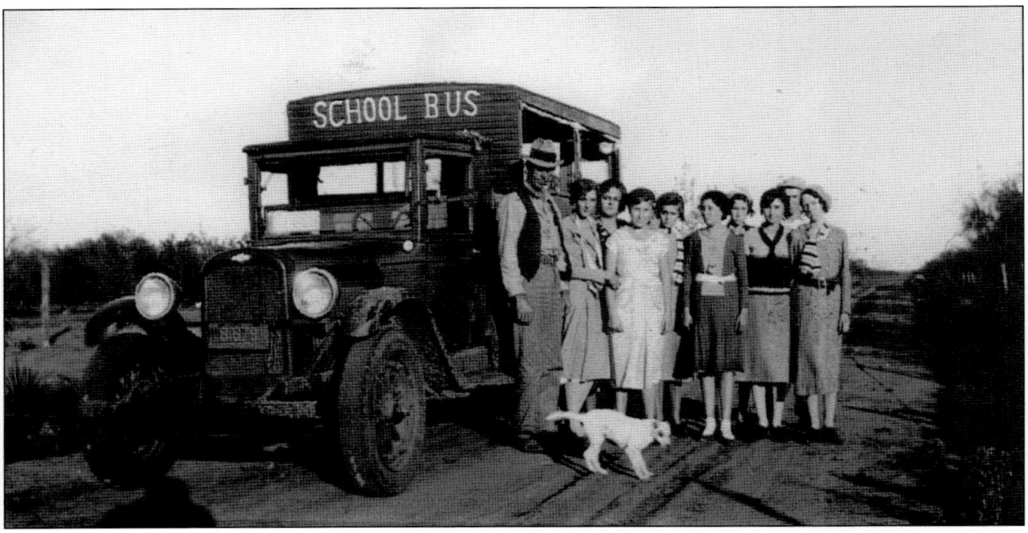

One of the Early School Buses. The Richland school bus, a luxury in the rural schools, was a 1928 truck owned by Arthur L. Nuckols, who drove the bus from 1930 to 1940. (Courtesy of Baylor County Museum.)

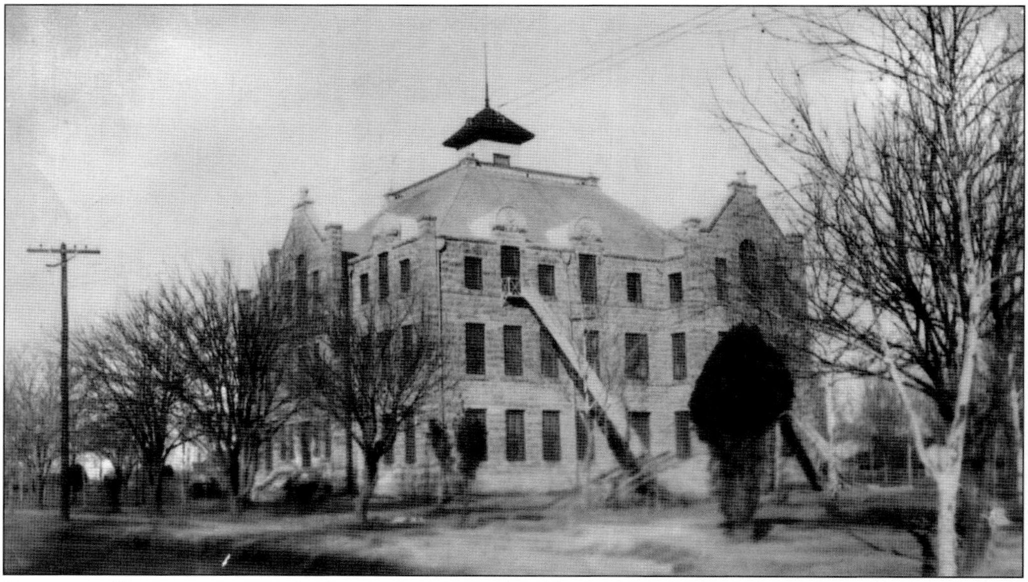

Seymour School, 1902. A three-story stone building served the educational needs for many years. In the early days, the first requirement of a male teacher was that he should be tough enough to lick his biggest pupil. Often in the early years, teachers would board in the homes of the students, and the single female teachers had a rather strict code of conduct to follow, which included no dancing or smoking. (Courtesy of Carolene Hash Stovall.)

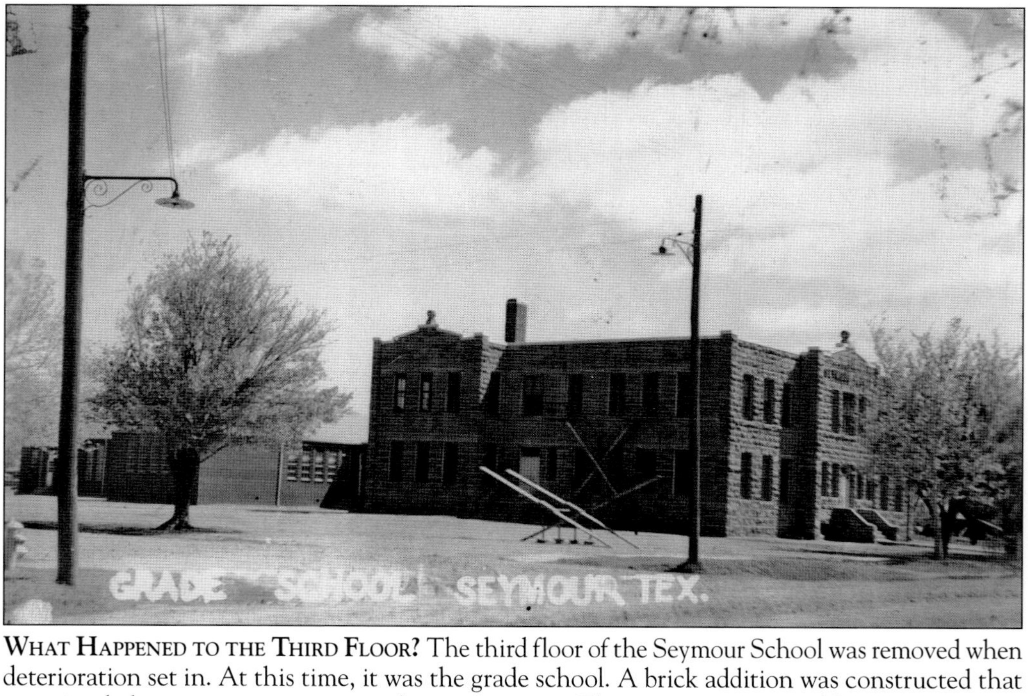

What Happened to the Third Floor? The third floor of the Seymour School was removed when deterioration set in. At this time, it was the grade school. A brick addition was constructed that contained classrooms, restrooms, and an auditorium. The stone section would serve until 1949, when new construction replaced that portion of the school. (Courtesy of John. L. Stallings.)

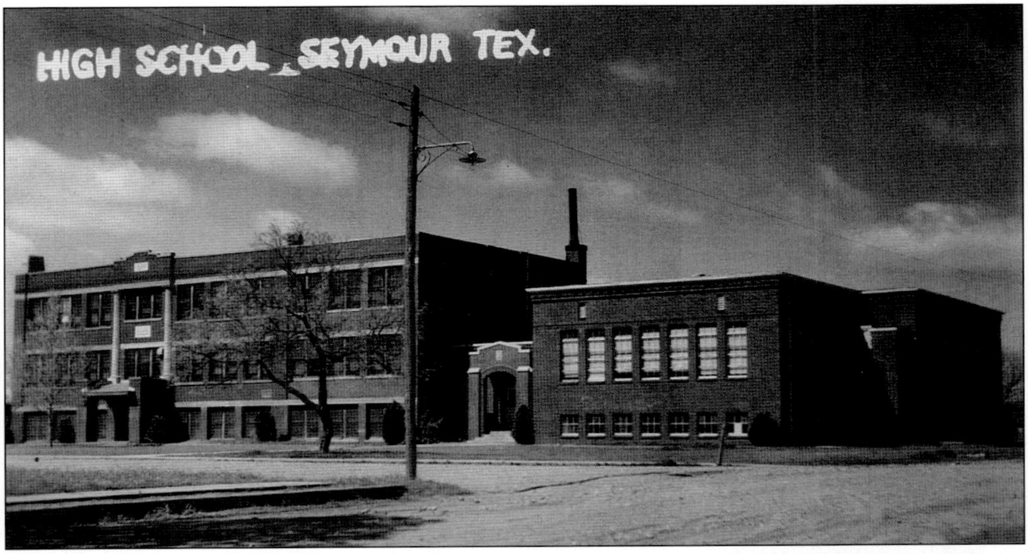

SEYMOUR HIGH SCHOOL, 1936. In 1917, the first portion of this school was built. In 1928, six rooms were added to the north end, and in 1936, the library and study hall were added to the north end as well. An auditorium and cafeteria were built in the early 1950s on the northwest side. The school and its additions would serve Baylor County students until 1991, when a new school was built "up on the hill." (Courtesy of John L. Stallings.)

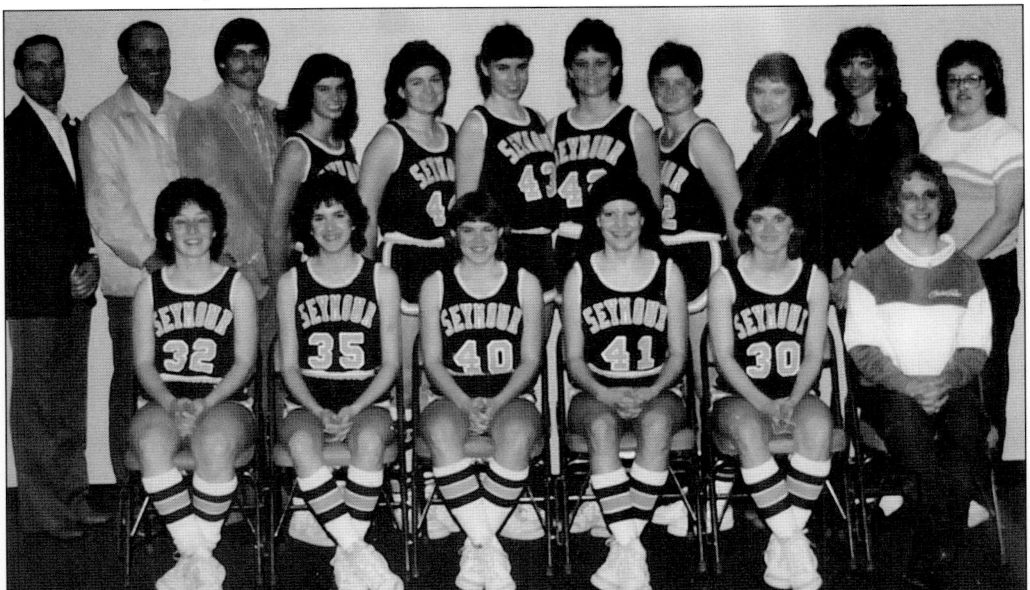

SPORTS EXCELLENCE IN SCHOOL. The Texas University Interscholastic League (UIL) was and is the largest interschool state organization of its kind in the world. In 1985, the Seymour High School girls' basketball team was a semi-finalist at the Class AA state tournament in Austin and the first Seymour High School team to reach this level. Pictured are, from left to right, (first row) Carrie Jackson, Judy Sullivan, Lorie Talley, Natalie Kuhler, Angie Richardson, and Cheri Conner; (second row) Randall Murry (coach), Billy Hardin (coach), Jerry Skelton (coach), Tina Donnell, Karri Worthington, Gena McClung, Jana Hays, Frieda Wirz, Charlotte Talley (manager), Stephanie Carter (manager), and Dian Sessions (manager). (Courtesy of Lorie Talley Stafford.)

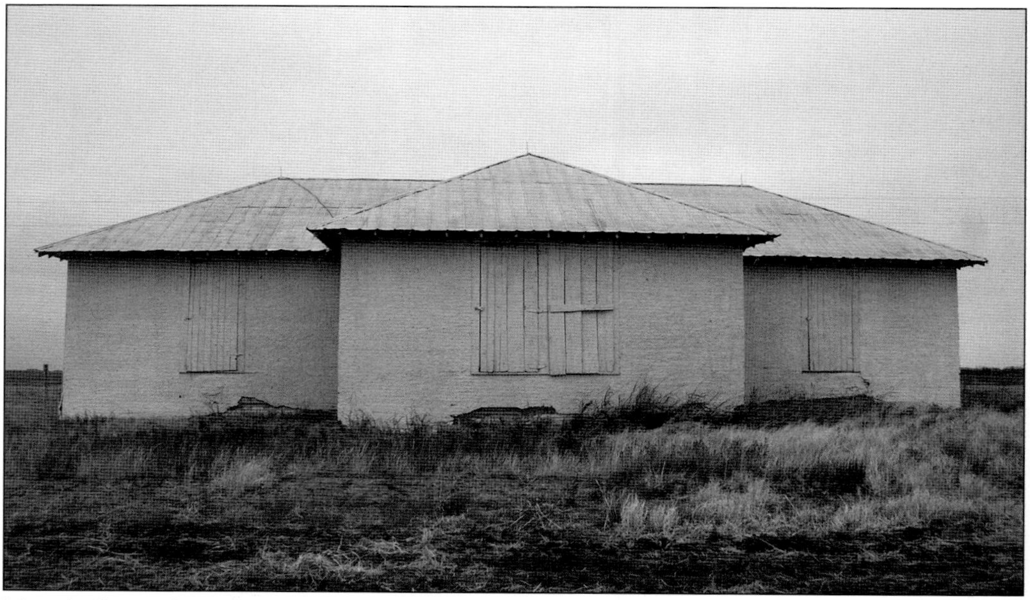

Mary's Creek Schoolhouse. The Mary's Creek Schoolhouse was built in 1908 as a one-room frame building. A second room was added in the 1920s, and the exterior of the building was stuccoed. The school is the last standing of the 38 schoolhouses that once served the county. It was awarded a Texas Historical Marker in 2006. (Courtesy of Carolyn Bomberger.)

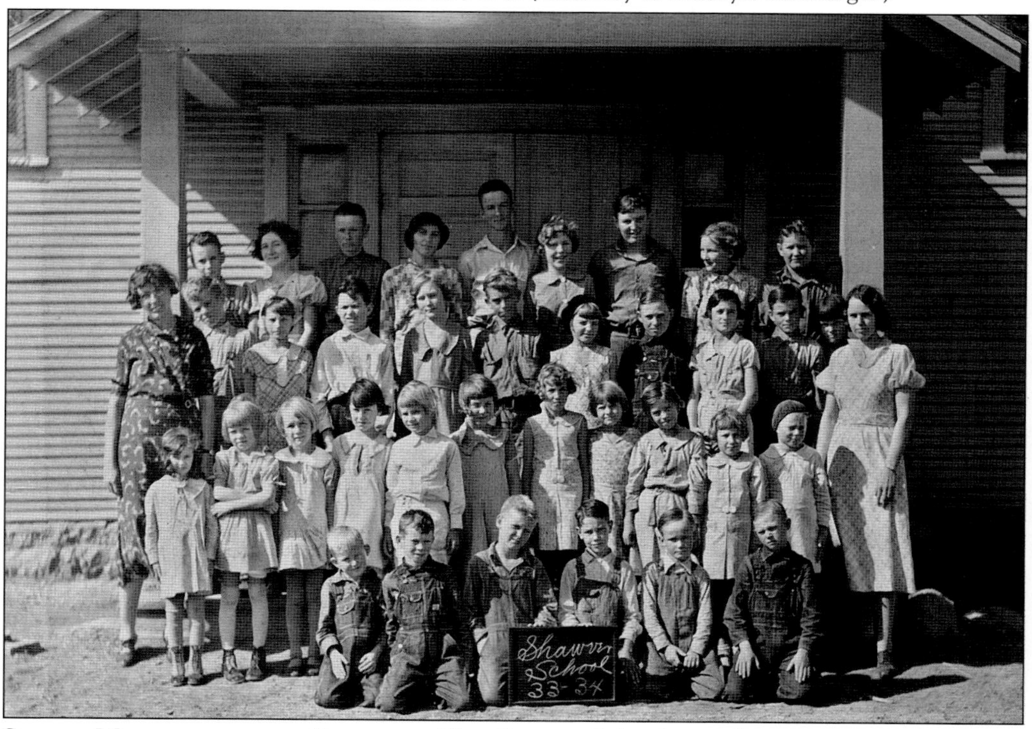

School Marms and their Students. The Shawver School served students in the southeast part of the county from 1911 to 1944. Peak enrollment was 89. Like other rural schools, declining numbers eventually forced its closing, with remaining students transferring to Seymour. (Courtesy of Baylor County Museum.)

Six

THE CULTURE OF CLUBS

The early years of the county saw social activities restricted generally to church activities and community socials and dances that were often held at the schoolhouses. Toward the end of the 19th century, sporting clubs—especially baseball—became popular. Community bands were another enjoyable activity.

As the 20th century progressed, continued prosperity and mechanization created more leisure time, leading to the organization of local clubs and civic organizations just for women. Sometimes, they were purely social, but most often they were educational in nature and promoted civic causes. The Pierian Club was one of the first civic clubs. In the first quarter of the 20th century, many home demonstration clubs were formed to serve the communities surrounding the rural schools. The Cache Creek and Plainview Home Demonstration Clubs were among the earliest in the county, both organizing in 1919. These clubs were under the supervision of the Texas Agricultural Extension Services. Initially, their focus was food production and preservation, but they adapted to the changing times, and sewing and quilting were added. The focus of quilting was often friendship quilts. Also added to the programs were 4-H clubs, and during World War II, victory gardens and victory canning were included in the demonstrations. One of the most lasting accomplishments of women's organizations has been the establishment of the Baylor County Free Library by the Pierian Club. Beginning in 1912, books were collected, and the library was kept open two afternoons a week by club members. From 1933 to 1936, a librarian's salary was paid by the Works Progress Administration (WPA). In the 1950s, the library became an arm of the county and was installed in the old courthouse. Today, the library occupies the northwest corner of the new courthouse.

Masonic and fraternal organizations were popular with men and women. Service clubs such as the Lions Club were also popular with men.

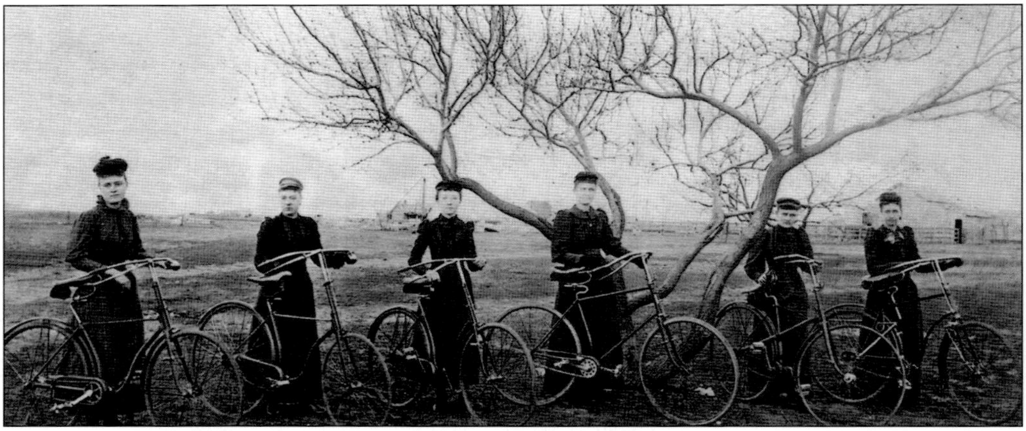

Seymour Bicycle Club, 1893. Community baseball teams and other sporting clubs were popular in the late 19th century. Social convention precluded women from participating in many of these sports. Bicycling, however, was considered appropriate and was a popular activity for ladies. From left to right are Hallie Hays Turney, Allie Elkins Lowry, Sadie Ray Britton, Anna Carmichael Pennington, Nettie Rupe Norwood, and Alice Lewis Boynton. (Courtesy of Baylor County Museum.)

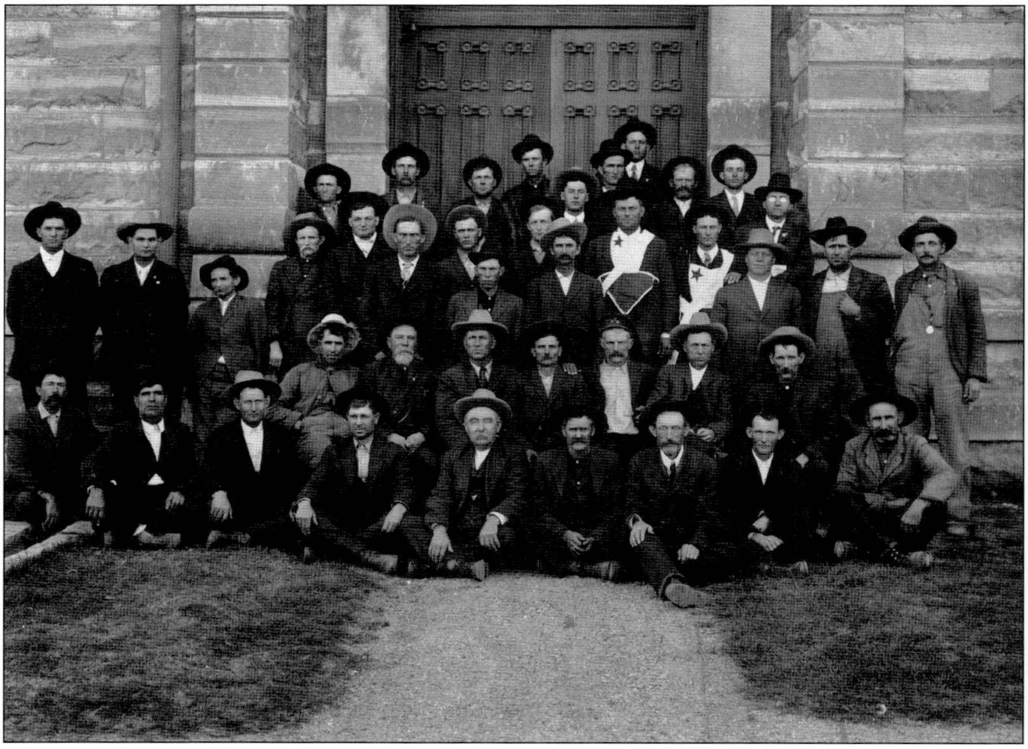

Woodmen of the World. Woodmen of the World is a fraternal society that was created in 1890. Many of the county's civic leaders, including Bert King, who was the county attorney in 1912, were members of either Woodmen of the World or a similar organization known as Modern Woodmen of America. Modern Woodmen, which was founded in 1883, is currently active in Seymour. (Courtesy of Baylor County Museum.)

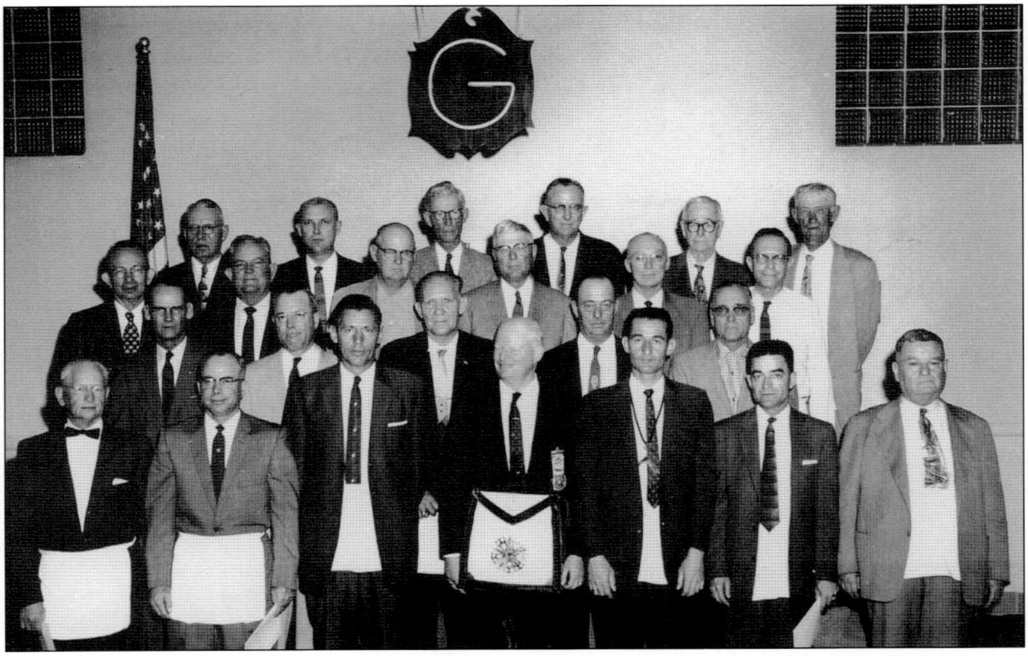

Past Masters of Seymour Lodge. This photograph was taken in 1958 at the Past Masters Night. Gene Robinson was worshipful master, Bob King was deputy grand master, and Cotton Moffatt was a past grand master. From left to right are (first row) Coleman Duggan, Sam Jones, Bob King, Cotton Moffatt, Gene Robinson, W.R. Whitley, and Ephriham Turscott Goss; (second row) Charles Richmond, L.S. Jones, J.K. Tidwell, W.A. Melear, and Carl Quisenberry; (third row) M.E. Tarver, T.E. Craddock, A.F. Wirz, W.L. Yoe, O.K. Hoyle, and E.F. Murphy; (fourth row) F.H. Bunkley, Jack Jones, J.D. Dickson, Earl Garrison, Joe Wheat, and Arthur McReynolds. (Courtesy of Baylor County Museum.)

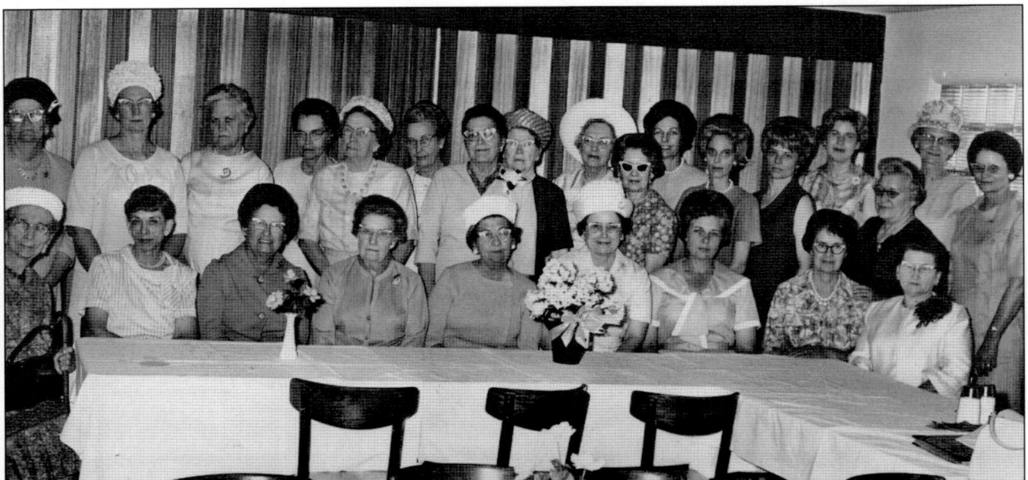

Seymour Pierian Club. The Pierian Club was organized in 1909 by Lottie Veal Wheat and Mrs. W.T. Britton. The name was taken from a couplet by Alexander Pope: "A little learning is a dangerous thing, / Drink deep, or taste not the Pierian spring." In 1910, the club became a member of the Texas Federation of Women' Clubs and joined the National Federation of Women's Clubs in 1914. The club was active until the 1990s. (Courtesy of Carolyn Bomberger.)

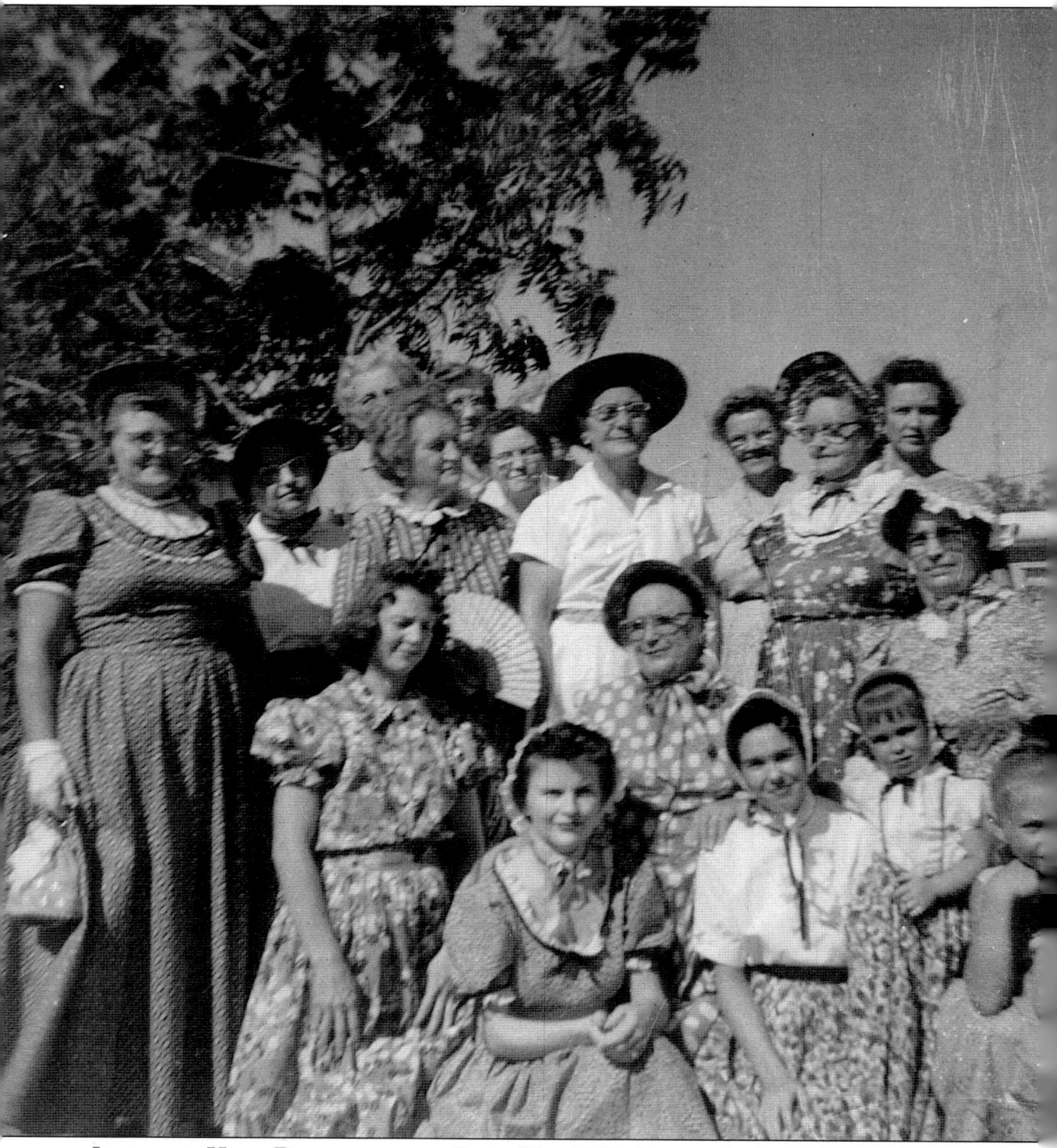

LEVELVIEW HOME DEMONSTRATION CLUB. This 1958 photograph shows the Levelview Home Demonstration Club posing for a photograph prior to mounting its float in the Old Settlers Rodeo and Reunion parade. Members are dressed in frontier-style clothes. Levelview had one of the first home demonstration clubs in 1919. It was organized by Bess Edwards, the first home demonstration agent in the county. Levelview was a community northwest of Seymour, not far from present-day Red Springs. (Courtesy of Dixie Peacock.)

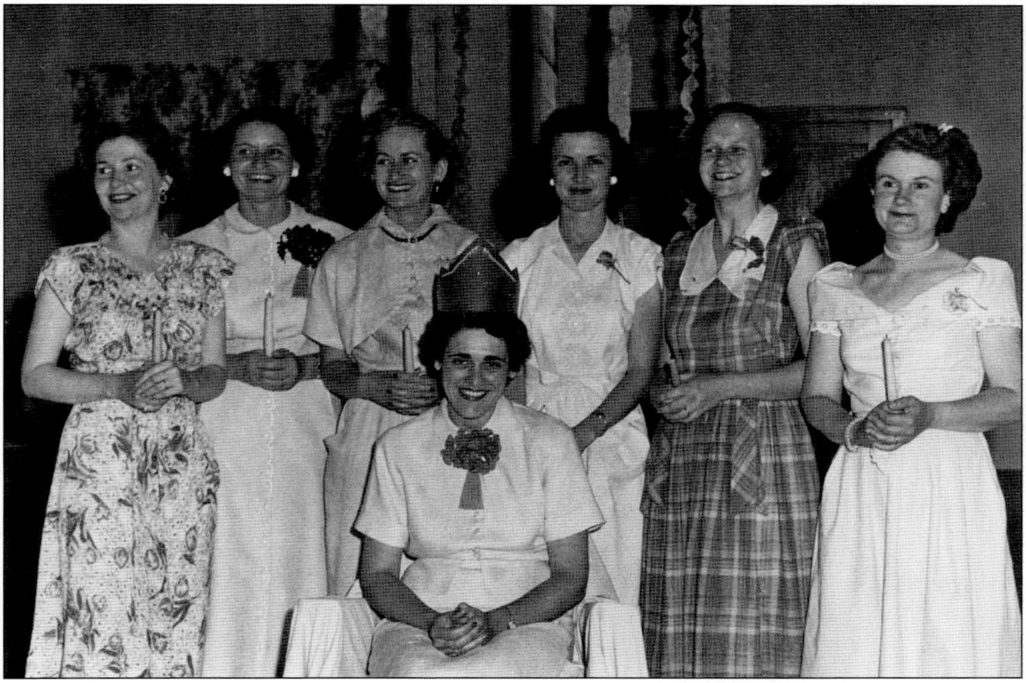

The Twentieth Century Club. This photograph is of the installation of the 1951 officers of the Twentieth Century Study Club at the country club. The club met to discuss and review books. Officers installed are, from left to right, Mrs. Gaines Edwards, Mrs. Norman Bryant, Mrs. John T. Farr, Mrs. Jim Richeson, Mrs. James Albritton, and Mrs. Geril Economeady. (Courtesy of Baylor County Museum.)

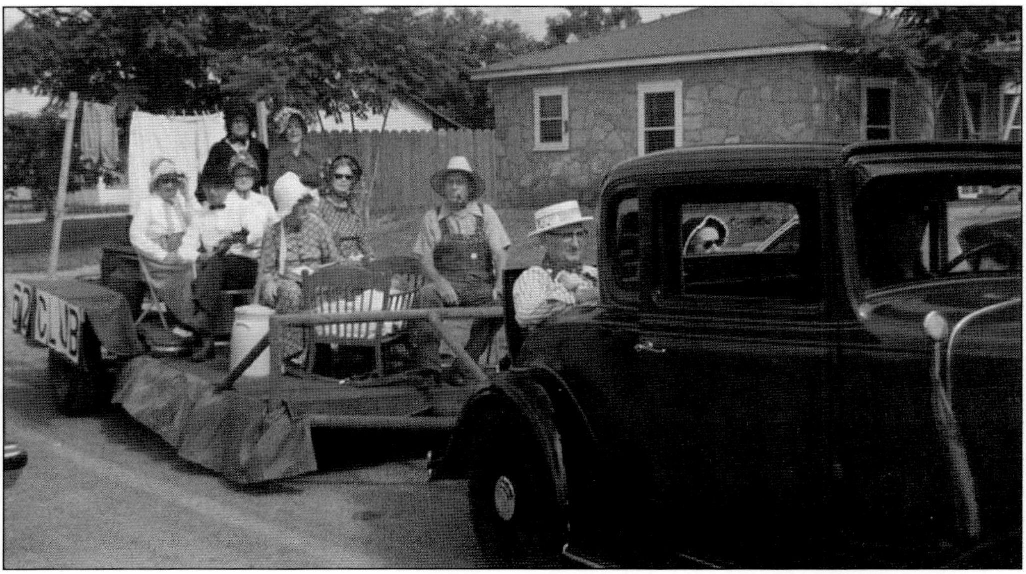

The 62 Club. The 62 Club was organized in conjunction with the Senior Citizens Center on August 14, 1967. It was a social organization for residents 62 and older. The club engaged in games, luncheons, and other activities at the Senior Citizens Center. In this photograph, members of the club wait to join the parade at the 79th Old Settlers Reunion and Rodeo in 1975. The float is being pulled by an unidentified vintage vehicle. (Courtesy of Larry Burnett.)

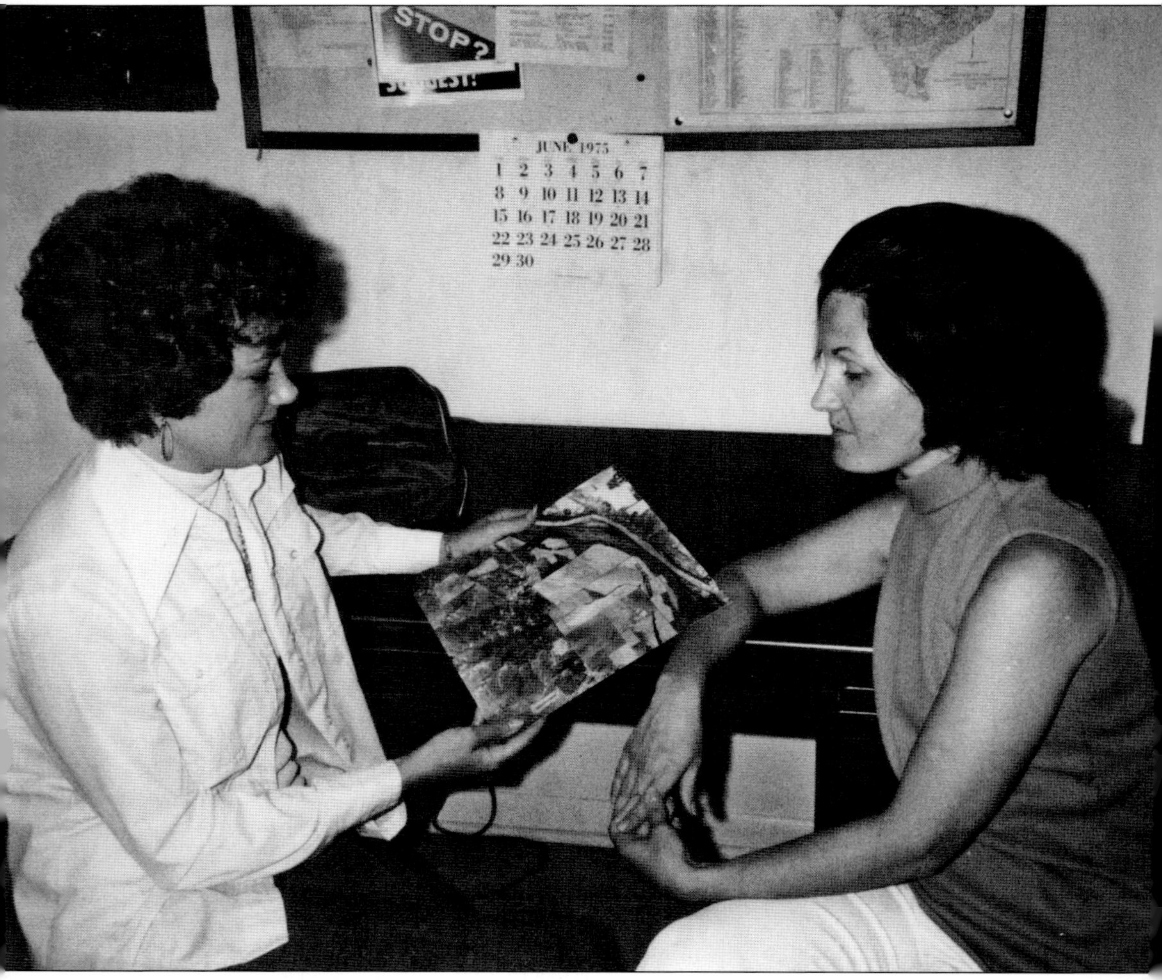

THE JUNIOR FORUM. In the spring of 1964, eight young women met to form a "helping hand" club. It was called the Junior Forum. Its object was to promote civic, social, and commercial improvements for the county. Founding members were Mrs. Jack Wright, Mrs. Bobby King, Mrs. Robert Clay, Mrs. Joe Dickson, Mrs. William Arledge, Mrs. James Styles, Mrs. Kenneth Gleghorn, and Mrs. Pat Lawrence. Mrs. Jack Wright was the first president. The club became a member of the Texas Federation of Women's Clubs in the Santa Rosa District on October 6, 1964. (Courtesy of Baylor County Museum.)

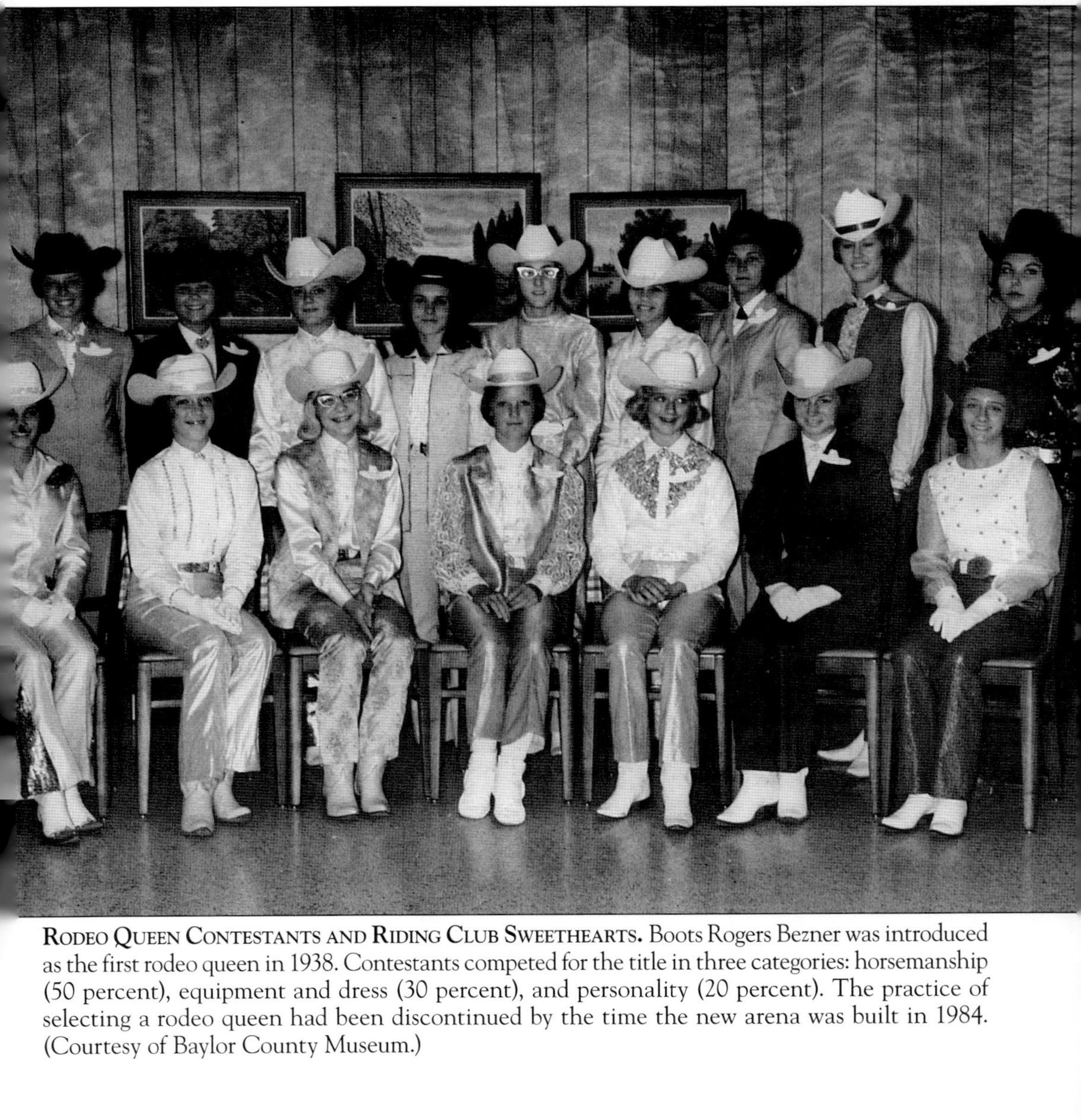

RODEO QUEEN CONTESTANTS AND RIDING CLUB SWEETHEARTS. Boots Rogers Bezner was introduced as the first rodeo queen in 1938. Contestants competed for the title in three categories: horsemanship (50 percent), equipment and dress (30 percent), and personality (20 percent). The practice of selecting a rodeo queen had been discontinued by the time the new arena was built in 1984. (Courtesy of Baylor County Museum.)

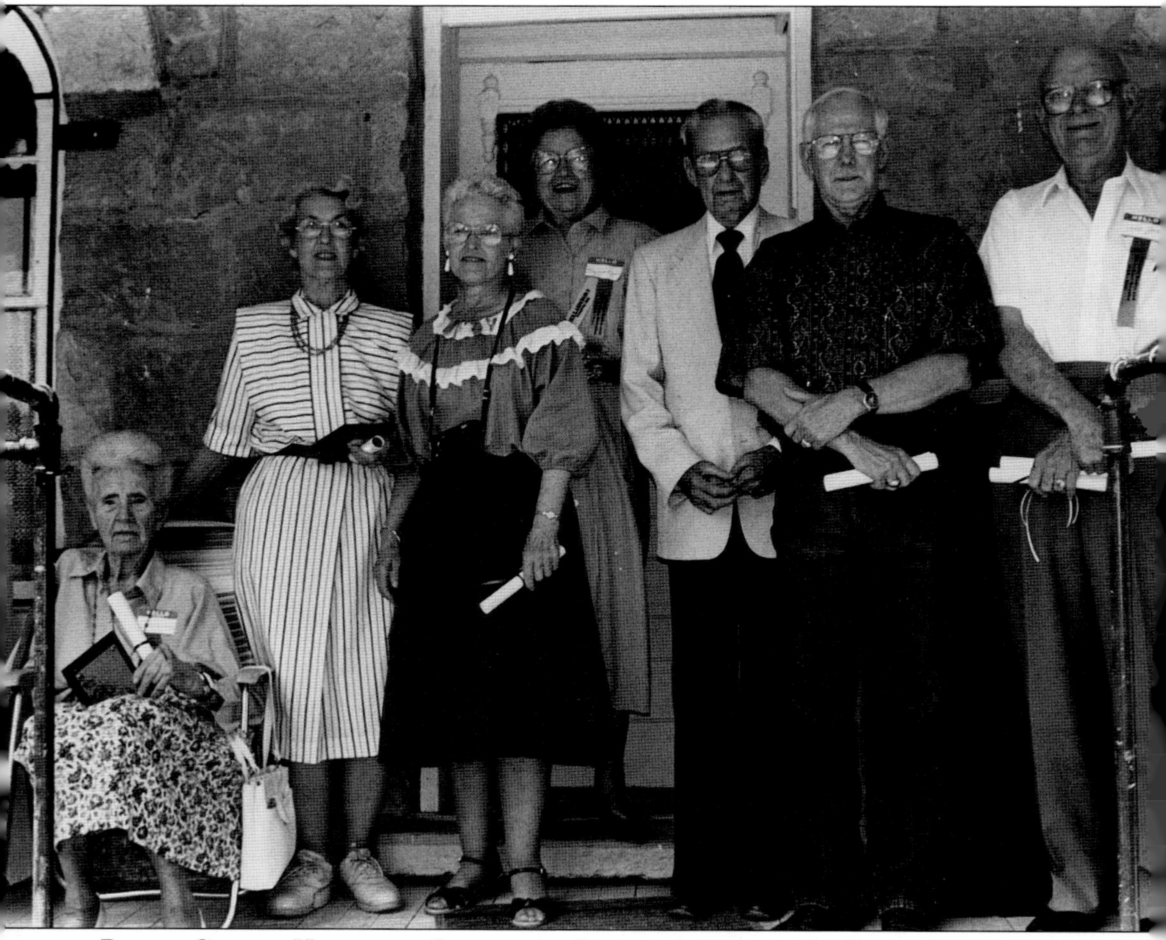

Baylor County Historical Commission Charter Members. The Baylor County Historical Commission administers the Baylor County Museum. The museum sprang from the activities of the Texas sesquicentennial. The commission produced a play about the history of Baylor County. The proceeds from the play and added donations were used to purchase the Morris house from the Harvey family for $3,000 for use as a museum dedicated to the pioneer history of the county. The Morris house was sold, and the museum, under the direction of Lloyd Fancher, moved to its current location at 116 North Washington Street in 2001. From left to right are Jette Howe Russell, Patsy Stout Cooper, Jo Alice Stout, Mary Ruth Higgins, Robert Fancher, Cyril Keith, and Jack Jones. (Courtesy of Baylor County Museum.)

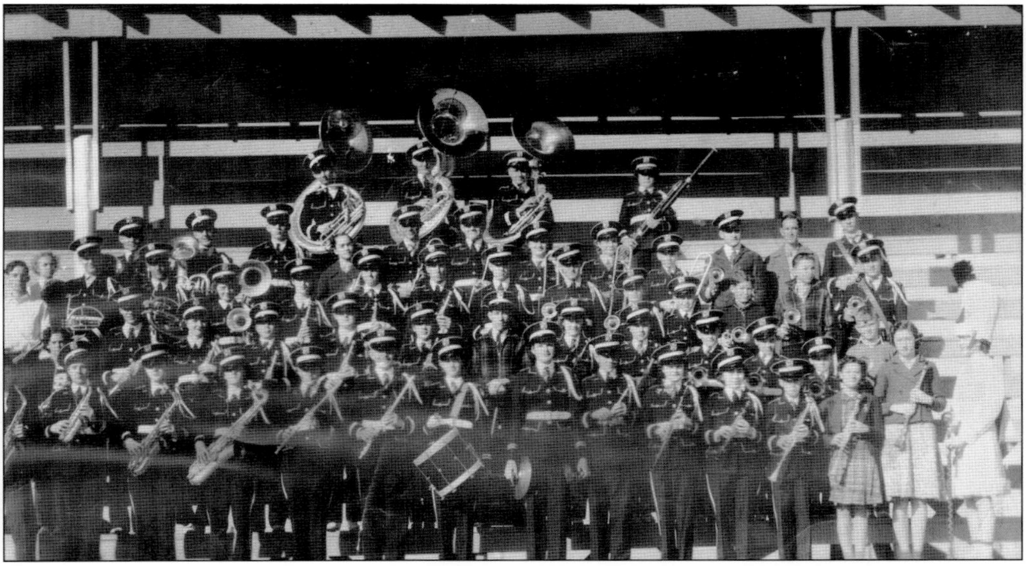

Seymour High School Band, 1942–1943. Community bands were popular in the late 19th and early 20th centuries. During the 1950s, Seymour listened to the melodies of a female singing group called the Blazers. The Seymour High School band had about 54 members in 1942–1943; Sonny Bench was the student director. (Courtesy of Tommie Lee.)

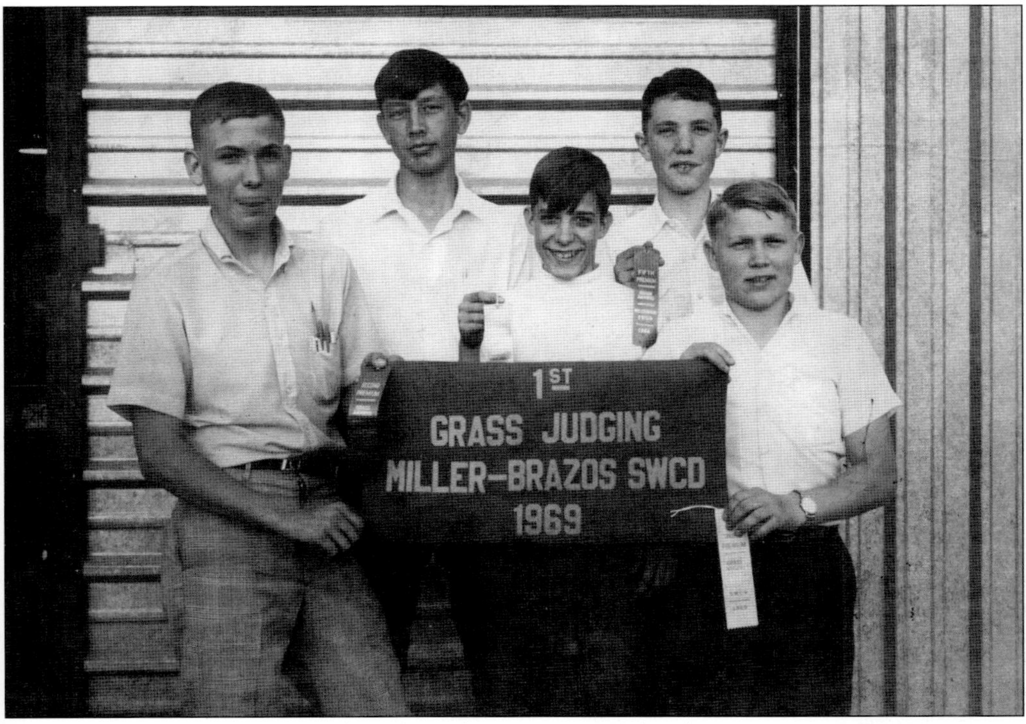

Future Farmers of America (FFA). Baylor County FFA has been an active club since it was organized September 4, 1941. FFA sponsors a variety of agriculture-related programs, events, and competitions. This photograph is from the grass-judging competition for the Miller-Brazos Soil & Water Conservation District. Members of the team are Tommy Ermis, Don St. Clair, Jack Bibb, Ed Hons, and Taylor Cade. (Courtesy of Baylor County Office of the USDA.)

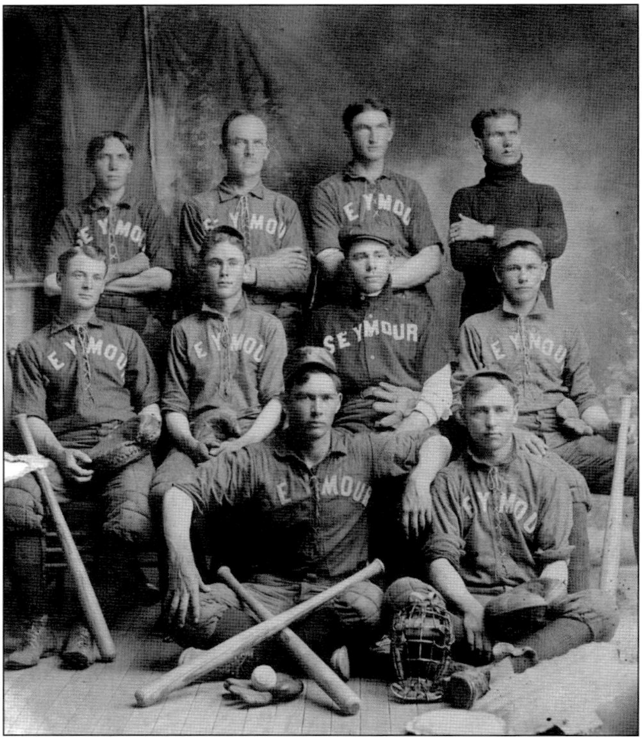

SEYMOUR BASEBALL TEAM, 1899. America's favorite pastime was as popular in Baylor County as it was in the rest of the nation. Members of the team are, from left to right, (first row) pitcher Powell Burkett and catcher Eck Wheat; (second row) Claude McKeen, Willie Baskin, Ross Lewis, and Ollen Newton; (third row) Roy Browning, S. Gorman, Ambrose Buie, and T.G. Easley. (Courtesy of Baylor County Museum.)

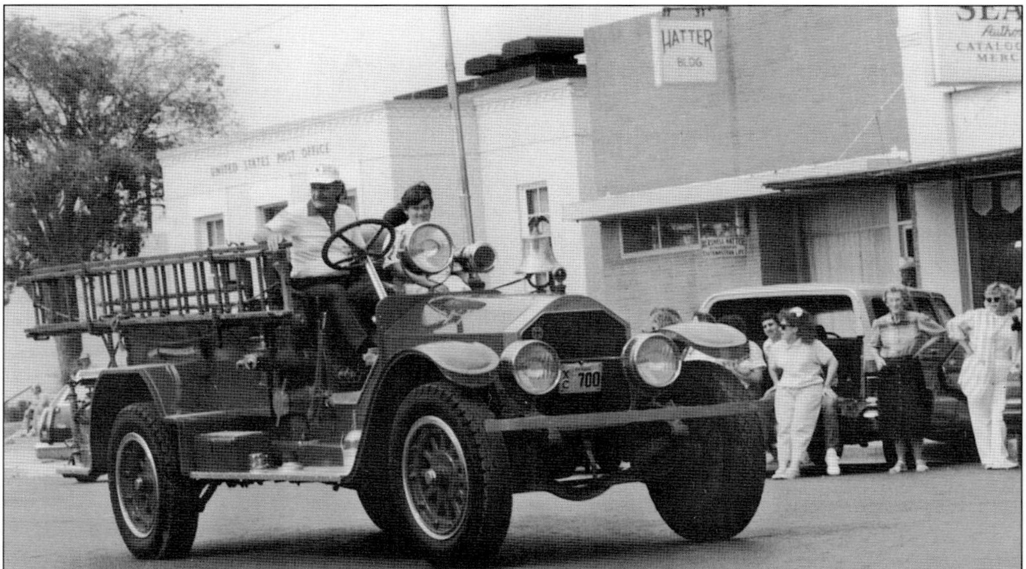

SEYMOUR VOLUNTEER FIRE DEPARTMENT. The Seymour Volunteer Fire Department was organized on September 4, 1909. Purchased in 1924, its first fire truck was an American LaFrance pumper. It is still in the fire department and referred to as "Ole Granny." Ole Granny was last used to fight fires in the late 1970s or early 1980s when the Shamrock station at the corner of Main Street and the Olney Highway burned. The fire truck is currently used for ceremonial purposes, mainly parades. In this photograph, it is driven by Gene Porter Robinson. (Courtesy of Randy Coltharp and the Seymour Volunteer Fire Department.)

Seven

People to See, Places to Go, and Things to Do

People are the glue that binds the rural fabric to create a tapestry of the past. The collective features and traits of individuals combine to form the essence of a unique community. It is hoped that these photographs will not only trigger recollections of good friends, favorite ancestors, and town personalities but will also preserve for future generations the way of the past.

The Permian period left Baylor County two priceless gifts; one was oil and the other was a wealth of fossils. Drilling for oil began in the county as early as 1919, but none was discovered until 1924. The Green Field was brought in during the 1930s, and in the early 1950s, wildcatters discovered oil on the 9,900 acres of Upshur School land in the southwest part of the county. This discovery led to the development of other fields in the southwest part of the county.

As the Gulf of Mexico receded from the high Texas plains 150 million years ago, what would become Baylor County was a narrow spit of marshland between two arms of the receding ocean. The declining waters left in their wake a paleontologist's dream of abundant fossilized flora and fauna. The discovery of a small intact fossil named *Seymouria baylorensis* for the location of its discovery put Seymour on the map in the world of paleontology. The Craddock ranch where the fossil was discovered, also knows as the Red Beds or the Craddock Bone Beds, is still being worked by paleontologists today.

For many years, Seymour received national attention for its Fish Day. Fish Day began in the mid-1920s after Lake Kemp was built and stocked with fish. It was held on May 1 every year to coincide with the opening of the fishing season, and the whole town closed up and went fishing.

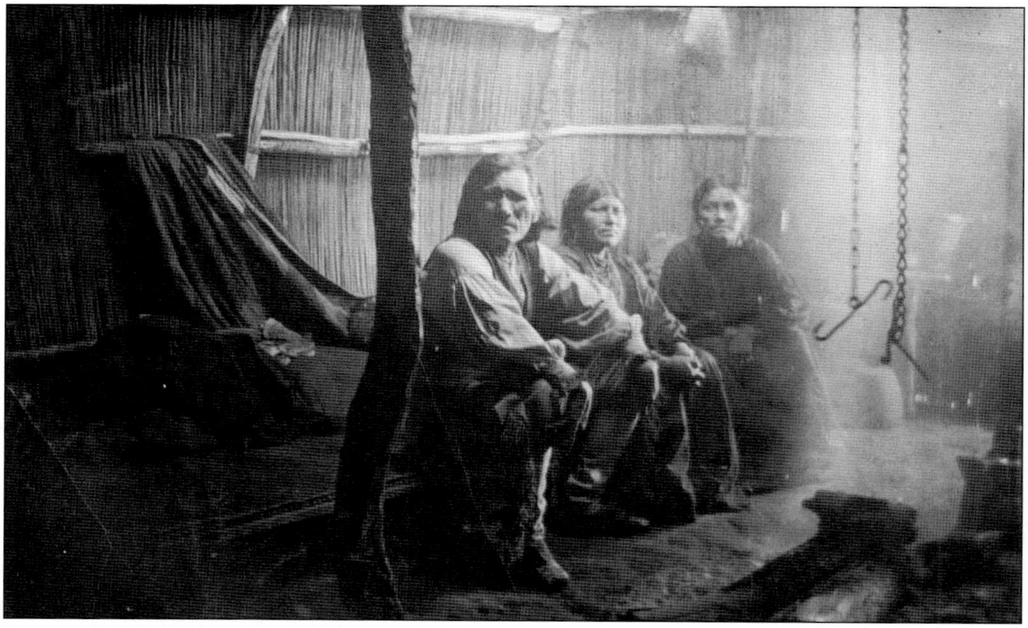

INTERIOR OF INDIAN DWELLING. We have no documentation concerning this rare photograph taken inside an Indian dwelling. The construction of the structure, however, bears a close resemblance to the homes of the Wichita Indians who lived in the area. These dwellings were dome-shaped, constructed of grass, and could be up to 30 feet in diameter. (Courtesy of Mary's Creek Ranch.)

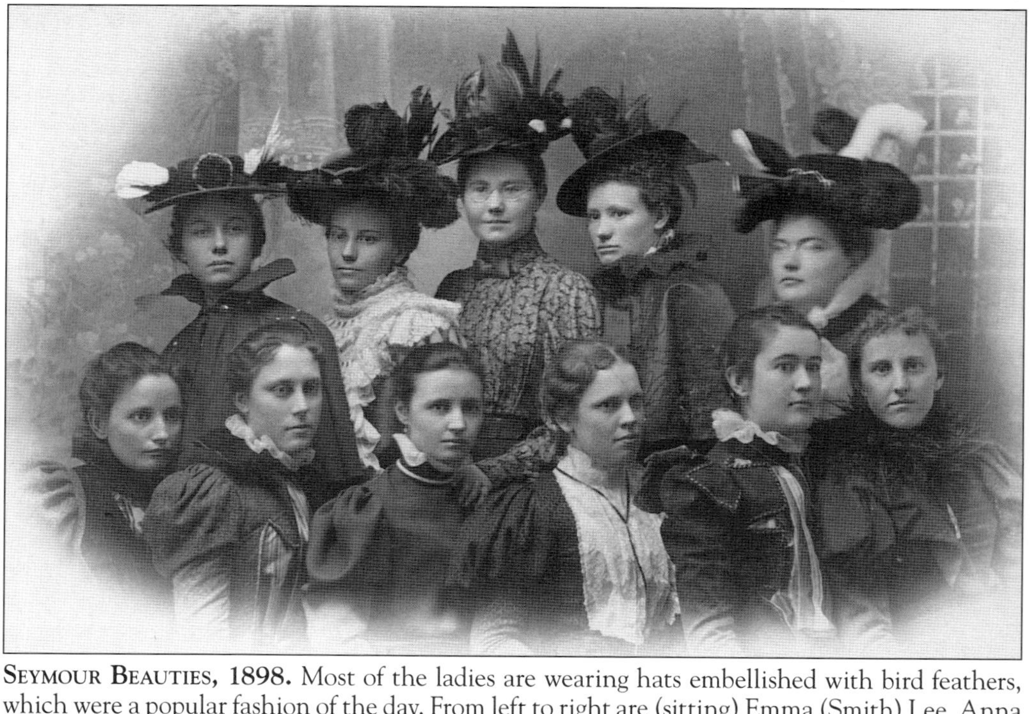

SEYMOUR BEAUTIES, 1898. Most of the ladies are wearing hats embellished with bird feathers, which were a popular fashion of the day. From left to right are (sitting) Emma (Smith) Lee, Anna Belle (Albright) Scruggs, Jennie Ranson, unidentified, music teacher Mamie Buster, and Helen (Peery) Briggs; (standing) unidentified, Eva Browning, Ethel (Hudson) Peery, Bert (Bellows) Browning, and teacher Willie Buster. (Courtesy of Baylor County Museum.)

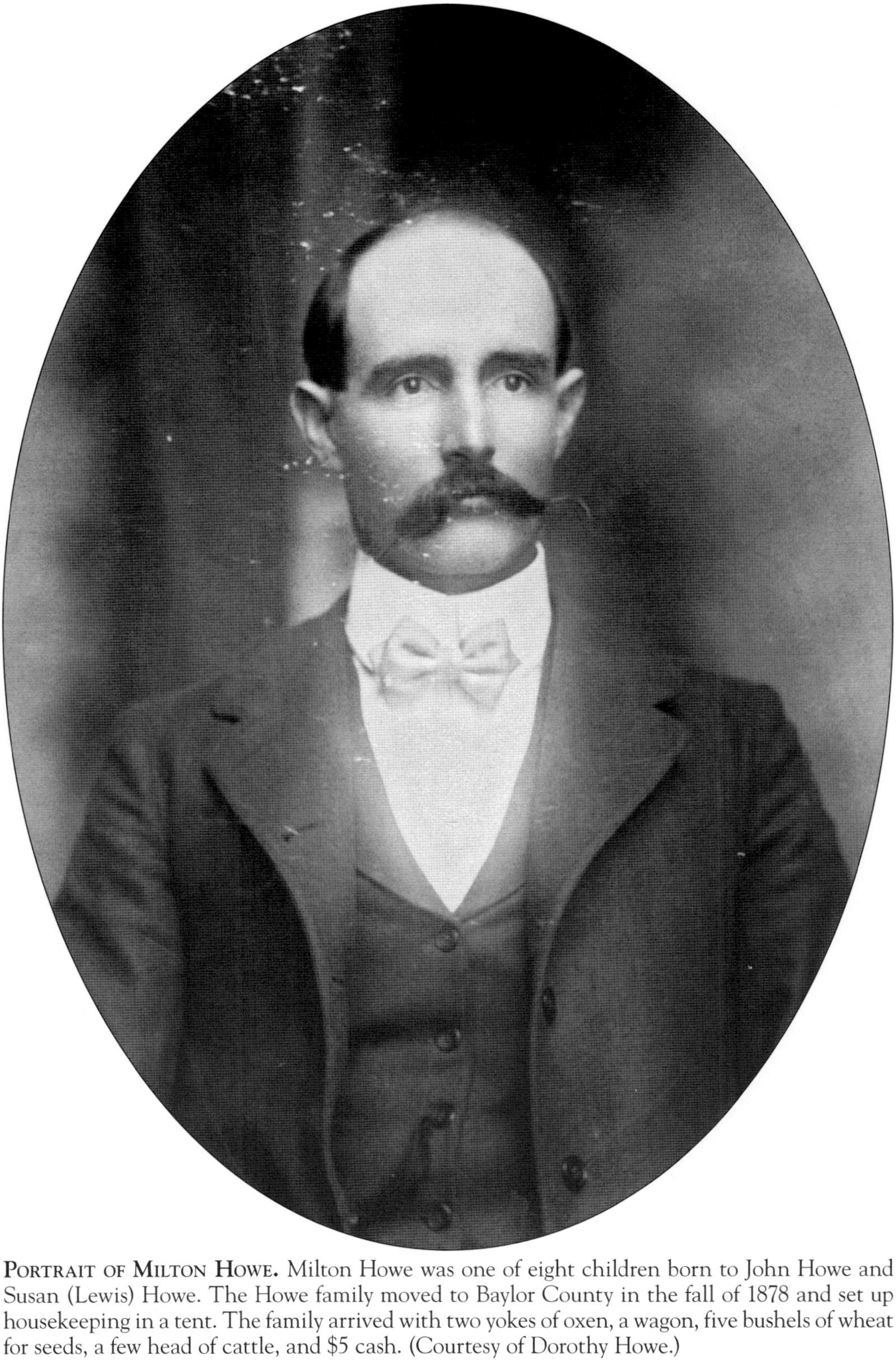

Portrait of Milton Howe. Milton Howe was one of eight children born to John Howe and Susan (Lewis) Howe. The Howe family moved to Baylor County in the fall of 1878 and set up housekeeping in a tent. The family arrived with two yokes of oxen, a wagon, five bushels of wheat for seeds, a few head of cattle, and $5 cash. (Courtesy of Dorothy Howe.)

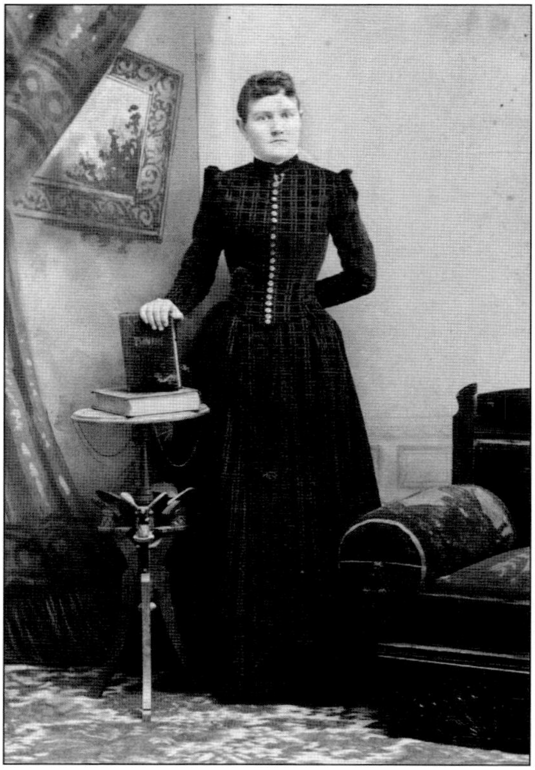

Studio Portrait of Clara Howe Porter. Clara was one of two daughters born to John Howe and Susan (Lewis) Howe. She married Charles Thomas Porter in 1895. This photograph was taken in the studio of J.C. Price. Seymour had a handful of early photographers. This studio was housed above the Ranson Hardware Store. (Courtesy of Dorothy Howe.)

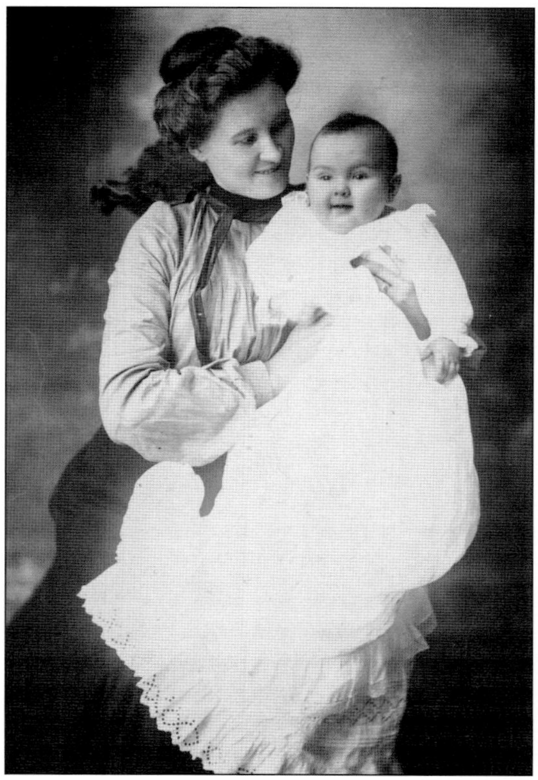

Lena Parker Howe and Infant Daughter. Lena Dell Parker married Lewis "Loo" Howe on December 25, 1901, in the Methodist church at Round Timber. Their daughter Jett, pictured as an infant, was one of the founders of the Baylor County Historical Society. This lovely photograph was taken by J.A. Hammock, another of Seymour's early photographers. (Courtesy of Dorothy Howe.)

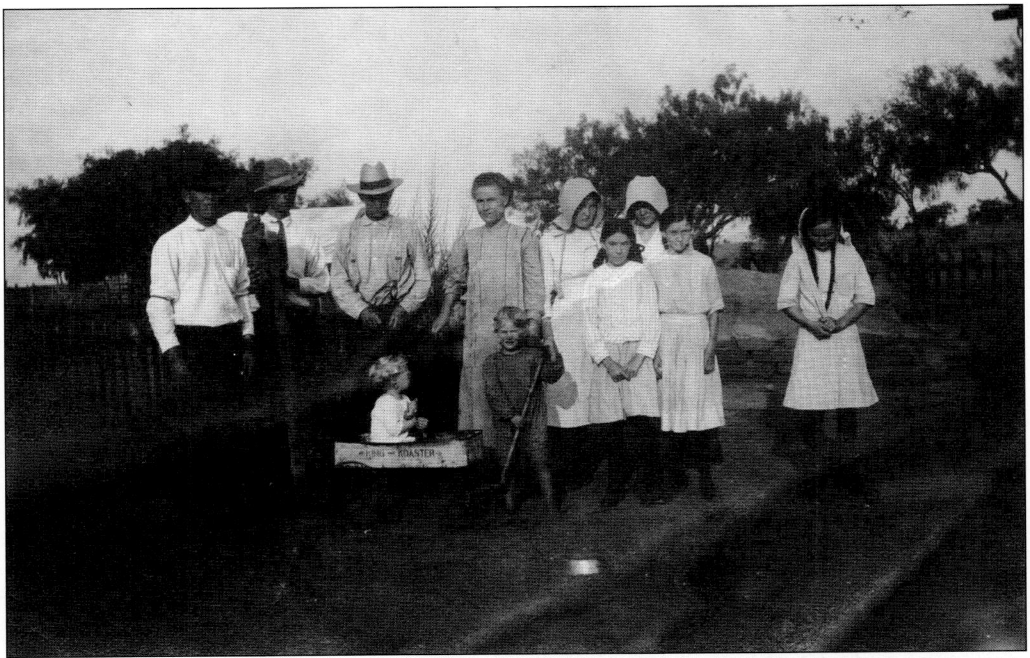

A Family Visits the Holmes. This photograph is of an unidentified family who went to visit Arch and Della Holmes in Clear Fork. They rode from Round Timber to Clear Fork in a covered wagon (barely visible in background). Clear Fork is near Albany in Shackelford County. (Courtesy of Dorothy Howe.)

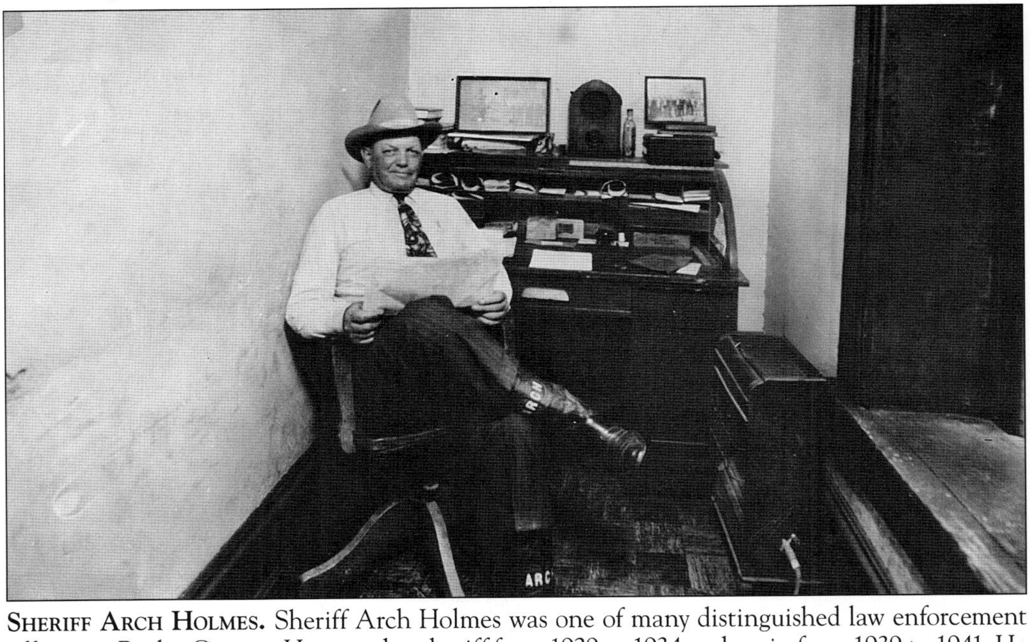

Sheriff Arch Holmes. Sheriff Arch Holmes was one of many distinguished law enforcement officers in Baylor County. He served as sheriff from 1929 to 1934 and again from 1939 to 1941. He went to New York City to retrieve a fugitive from justice and created such a stir in his 10-gallon hat and Western boots that the management of the Lincoln Hotel where he was staying photographed him for publicity purposes. He is shown in his office in the courthouse wearing custom boots that sport his first name. (Courtesy of Margaret Higgins Johnson.)

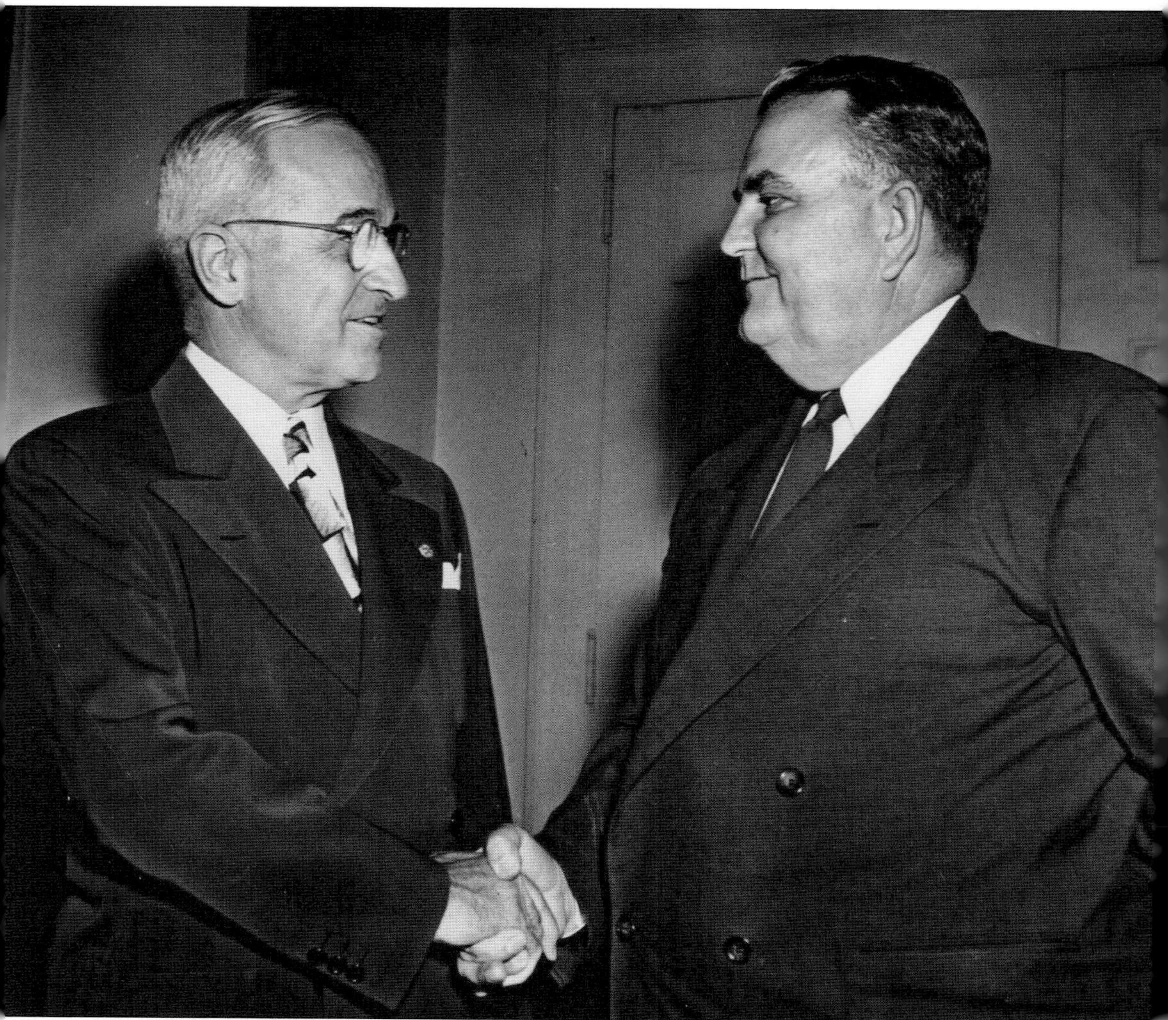

President Truman and Tom Craddock. Rural electrification in Baylor County began in 1938 when Craddock, as a city official, played a key role in helping Seymour secure the first loan for a rural electric cooperative. A friend of many national leaders, he was acquainted with Franklin Roosevelt, Harry Truman, John F. Kennedy, Lyndon Baines Johnson, and Speaker of the House Sam Rayburn. (Courtesy of Baylor County Museum.)

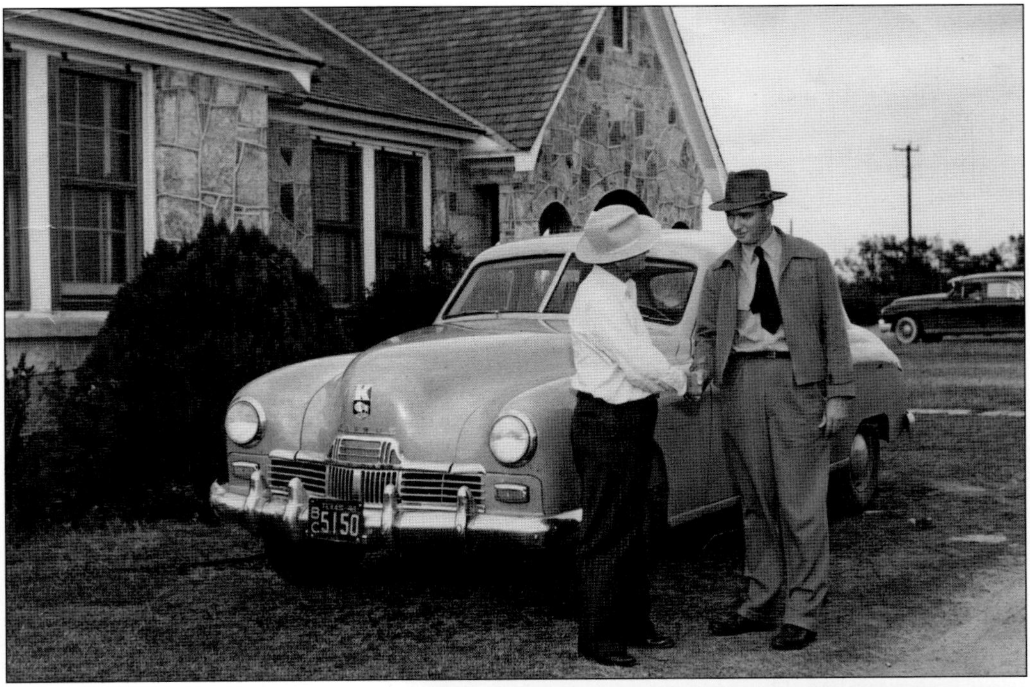

A.B. Martin and Elmo Brown. A.B. Martin (left) accepts congratulations from Brown on winning a trip to the Kaiser-Frazer automobile plant in Detroit, Michigan. Later, Martin was to be a guest of Guy Lombardo and his Royal Canadian Orchestra in New York. The Kaiser-Frazer dealership in Seymour was owned by Elmo Brown. (Courtesy of A.B. Martin.)

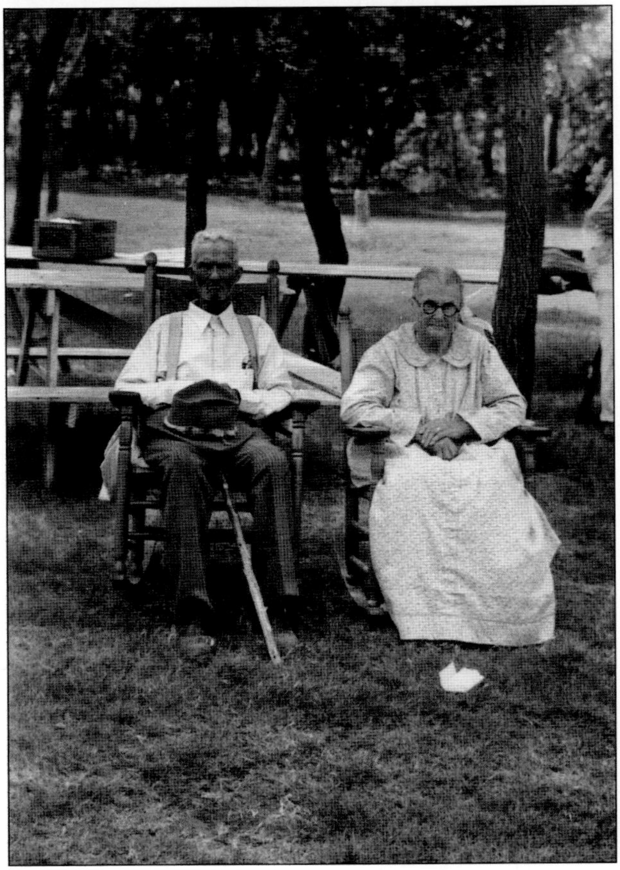

Mr. and Mrs. Stout. The J.P. Stout family arrived in Baylor County in 1887. The Stouts settled on land four miles south of Round Timbers, across the river in Throckmorton County. In 1925, they rented out their farm and moved into Seymour, where they spent the remainder of their lives. This photograph was taken on their 60th wedding anniversary. (Courtesy of Mac Stout.)

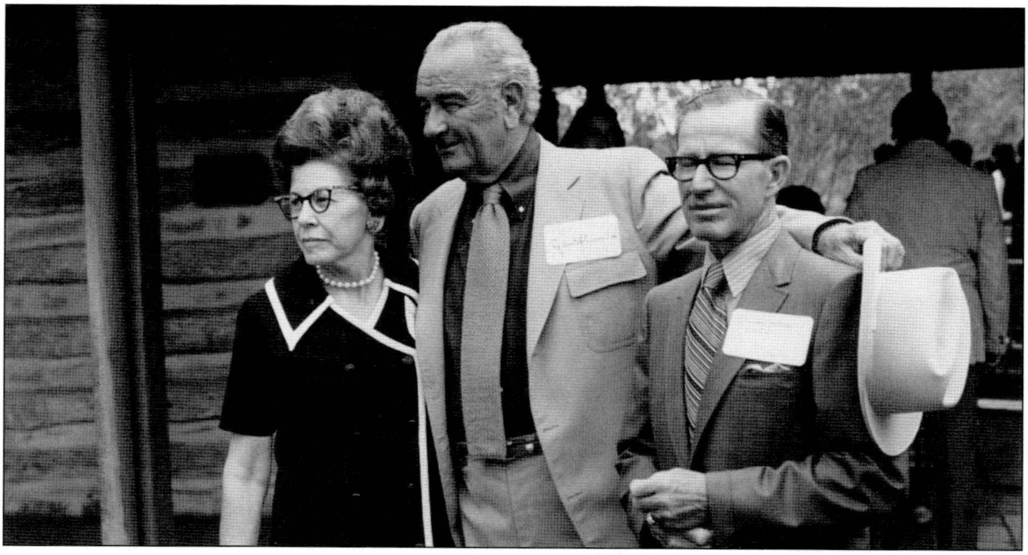

Mr. and Mrs. Hobbs. In this photograph, Charles and Fannie Hobbs are standing with former president Lyndon Baines Johnson (center). The picture was taken October 15, 1971 at LBJ Park in Johnson City, Texas, at the Lady Bird Johnson Beautification Awards Ceremony. Seymour was recognized for its work in landscaping the approach to the Brazos River Bridge in Seymour. (Courtesy of Baylor County Museum.)

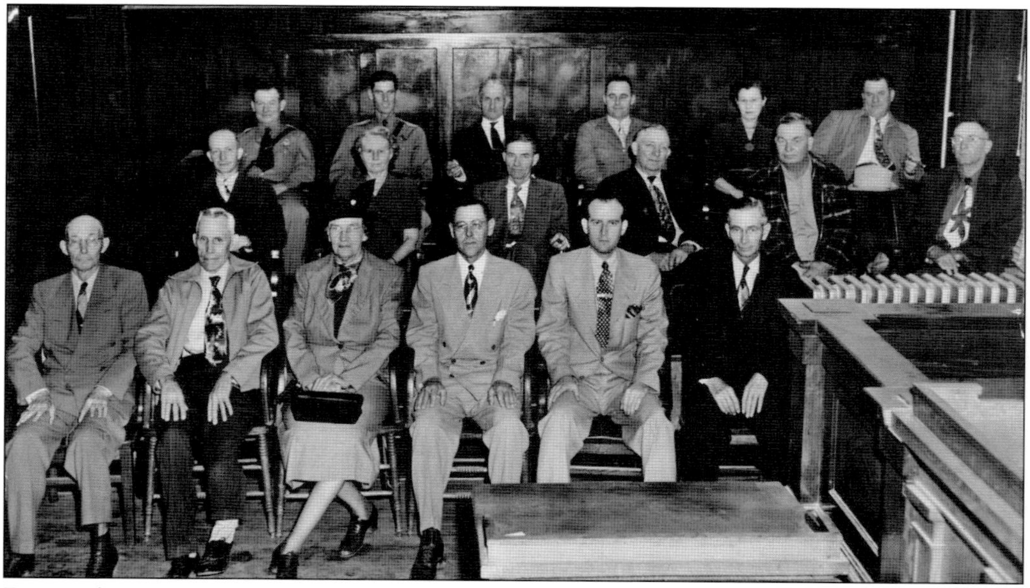

Elected Officials, 1951. This photograph pictures the elected officials and other individuals necessary to the functioning of the county. They include, from left to right, (first row) justice of the peace C.C. Fancher, county treasurer W.R. Hart, county school superintendent Hallie Longley, county judge James F. Lester, state representative Clyde Whiteside, and county attorney Thomas F. Glover; (second row) county and district clerk Wilburn Redwine, deputy in county clerk's office Flossie White, Precinct 4 commissioner Carl Snyder, Precinct 1 commissioner Joe Cox, Precinct 3 commissioner C.D. Devrow, and Precinct 2 commissioner F.J. Cooper; (third row) Texas Highway patrolmen Red Berry and George Leedy, constable Collie Jeter, deputy Wesley Styles, deputy Hattie Robinson, and sheriff Lott Keffer. (Courtesy of Baylor County Museum.)

June Prichard, Miss Texas 1955. The caption from this United Press Telephoto reads, "Miss Texas (June Prichard, 23) stole the show in the annual Miss America parade on a borrowed horse. The Seymour, Texas, beauty brought down the house when she rode a palomino down the famed boardwalk." (Courtesy of Baylor County Museum.)

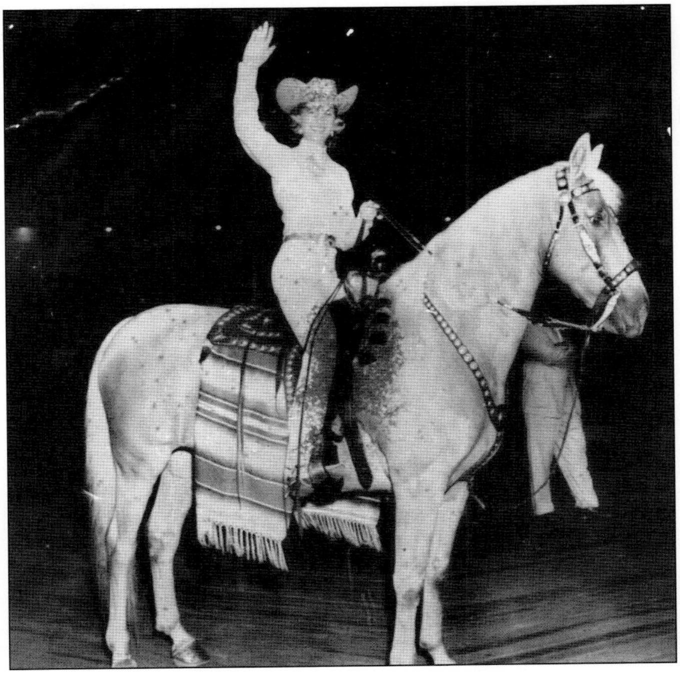

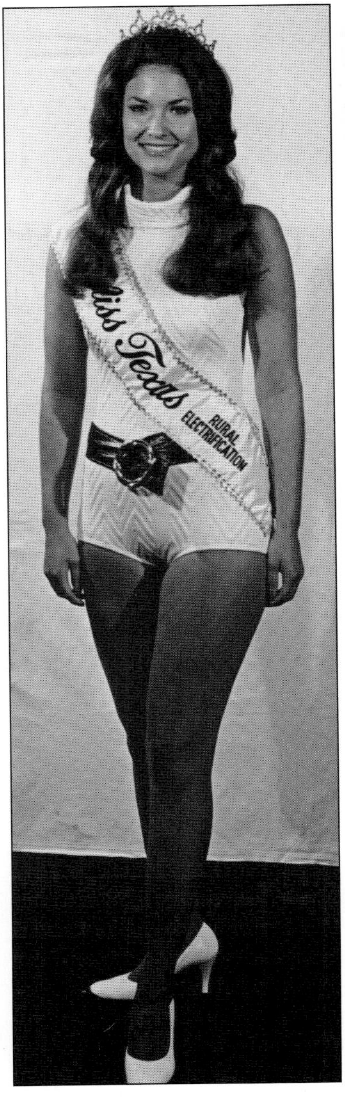

Miss Texas Rural Electrification. Selecting beauty queens and club sweethearts was a civic ritual from the late 1930s to the mid-1970s. Contests were held for Miss Lake Kemp, Rodeo Queen, and just about anything else organizers could think of. In this photograph, Susie Howard, Miss Texas Rural Electrification, is a physical embodiment of a political subject. (Courtesy of Baylor County Museum.)

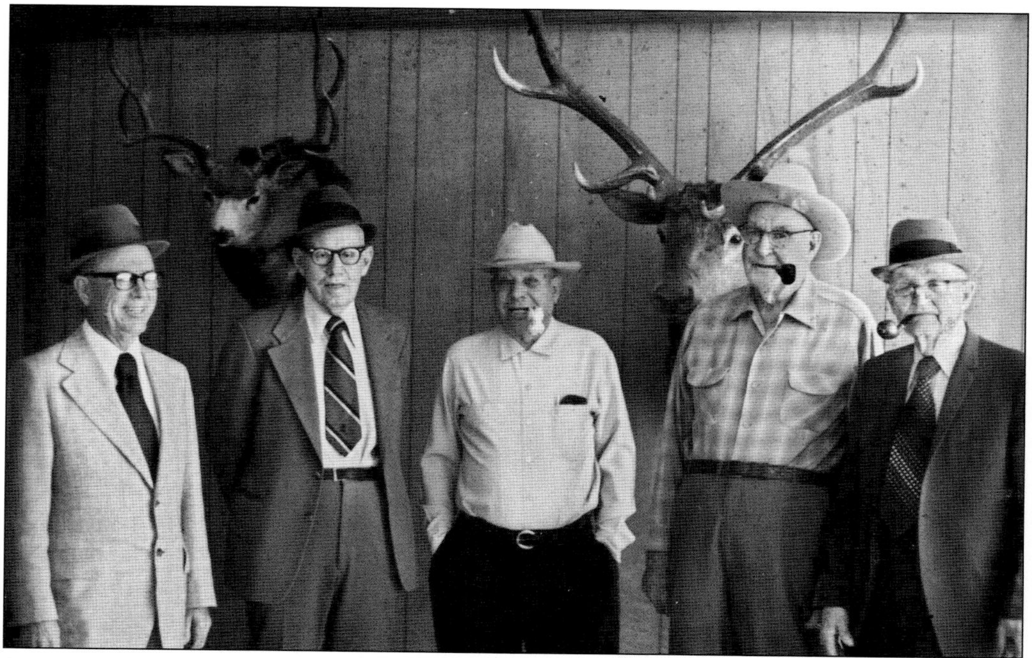

SEYMOUR BUSINESS LEADERS. The men in this photograph represent the insurance, mercantile, ranching, and oil enterprises in Seymour and Baylor County. They were all leading citizens and supporters of the town. From left to right are Lloyd D. Jones Sr., Foster Bunkley, Charles Randall, Buck Wallace, and Frank Davis. This undated photograph was taken in Randall's office. (Courtesy of Baylor County Museum.)

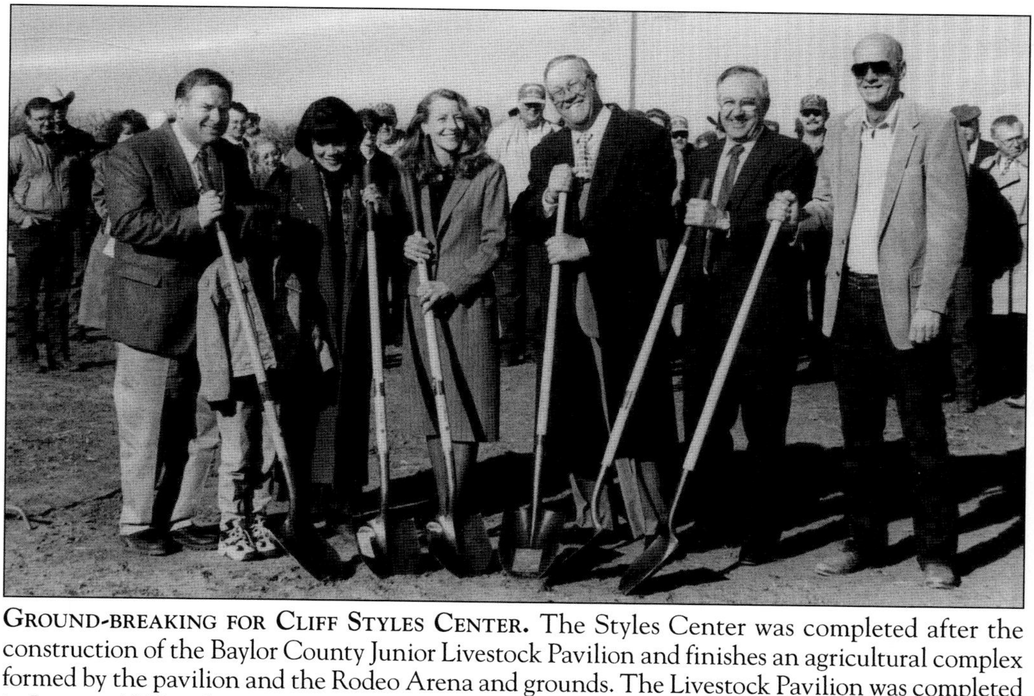

GROUND-BREAKING FOR CLIFF STYLES CENTER. The Styles Center was completed after the construction of the Baylor County Junior Livestock Pavilion and finishes an agricultural complex formed by the pavilion and the Rodeo Arena and grounds. The Livestock Pavilion was completed in January 1991 and measures 100 feet by 200 feet. It was constructed by Herring Construction of Munday, Texas, assisted by local Seymour contractors. (Courtesy of Baylor County Museum.)

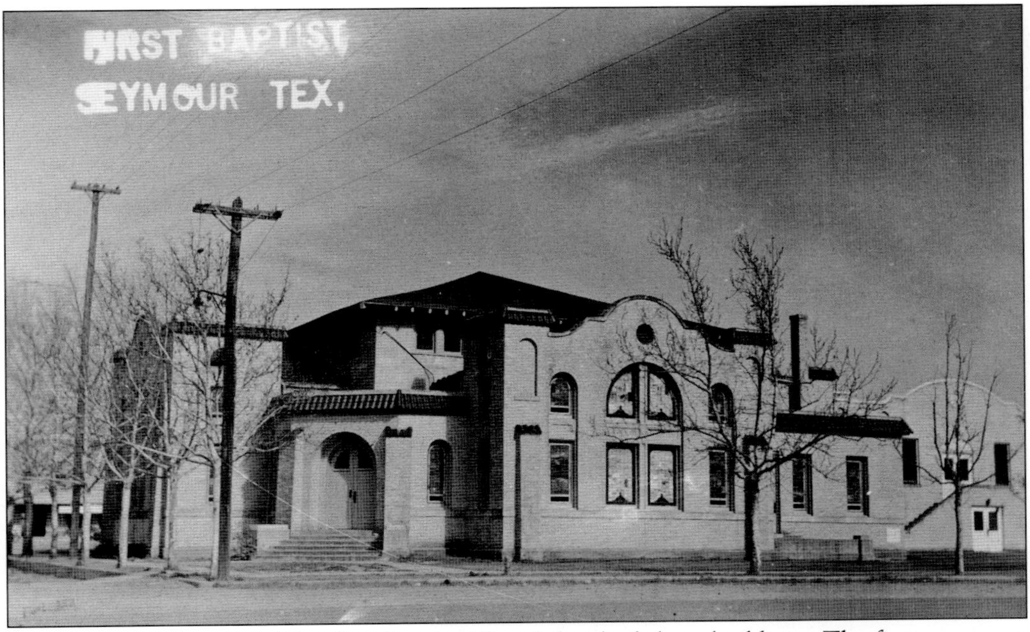

FIRST BAPTIST CHURCH. The First Baptist Church has had three buildings. The first one was a small frame church built in 1891. This structure was moved and became the Catholic church. The second church, pictured, was built in 1916 at the corner of Washington and Nevada Streets. The third and current sanctuary was built in 1959–1960 on the site of the second church. (Courtesy of Baylor County Museum.)

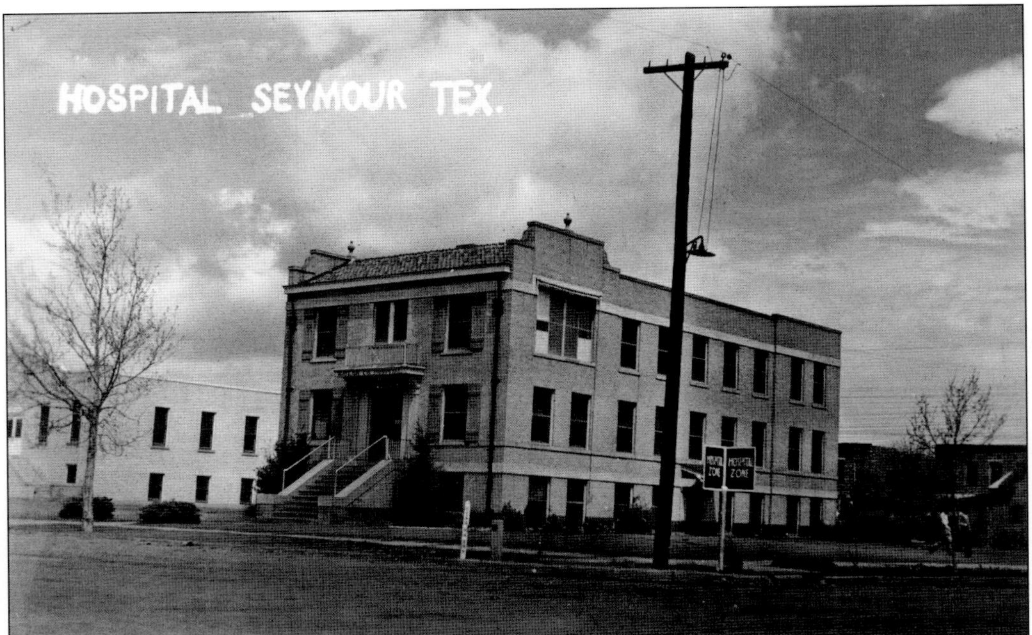

SEYMOUR MEMORIAL HOSPITAL. The old hospital was built at a cost of $50,000 in 1925 as a memorial to Baylor County's veterans. It was a three-story building with 20 patient beds. In 1948, it was remodeled and expanded to a 43-bed capacity. The site of the old hospital was later purchased by the First Baptist Church for its gymnasium. (Courtesy of Baylor County Museum.)

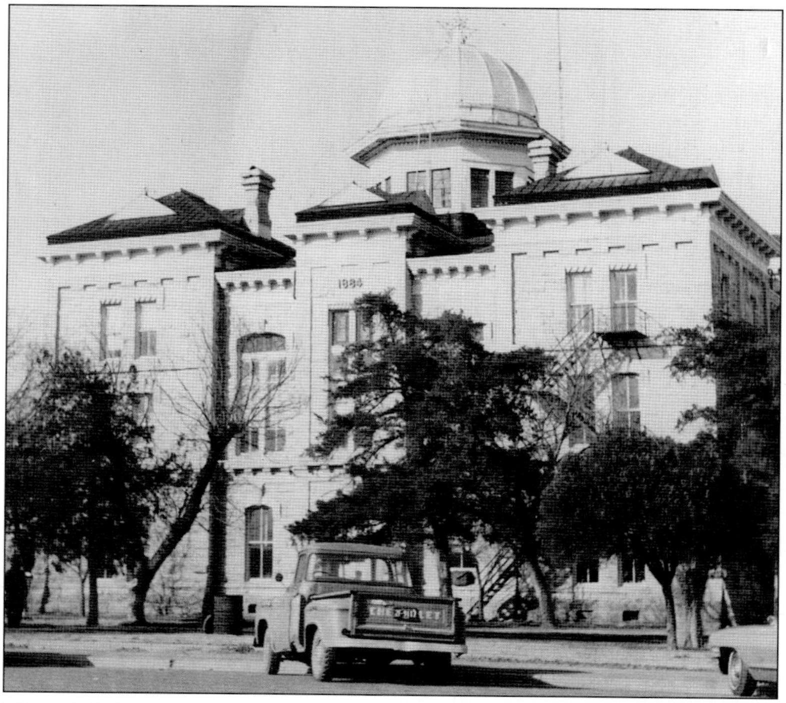

BAYLOR COUNTY COURTHOUSE. The old courthouse occupied the town square. The grounds were tree-shaded and provided a convivial meeting place for gentlemen to visit, exchange ideas and opinions, hear the latest news, and engage in the gentle art of storytelling. The date the courthouse was completed, 1884, can be seen clearly in this photograph. (Courtesy of Baylor County Museum.)

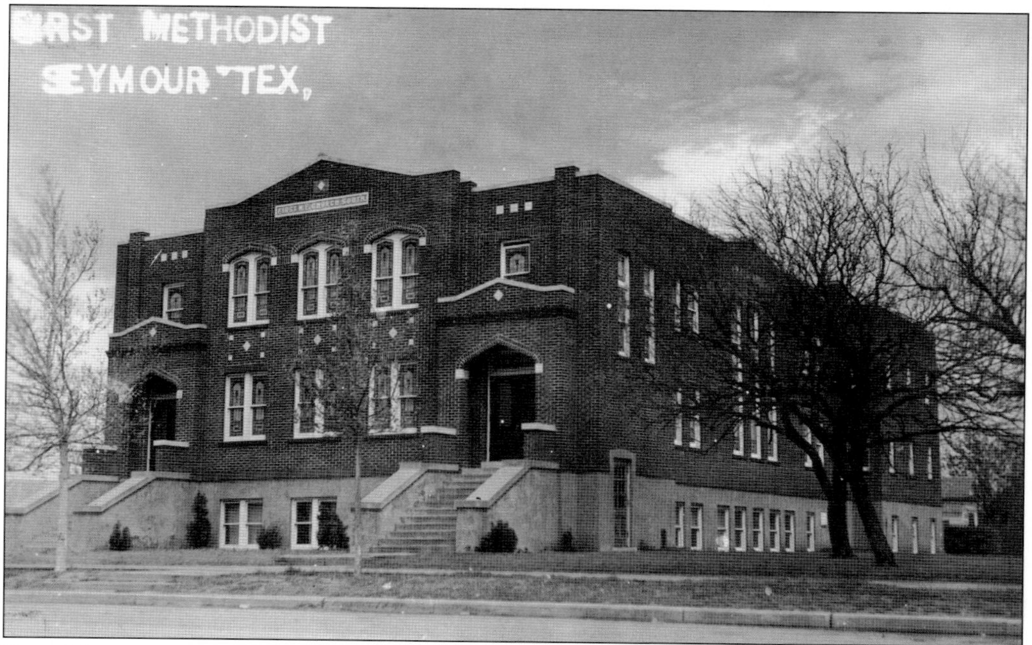

FIRST METHODIST CHURCH. In the spring of 1880, L.A. Donnell invited Rev. J. Farmer to preach a sermon in Seymour. The service was held in the basement of the Donnell house, and the decision to create a Methodist church was presented at this time. In 1883, the first church built in Seymour was constructed by the Methodist congregation. In January 1927, dirt was broken for the brick building pictured in this photograph. In 1964, this new structure was sold to the Assembly of God congregation, and a modern church was built on the Lubbock Highway. (Courtesy of Baylor County Museum.)

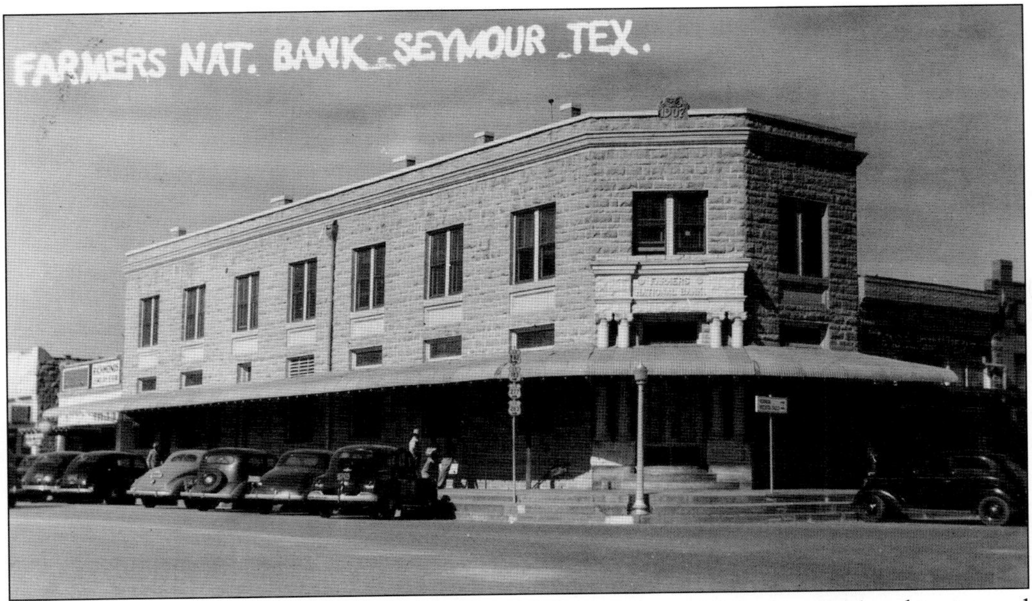

FARMERS NATIONAL BANK. The Farmers National Bank was established in 1906 and is pictured prior to the interior and exterior renovations made in 1952. In 1962, the building was torn down and replaced with the current modern structure. At the time of the new construction, a "motor bank tele-video drive in" was installed. It was the second drive-in bank in Texas. (Courtesy of Baylor County Museum.)

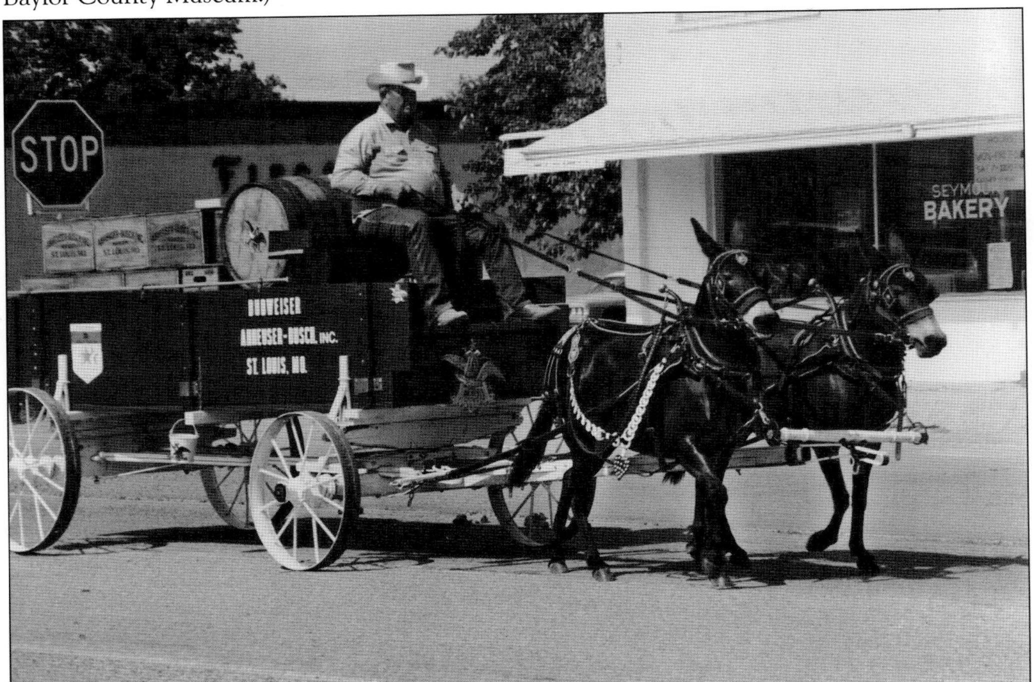

OLD SETTLERS REUNION AND RODEO PARADE. The rodeo is not large enough to command the appearance of the Budweiser Clydesdale horses, so a Baylor County tongue-in-cheek version using miniature mules was created for the 1982 rodeo parade. The driver is Wayne McCauley. The window of the Seymour Bakery can be seen in the background. (Courtesy of Sue Cooper.)

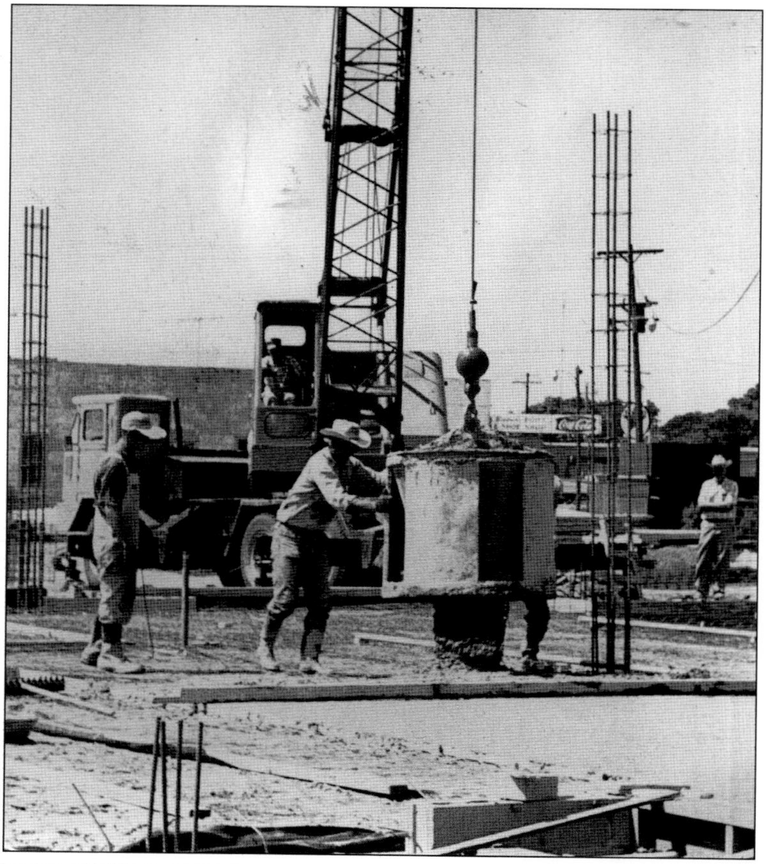

NEW SEYMOUR HOSPITAL. In 1968–1969, a new hospital was constructed on Fair Park Hill west of the stadium. It contained 50 beds, cost nearly a million dollars, and was financed with revenue bonds through the Department of Housing and Urban Development. The architect was Wingler and Sharp, of Wichita Falls, Texas, and the contractor was H.A. Padgett, of Lubbock, Texas. This hospital continues to serve Baylor County. (Both, courtesy of Baylor County Museum.)

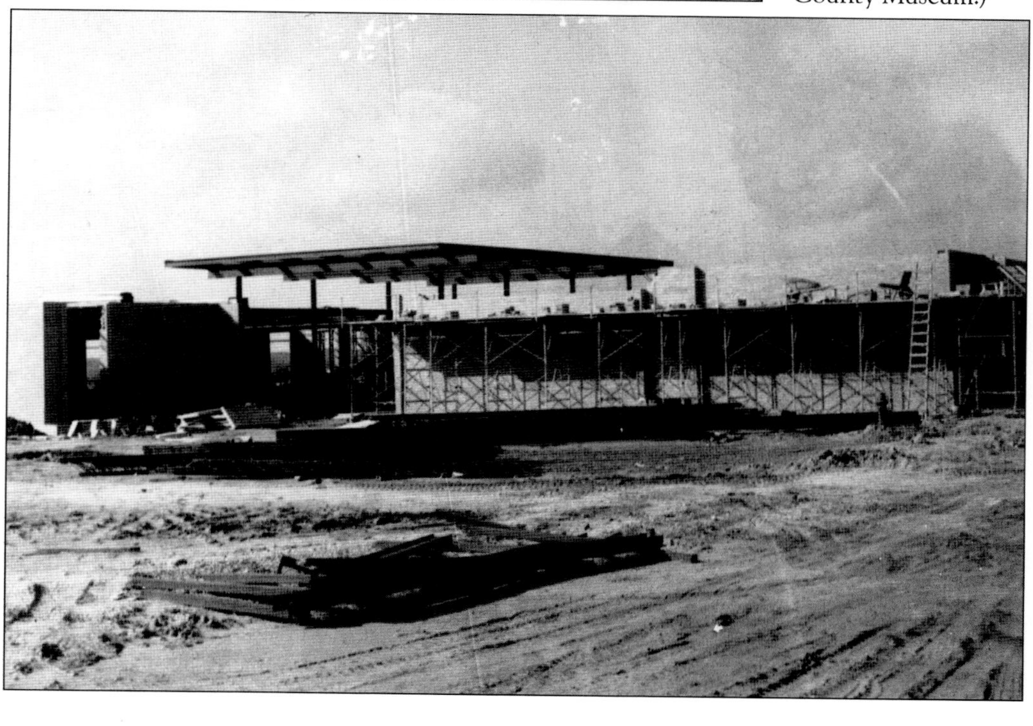

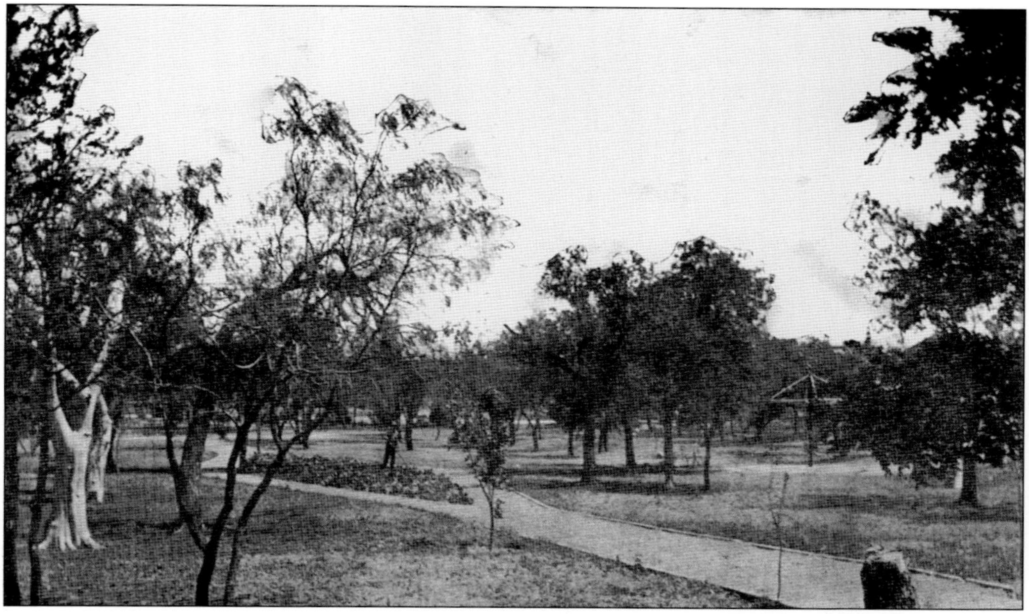

Seymour Municipal Park. In 1921, plans for a municipal park were initiated. The 87-acre park is located in the city limits on the east edge of town near Seymour Creek. The land where the park is located was known as the McClain grove because of its wonderful growth of live oaks. Fair Park Stadium and the bathhouses along with the rock walls that border the perimeter of the park were built by the WPA. (Courtesy of Baylor County Museum.)

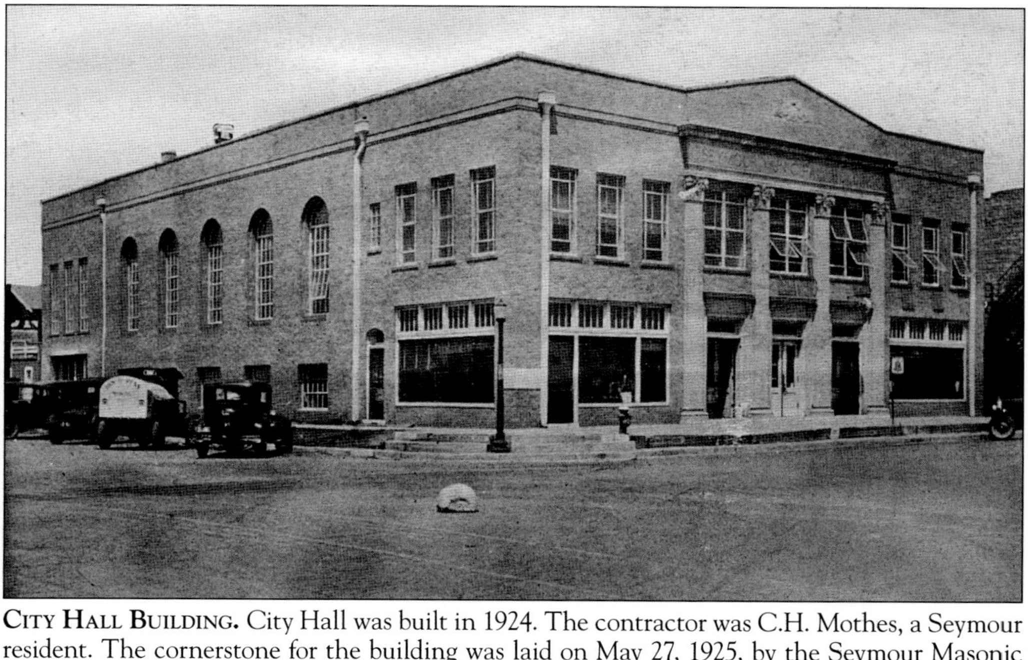

City Hall Building. City Hall was built in 1924. The contractor was C.H. Mothes, a Seymour resident. The cornerstone for the building was laid on May 27, 1925, by the Seymour Masonic Lodge. The building was equipped with a beautiful auditorium, the site of many piano recitals and graduation ceremonies. (Courtesy of Baylor County Museum.)

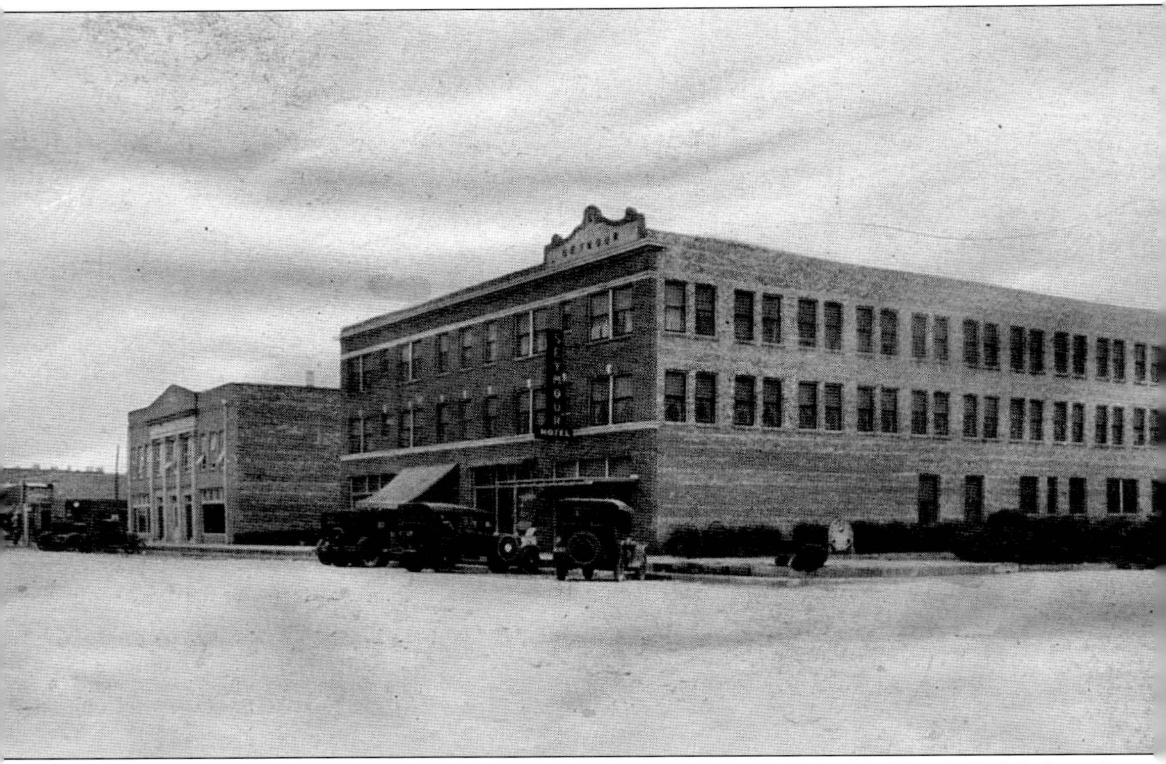

SEYMOUR HOTEL. The Seymour Hotel was another building constructed by C.H. Mothes. It was three stories tall, had 50 guest rooms, 30 private baths, and an elevator. Rooms were $3 a night ,and dinner was 50¢. It was considered one of the finest small hotels in the state and was patronized by salesmen. The hotel was purchased by the City of Seymour on March 3, 1971, and eventually torn down. (Courtesy of Baylor County Museum.)

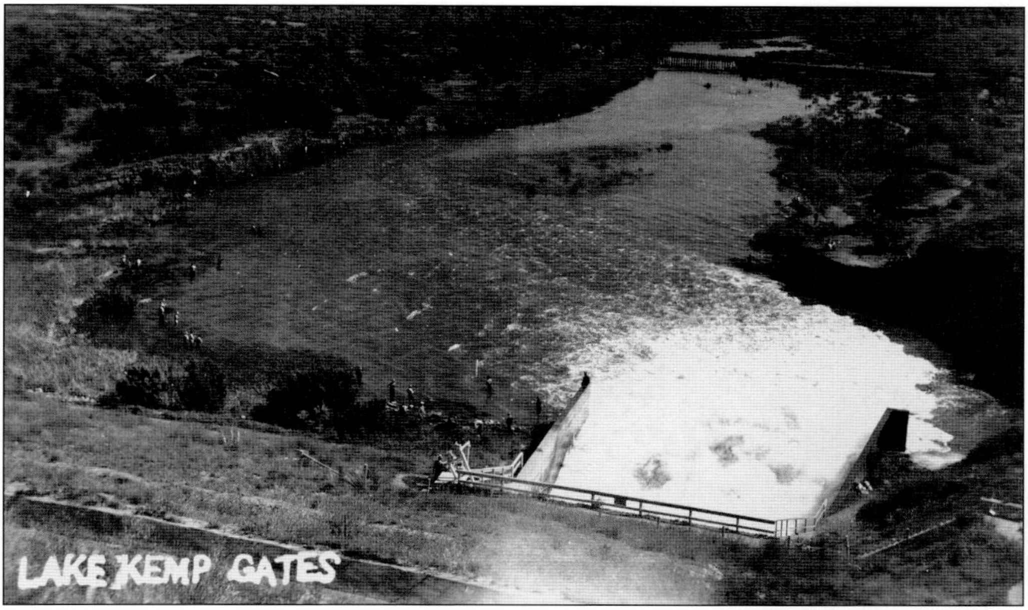

Lake Kemp Gates. Lake Kemp is located entirely in Baylor County. It was built in the early 1920s at a cost of $4.5 million and covers about 25 acres. Water from the lake is released through floodgates and flows down the Wichita River, intended to irrigate land. Lake diversion was created later to help prevent flooding in Wichita Falls. (Courtesy of Baylor County Museum.)

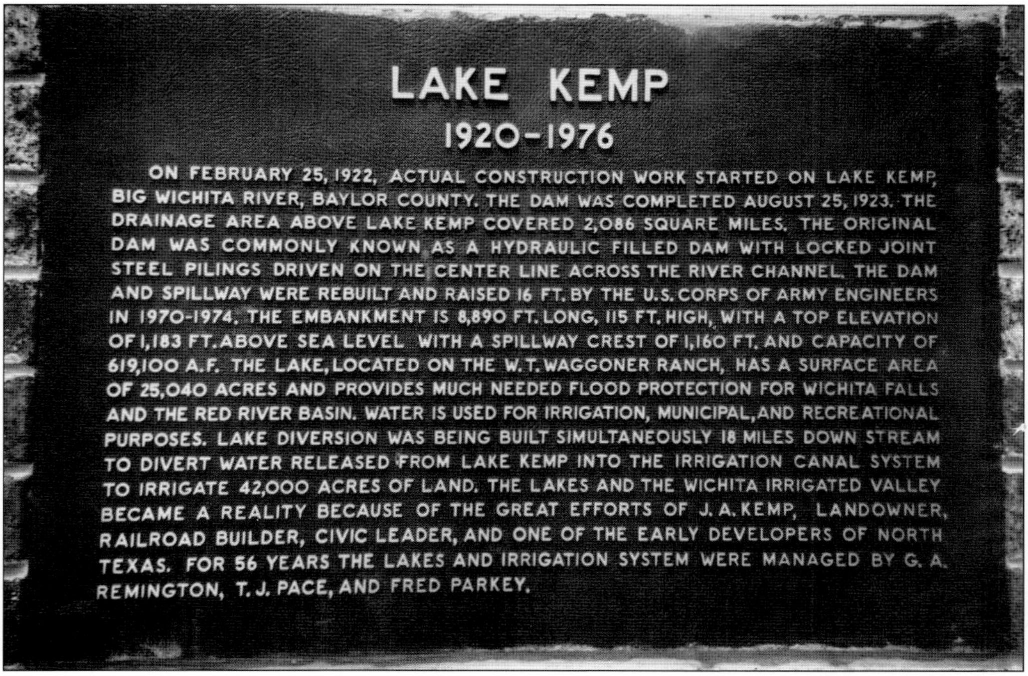

Lake Kemp Marker. Lake Kemp provides recreation for Baylor County and is the home of Fish Day. At its peak, Fish Day received national attention. The entire town closed up and went fishing. Construction on Lake Kemp began February 25, 1922. The original damn and spillway were rebuilt and raised 16 feet during the years 1970–1974 by the United States Corps of Engineers. This photograph probably dates from this period. (Courtesy of Baylor County Office of the USDA.)

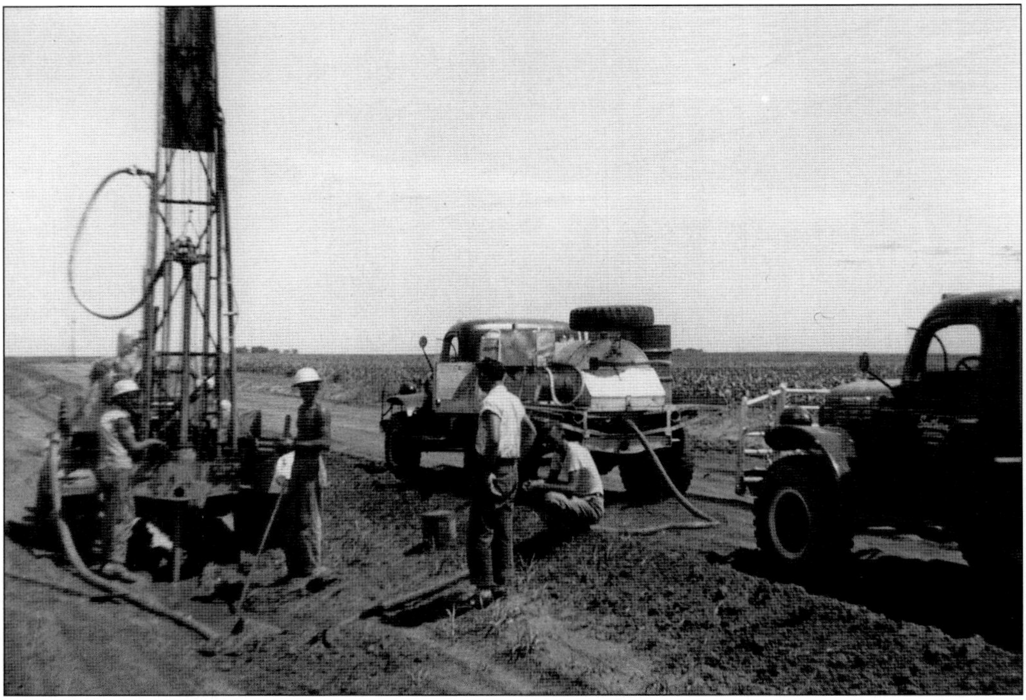

Seismographic Crew. Measuring earth tremors or sound waves was one of the early methods of searching for oil. Seismographic measurements help the geologist determine the geological and oil-bearing structure. The Permian period left Baylor County invaluable gifts of oil and fossils. Drilling for oil in the county began in 1919. (Courtesy of Betty and Don Welch.)

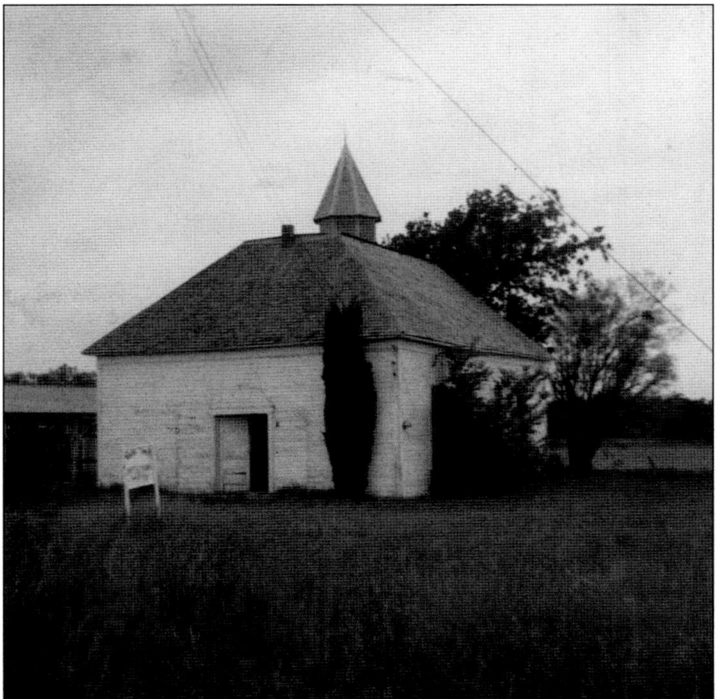

Round Timber Baptist Church. The Round Timber Baptist Church was built in 1897 by the Methodists and sold to the Baptists in 1933. The burial ground dates from 1870, making it one of the oldest cemeteries in the county. The church collapsed in 2006. In 2009, the site was issued an Official Texas Historical Marker. (Courtesy of Betty Welch.)

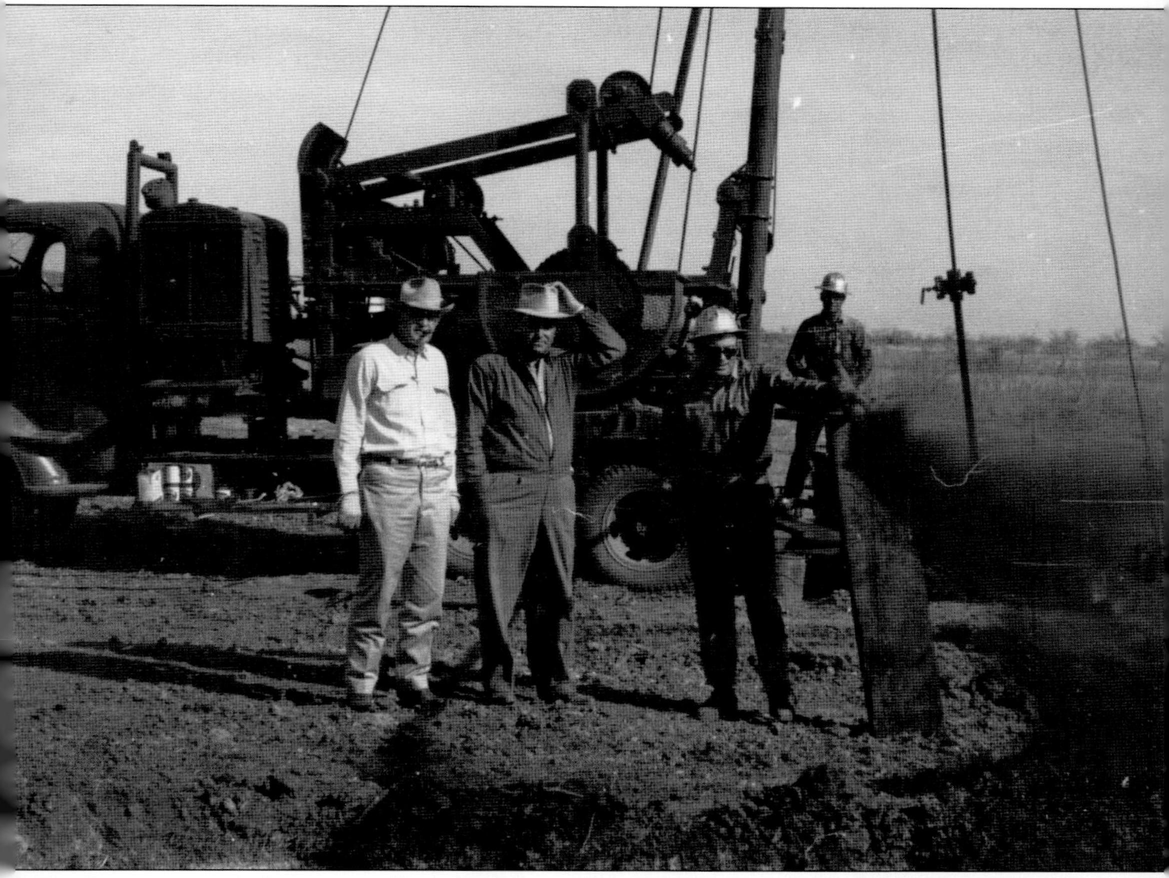

Oil Discovered. A discovery well was brought in the southwest part of the county in December 1953. This field became known as the Baylor County Regular Field. It added needed income to the county after several years of severe drought and financial hardship in the farming and ranching communities. (Courtesy of Mary's Creek Ranch.)

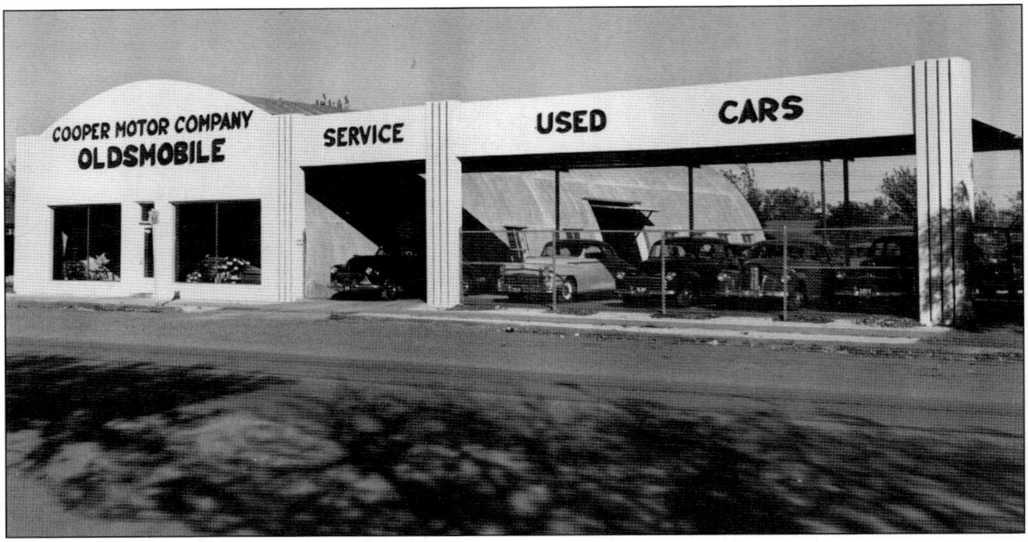

COOPER MOTOR COMPANY. Cooper Motor Company was purchased by W.R. Cooper in the 1940s. James Cooper, one of W.R.'s sons, began working there in 1953 and assumed the position of dealer in October 1955. The dealership handled Oldsmobile and Cadillac lines. The original location on the east side of Washington Street burned, and the business was relocated directly across the street. (Courtesy of A.B. Martin.)

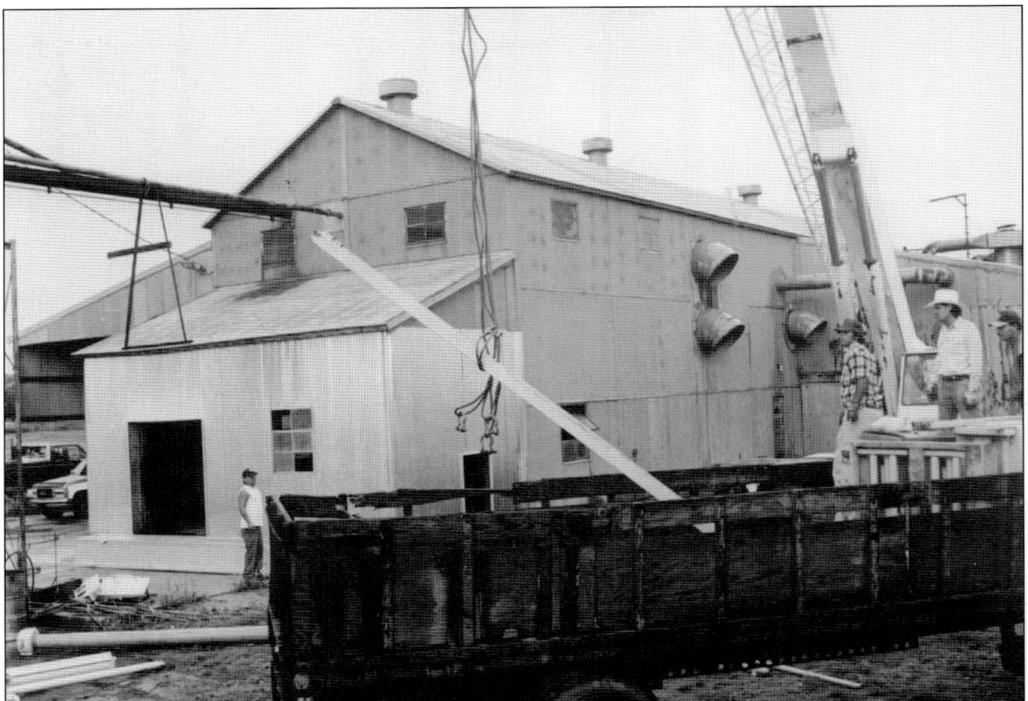

WEST TEXAS CULVERT COMPANY. In the early 1970s, West Texas Culverts was established by John Horn. The first location of the business was across from the bus barn. In the early 1970s, the plant was moved to its current location on the Wichita Highway. In 2007, the plant was sold, and the name changed to ConTech. This photograph was taken during the refitting of the old gin prior to West Texas Culverts' move. (Courtesy of Baylor County Museum.)

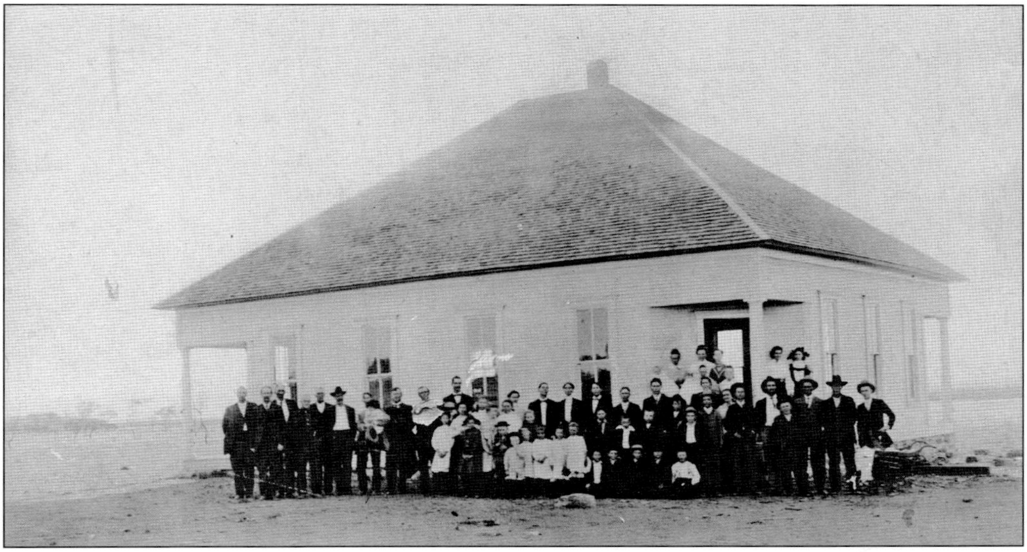

Rendham Church, 1906. The Rendham settlement was east of Seymour. At one time, it had—besides the church—a gin, a grain elevator, cattle pens, and a depot. The town received the name of Rendham from the United States Post Office Department when Thomas Haddox applied for a post office to be located in his store. (Courtesy of Baylor County Museum.)

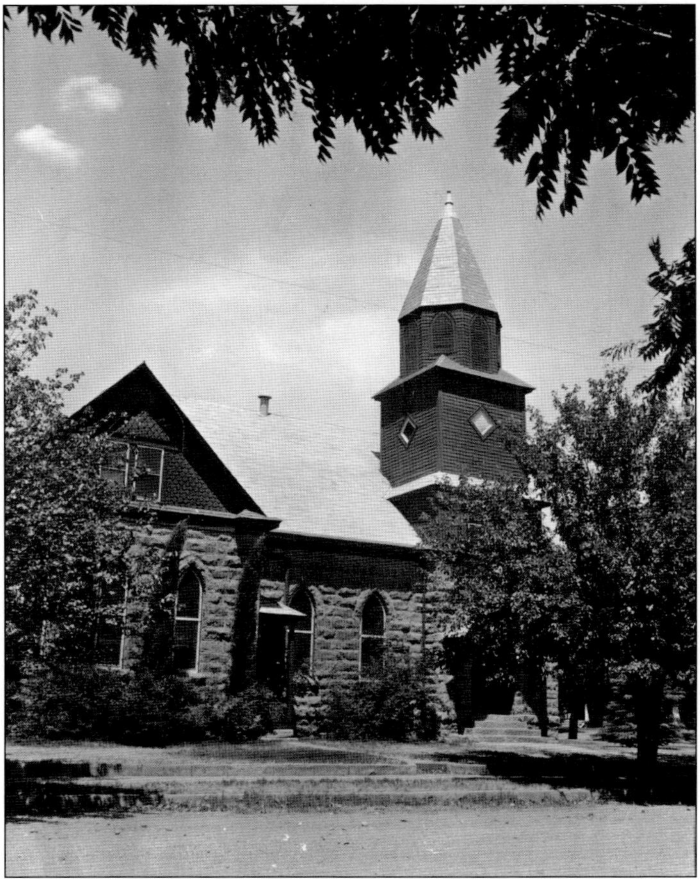

First Christian Church. The First Christian Church was organized in 1880. The congregation met in the courthouse for several years and eventually built a two-story house. The masons used the upper story, and the church services were held in the lower story. The current Gothic-style structure was built in 1906–1907 of native stone and is the oldest church building in the town. It was awarded a Texas Historical Marker in 1970. (Courtesy of Baylor County Museum.)

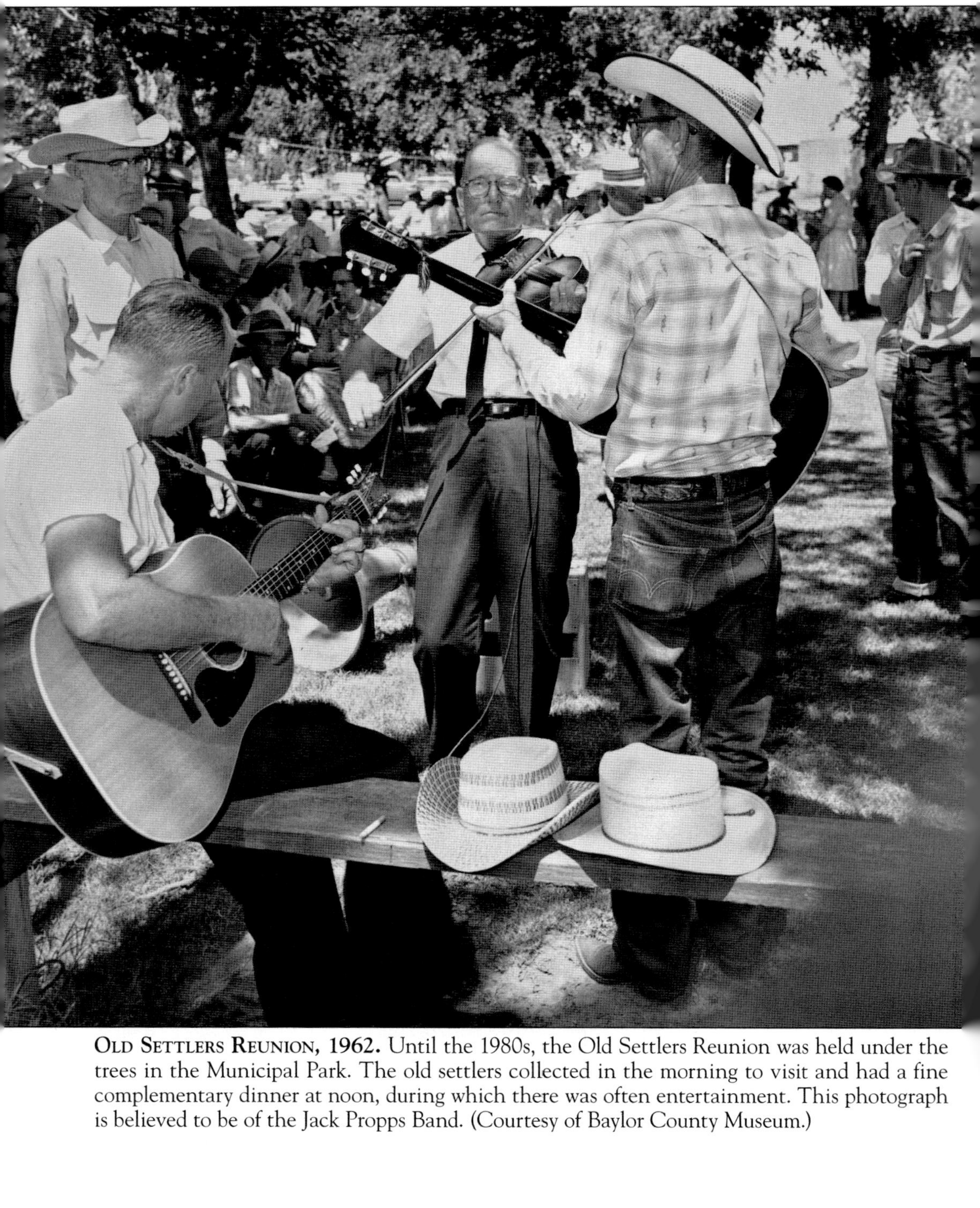

Old Settlers Reunion, 1962. Until the 1980s, the Old Settlers Reunion was held under the trees in the Municipal Park. The old settlers collected in the morning to visit and had a fine complementary dinner at noon, during which there was often entertainment. This photograph is believed to be of the Jack Propps Band. (Courtesy of Baylor County Museum.)

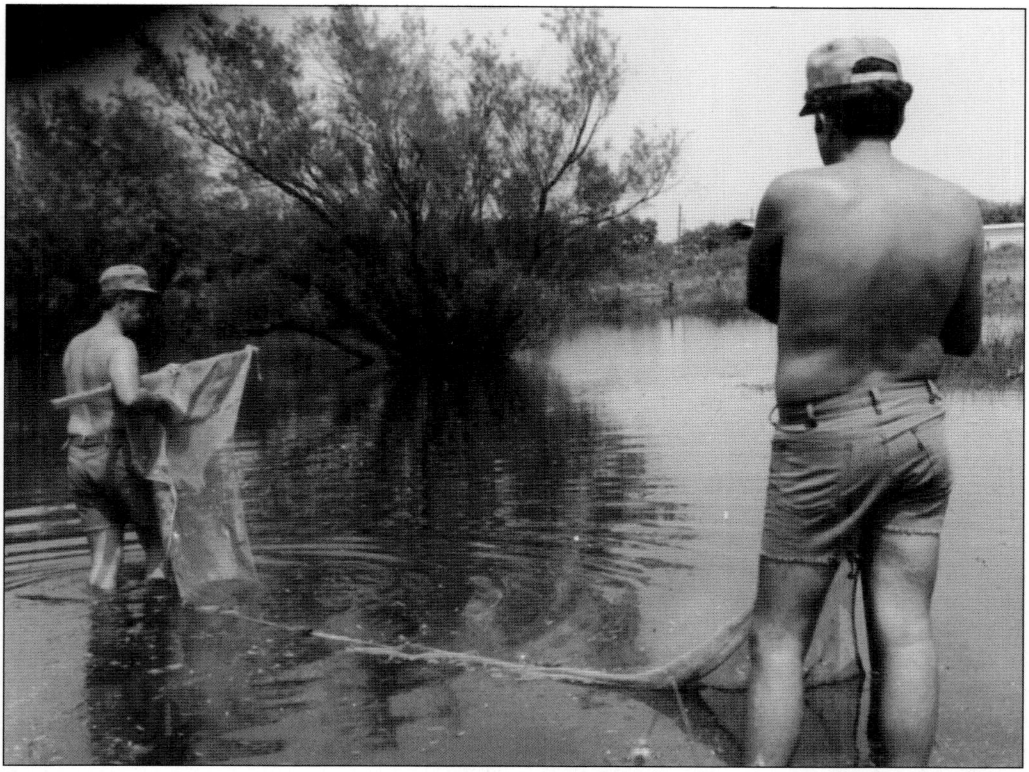

Seining in a Stock Tank. Opportunities to fish in Baylor County are available at Miller Creek, Lake Kemp, private stock tanks, and occasionally the Brazos River. Catfish weighing 50 to 60 pounds used to be taken out of Miller Creek. (Courtesy of the Baylor County Office of the USDA.)

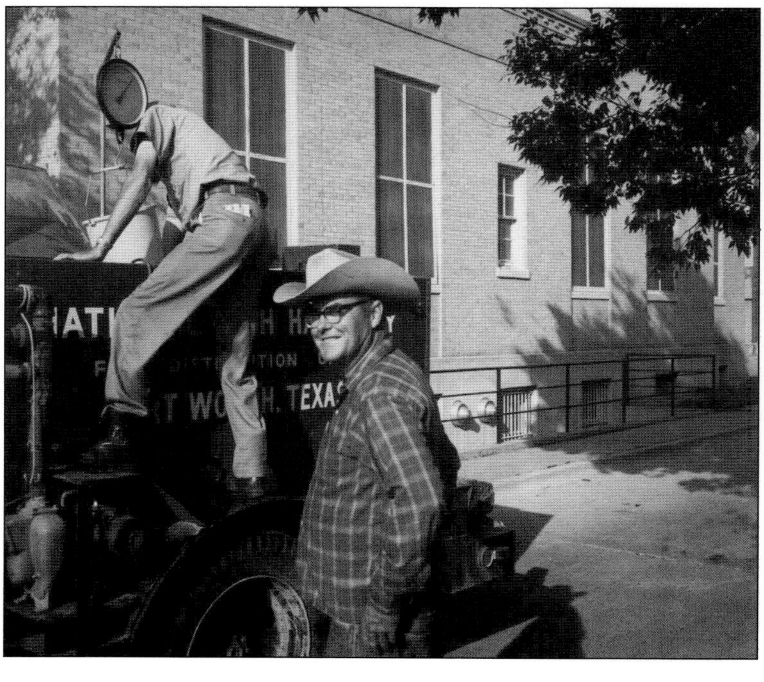

Fish Hatchery Delivery. Stock tanks in Baylor County are often filled with sport fish. Fish and the ecosystem they help create make the tanks a suitable habitat for a variety of animals. Dug to catch water for cattle, these tanks also water a variety of wildlife, including deer. (Courtesy of Baylor County Office of the USDA.)

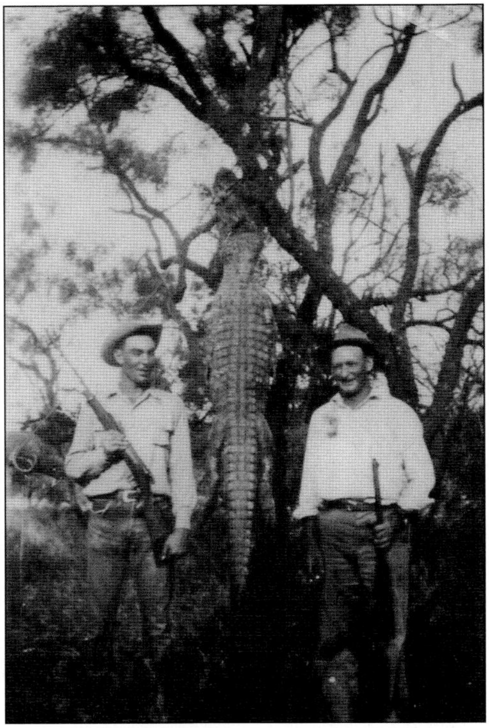

Alligator Found on Hunt Ranch. Ernest Hunt (right) and ranch hand Lige Parrot stand beside the alligator that was killed on the Hunt Ranch by Winslow Whitten of Red Springs with a 30-30 Winchester rifle. The alligator measured eight feet, five inches long and weighed 140 pounds. It was killed at a tank on Hunt Ranch land about six miles from the Brazos River. (Courtesy of Baylor County Museum.)

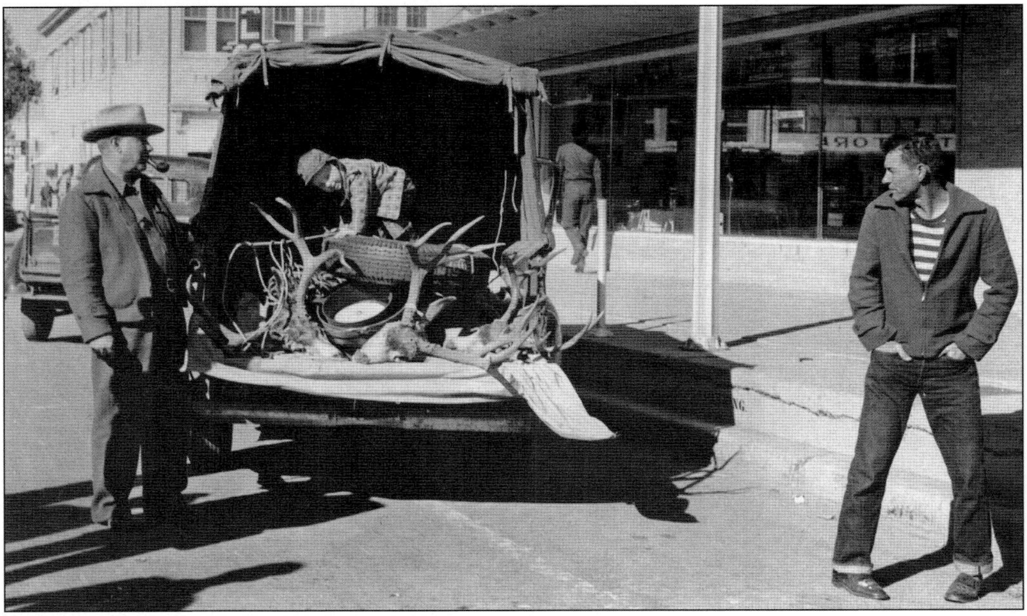

Morris Randal and Grandson. When the ranchers and settlers first came to Baylor County in the late 19th century, wild game was abundant in the area. Conversion of the land to farming and hunting for food took its toll, and slowly the numbers reduced. However, in recent years, careful wildlife management practices have enlarged the populations again, and recreational hunting adds much-needed revenue to the county. In this late-1940s or early-1950s photograph, Morris Randall supervises his grandson as he plays in the back of a truck loaded with antlers. The man at right is unidentified. (Courtesy of Baylor County Museum.)

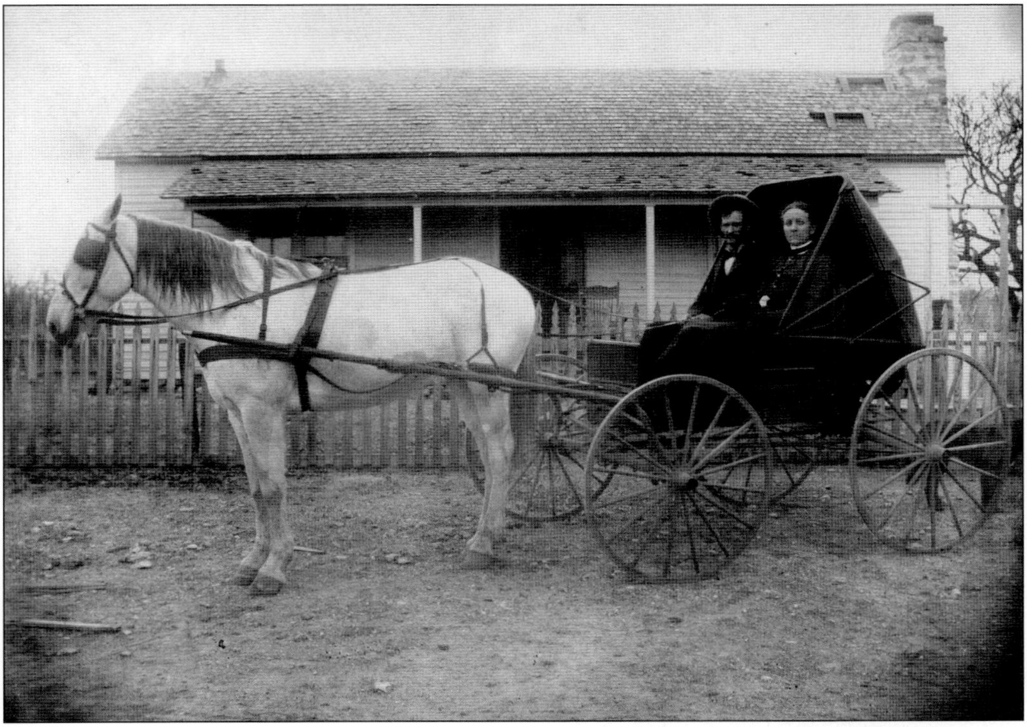

COURTING IN A ONE-HORSE SHAY. The one-horse shay was a fashionable conveyance in the early days of Baylor County. A shay is a light, covered two-wheel carriage drawn by a single horse. It seated two people and was popular with ladies, doctors, preachers, and courting couples. (Courtesy of Baylor County Museum.)

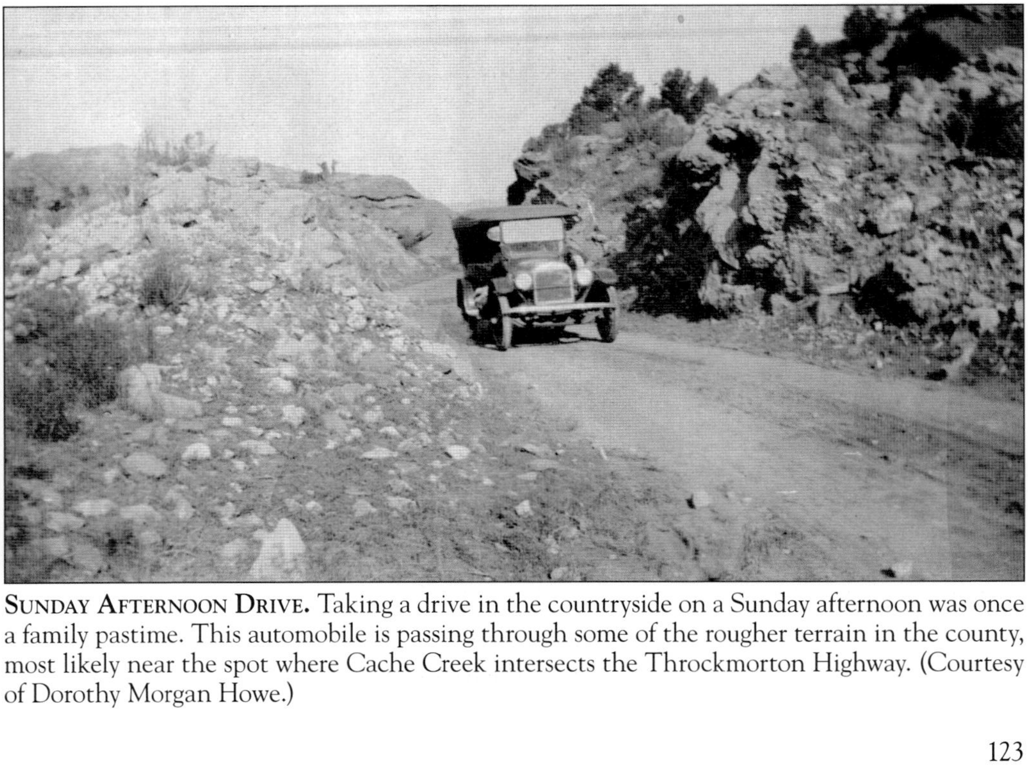

SUNDAY AFTERNOON DRIVE. Taking a drive in the countryside on a Sunday afternoon was once a family pastime. This automobile is passing through some of the rougher terrain in the county, most likely near the spot where Cache Creek intersects the Throckmorton Highway. (Courtesy of Dorothy Morgan Howe.)

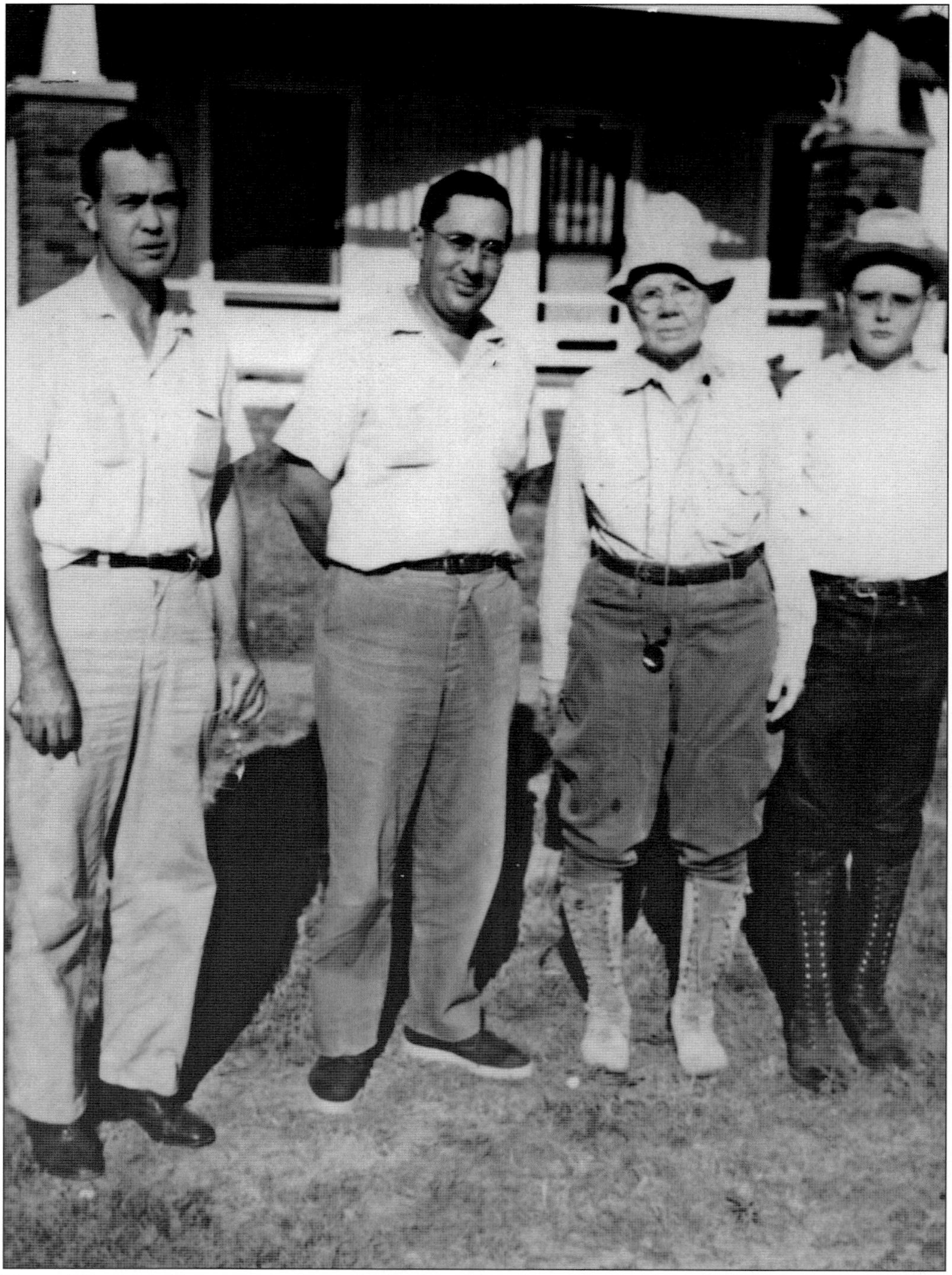

Fossil Hunting Expedition. Augusta (Mrs. J.F.) Kemp was a noted local amateur paleontologist. Dr. Sergius H. Mamay was a renowned United States Geological Survey paleobotanist and research associate at the Smithsonian. This photograph was taken as they were preparing to leave on an expedition to study fossils in Baylor County sometime in the mid-1950s to mid-1960s. From left to right are Arthur D. Watt, Dr. Mamay, Augusta (Mrs. J.F.) Kemp, and Bob Hayley Jr. (Courtesy of Baylor County Museum.)

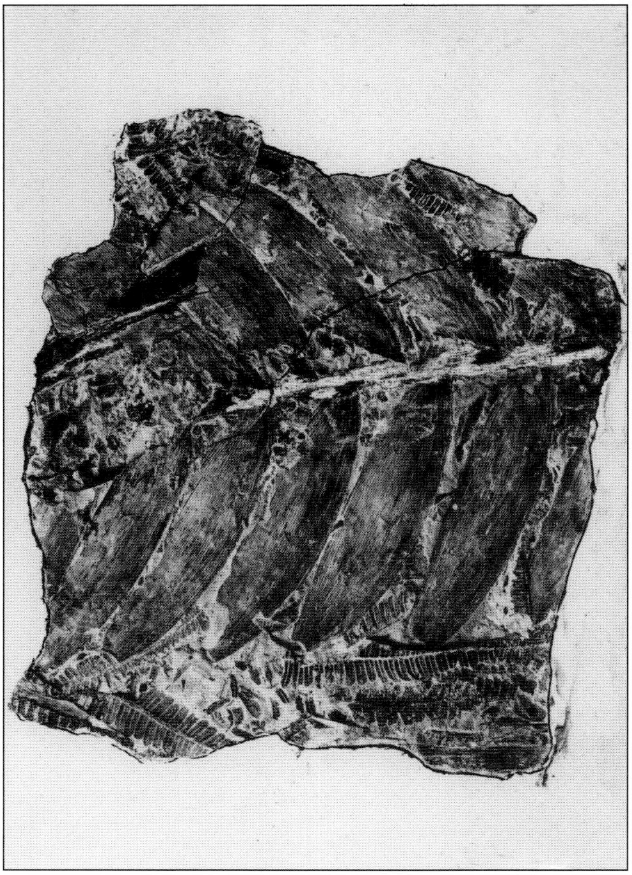

RUSSELLITIES TAENIA FOSSIL. Baylor County contains one of the richest variety and concentration of Permian period plants in North America. The above leaf fossil is from the Emily Irish deposit in Baylor County. The plant bearing the palm-like leaf in the photograph is found nowhere else in the world, and was named in honor of Mart and Jet Russell. (Courtesy of Baylor County Museum.)

OMA HASH'S AIRPLANE. Carl and Oma Hash were both licensed pilots. They built the Seymour Airport and Flying School on the Olney Highway, northeast of the cemetery. After World War II, pilots needed work, and the Hashes hired them as flight instructors for the school and as crop dusters for the community. The airport blew away during a spring storm. (Courtesy of Carolene Hash Stovall.)

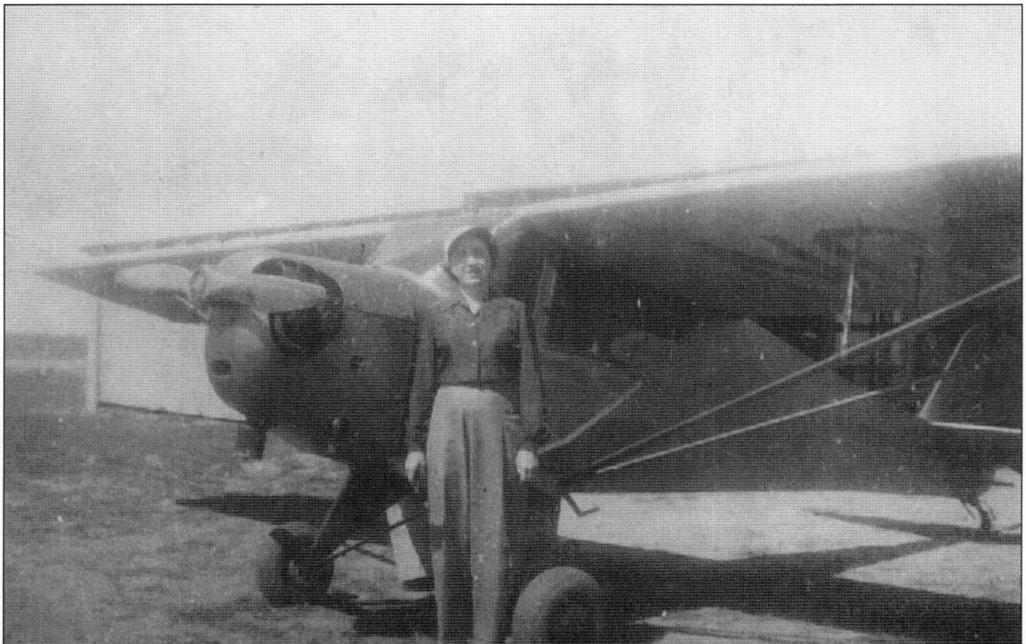

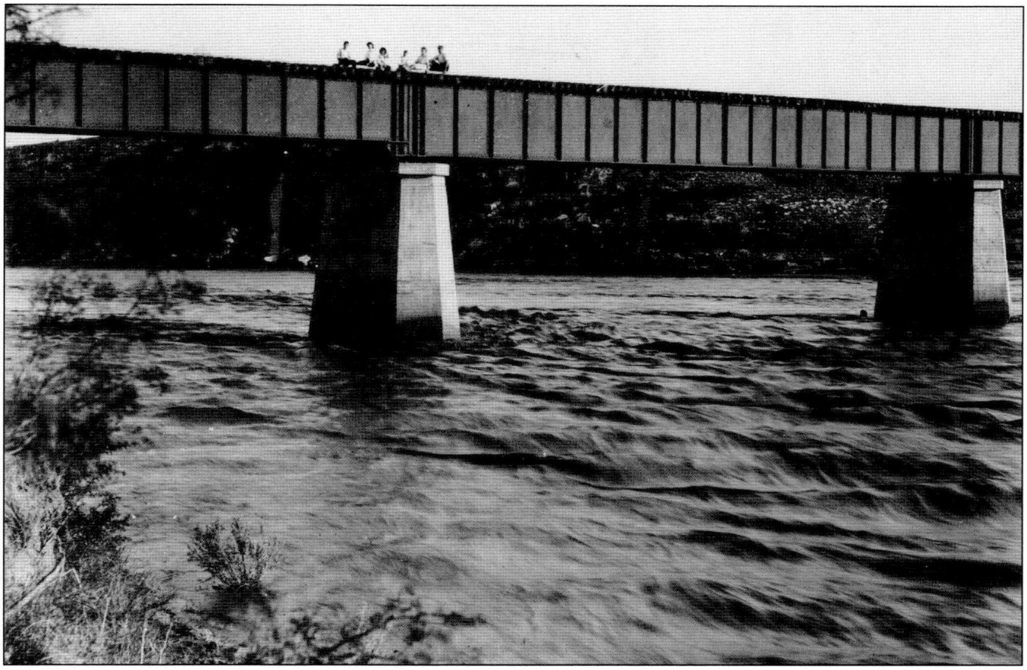

Brazos River Railroad Bridge. The first passenger train across the Brazos River was in 1907. This photograph was taken August 7, 1909. (Courtesy of Baylor County Museum.)

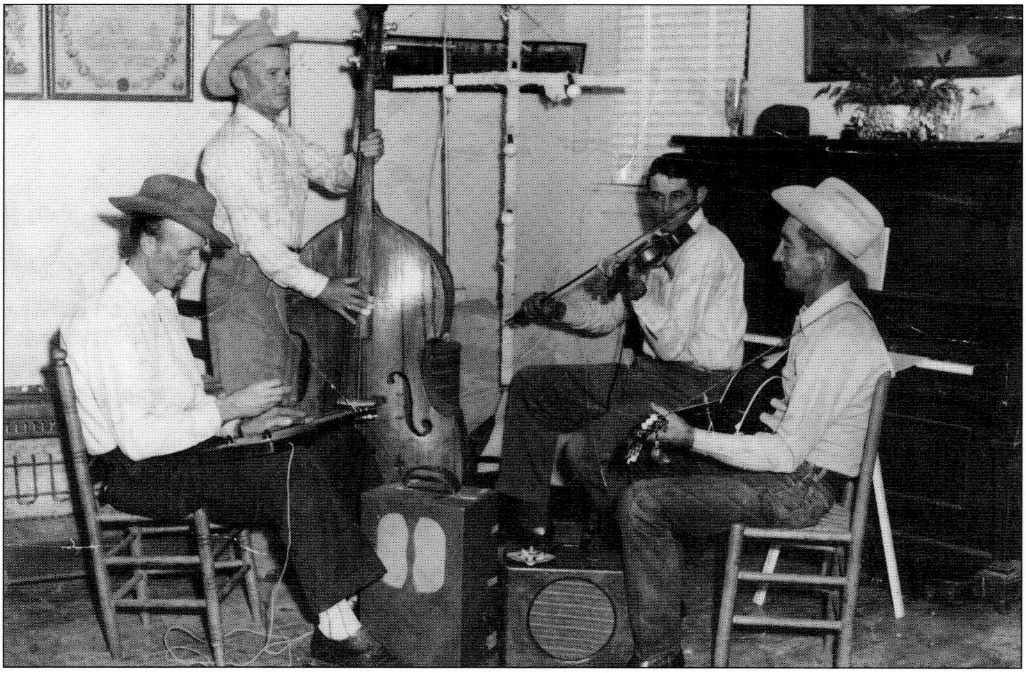

Perk and the Perkolators. Music has always been a popular form of entertainment in the county. Perk and the Perkolators was a group of friends who got together and played for their own enjoyment and the occasional social activity. The band includes, from left to right, John Perkins, Al Latham (from Munday), Bill Glover, and Buster Ryan. Member Louis Kubala is not pictured. (Courtesy of Baylor County Museum.)

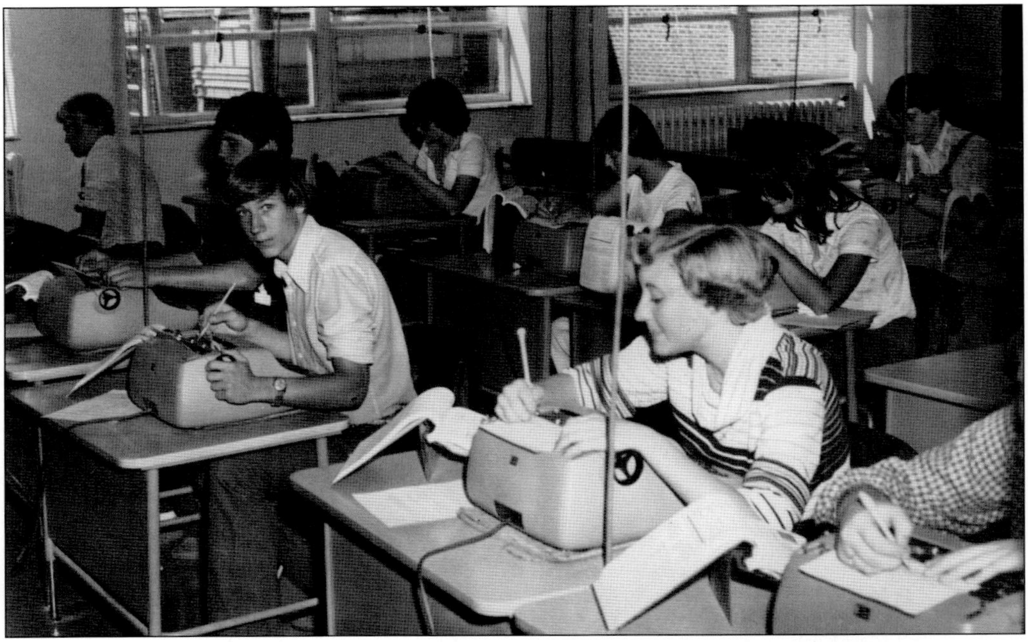

Typing Class at Seymour High School. Prior to the development of the personal computer, typing was a practical and necessary skill. These students have an advantage, as they are learning to type on electric rather than manual typewriters. (Courtesy of Baylor County Museum.)

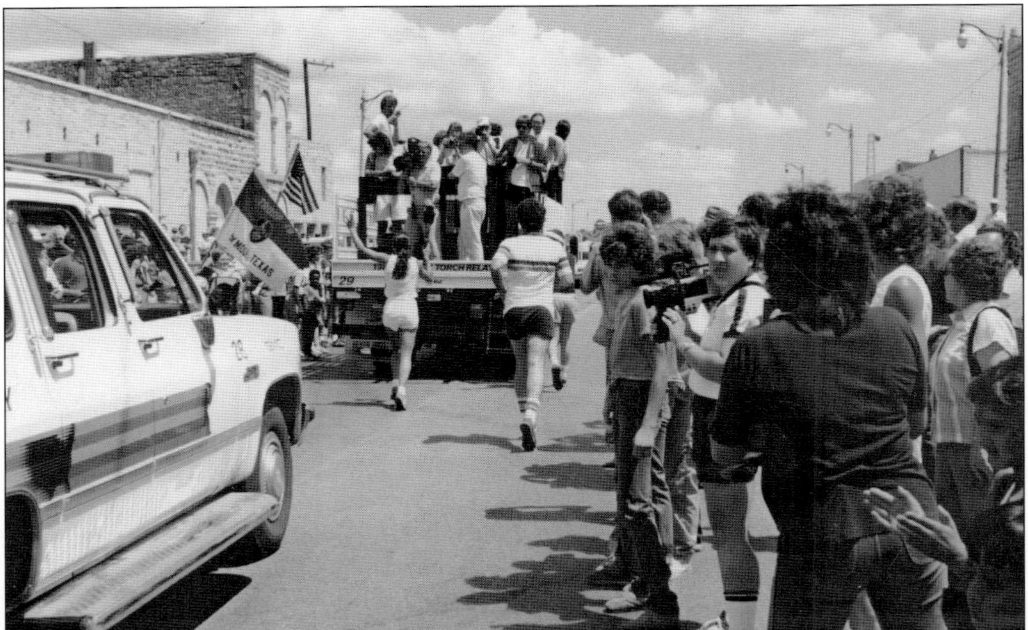

Olympic Torch, 1984. The Olympic torch passed through Seymour on its way to the 1984 Summer Olympics in Los Angeles, California. The town received national media coverage, and people from Seymour and surrounding counties lined the streets for this historic occasion. The torch was met on the outskirts of town by B.F. Tucker and Mindy Morris, who was mounted on horseback and held the United States and Texas flags. (Courtesy of Janice Vita Thornhill.)

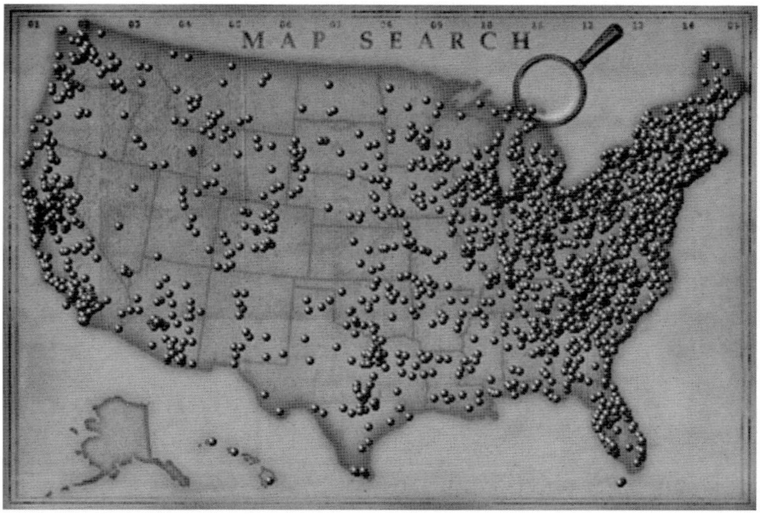
MAP SEARCH